Leisure and Recreation Studies
Series Editors: Stanley Parker and Sarah Gregory

1   Leisure Identities and Interactions

Leisure and Recreation Studies

2 LEISURE AND WORK
   by Stanley Parker

Leisure Identities and Interactions

John R. Kelly
University of Illinois

London
GEORGE ALLEN & UNWIN
Boston   Sydney

George Allen & Unwin (Publishers) Ltd,
40 Museum Street, London WC1A 1LU, UK

George Allen & Unwin (Publishers) Ltd,
Park Lane, Hemel Hempstead, Herts HP2 4TE, UK

Allen & Unwin, Inc.,
9 Winchester Terrace, Winchester, Mass. 01890, USA

George Allen & Unwin Australia Pty Ltd,
8 Napier Street, North Sydney, NSW 2060, Australia

First published in 1983

British Library Cataloguing in Publication Data

Kelly, John R.
    Leisure identities and interactions. – (Leisure and recreation studies; I)
1. Leisure
I. Title   II. Series
306'.48   GV174
ISBN 0-04-301150-0

Library of Congress Cataloging in Publication Data

Kelly, John R. (John Roberts), 1930–
    Leisure identities and interactions.
(Leisure and recreation studies; no. 1)
Includes index.
1. Leisure – Psychological aspects. 2. Leisure – Social aspects. I. Title. II.
Series.
GV14.4.K44 1983   790'.01'32   82-25278
ISBN 0-04-301150-0

Set in 10 on 11 point Bembo by Computape (Pickering) Ltd
and printed in Great Britain by Biddles Ltd, Guildford, Surrey

Contents

Preface

This book is intended to do more than review and summarize current research and theory in the study of leisure. It offers what is intended as a coherent and integrated argument. However, no finality or closure is assumed or desired. Rather, the presentation moves through some of the accomplishments and limitations of sociological and social-psychological approaches to leisure to the development of an 'existential' mode of analysis. This mode should be understood as a springboard for further work rather than a final answer to researchable questions.

Further, those who are engaged in the study of leisure are now in a position to undertake a more systematic dialogue with their disciplines in the social sciences. This dialogue need not be apologetic or tentative. There is now ample evidence that leisure is a major element in human life. Giving attention to understanding this phenomenon is not frivolous and may properly receive the investment of able scientists of many disciplines and theoretical persuasions.

Leisure is simply too important to too many people to be trivial. A social-psychological approach to understanding leisure incorporates both the social context of the roles that change through the life course and the development of identities in and through those roles. In social systems with considerable rigidity in how many roles are defined and enacted the relative freedom of leisure often offers the richest opportunities for the development of satisfying selfhood and identities. When developmental dilemmas constrict personal expression and the exploration of significant dimensions of interpersonal relationships, leisure may be the social space in which there is openness for important new interactions and self-definitions.

The final chapter in this book incorporates the presentation first developed in the December 1981 special issue of *Social Forces*. For more detailed analysis of some of the specific contexts of leisure, the reader is referred to the author's recent book *Leisure*. However, *Leisure Identities and Interactions* goes far beyond that in its development of the dialogue between sociology and leisure studies. While every effort is made not to burden the reader with needlessly complex vocabulary and concepts, this book is intended for those who desire more than an introduction to the study of leisure.

I am grateful to all who have enriched my understanding of life and leisure through the years. They include not only scholars who have informed my views in formal and informal exchange, but so many whose experiences and interpretations have been absorbed even though the source of the insight has been forgotten. I dedicate this work to that international community of leisure scholars who have taken the risks of investing themselves in this area of study and to the future of our work together.

JOHN R. KELLY
University of Illinois

Leisure Identities and Interactions

1

Meanings of Leisure:
an Introduction

In leisure the same activity may have many meanings:

- For one young mother, her art class is primarily a social event in which she is released for two hours from home and childrearing for conversation during the class and the coffee break that follows. For another woman of about the same age, her engagement with art is a demanding discipline begun in school and focused on a development of a mastery of techniques and styles that is both the aim and the satisfaction of painting.

- On the golf course at the same time there is a student striving to improve his game for tournament play, another young man using the outdoor environment for purposes of courting a young woman whom he expects to marry, a salesman courting customers for his new life insurance plan and a group of 'regulars' who take both the game and their friendships seriously.

- On a Friday evening at the local public house the crowd includes groups of men seeking the relaxation of a pint or two and conversation unimpeded by the noise of factory machinery, at least three groups of adolescent men and women who use the pub as a meeting-place and who will soon be off in their cars, and a large group of couples who come together more or less regularly in an informality and ease that does not require the preparation and scheduling of entertaining friends at home where space is more limited. On the fringes of the pub groups there are also a number of individuals who have come alone and who appear to be more serious about their drinking.

However, different activities may have much the same meanings to participants:

- For devotees of both ceramics and squash, the development of a measured mastery and skill may be central to the experience that draws men and women back for regular engagement.

And one event may include many modes of behavior:

- A social event such as a party may also be a demonstration of skill for the organizers, an opportunity to explore new relationships for some and to cultivate old ones for others, an experience of ease and grace in communication for some and of extreme effort bordering on anguish for others, and a mixture of meanings and experiences for most partygoers.

Further, the same activity may have different meanings at different times for the same person:

- A tennis player may be on the court in an intense skill-honing session one afternoon, in a parental combination of teaching and companionship the next morning and in a very social and non-competitive mixed doubles game that evening. The meanings move from competence-building and testing to relationship-building to social expressivity.
- Reading at home may be for the teacher a complement to work, sheer escape, general 'keeping up with the world' and an intense and engrossing immersion with the literature at various times depending on what is read, her mood and orientations.
- An encounter on Saturday at the shopping center may be a passing and relatively meaningless exchange of greetings, a pleasant opportunity for more prolonged conversation, or, for a group of teens, the main purpose of going to town.

In general, both activities and their meanings may vary in a seemingly limitless possibility of combinations.

'Is It Leisure?'

Not only is there a variety of kinds of activity that may be leisure and of the meanings of those activities to participants, but leisure would appear to be diffused through time and space. When the question 'is it leisure?' is asked of an activity, be it reading or football, the appropriate answer would appear to be 'sometimes'. Swimming may be primarily social interaction on the beach, fierce competition, hours of disciplined effort, physical conditioning, a job skill for the pool staff, or a relaxing experience of buoyancy. Walking may be a health-preserving regimen, transportation to the shops, a companionable stroll, or immersion in an absorbing natural environment. Conversation, the essential content of much social leisure, may take place almost anywhere. In fact, variety and diffusion would appear to be integral to the experience of leisure in our culture and era.

There is variety in activity – from daydreaming to scheduled cello practice.

There is diffusion in environments – from home to shopping center, from store and sidewalk to forest and concert hall and even from factory and office to beach and boat.

There is a multiplicity of social contexts – from solitary occupation to the coached meshing of positions in team sports, from one-dimensional interaction in an activity group to the complex relationships and expectations of leisure with a primary group such as the family.

There is variety in meanings – from the 'pure' experience of engagement in which all sense of time and place seem to disappear to a carefully adjusted set of communications and interactions responding to the complex requirements of an event combining social and action components, from autotelic and self-contained moments to conscious role complementarity.

Meanings of Leisure

In a number of research approaches people have been asked both directly and indirectly about the meanings they find in their leisure. In one of the earliest such studies Robert Havighurst and his associates asked Kansas City adults about their favorite activity.[1] The most common responses were:

'I like it just for the pleasure of doing it.'
'It's a welcome change from my work.'
'I like it because it brings me into contact with friends.'
'It gives me a new experience; I learn something from it.'
'It gives me a chance to achieve something.'
'I feel I am being creative.'
'I like to do things that will benefit society.'
'It makes the time pass.'

More recently research into leisure roles and environments in three North American communities produced the following ranking of satisfactions among adults for the five or six activities they valued most:[2]

'I like it.'
'I enjoy the companions.'
'I feel relaxed.'
'It strengthens a relationship.'
'I grow as a person.'
'It's restful.'

'It's exciting.'
'It's my self-expression.'
'It's healthful.'
'I like doing it well.'
'It's different from my work.'
'It's active exercise.'
'I like developing a skill.'
'I feel I belong.'
'I like being of help to others.'

Reasons expressing a sense of obligation or duty to family or friends, enjoying the contest or being outdoors, receiving the approval of others and taking up time were less important to the respondents. In general, social satisfactions, rest and relaxation, and engagement with the experience or mastery of an activity, were all found to be significant meanings of leisure.

A compilation of motivations identified from the employment of social-psychology scale items by several investigators yields the following list of meaning dimensions not ranked by importance:[3]

(1) Enjoying nature, escaping civilization; (2) Escape from routine and responsibility; (3) Physical exercise; (4) Creativity; (5) Relaxation; (6) Social contact; (7) Meeting new people; (8) Heterosexual contact; (9) Family interaction; (10) Recognition, status; (11) Social power; (12) Altruism; (13) Stimulus seeking; (14) Self-actualization, feedback, self-improvement; (15) Achievement, challenge, competition; (16) Killing time, avoiding boredom; (17) Intellectual aestheticism.

While the results of research on the meanings, motivations, or satisfactions of leisure reflect both the methods employed and the cultural setting of the population, the main point is clear: leisure has multiple meanings as well as a wide spectrum of activities and environments. It is multidimensional and multivalent.

Then Just What Is Leisure?

Leisure may be a complex phenomenon. Nevertheless, any use of the term presupposes some agreement on its parameters. At least in a general way, there must be characteristics that distinguish leisure from other human action. Several models of leisure provide approaches to grasping the dimensions of leisure as a human phenomenon. However, there are two dimensions that call for prior attention.

Leisure as an Existential Reality

The persistent element in defining leisure throughout the history of

Western civilization has been relative freedom of choice.[4] From Aristotle[5] to contemporary analysis, the perennial defining dimension of leisure has been freedom. Leisure is existential in this insistence on 'chosenness' in its realization.

Sociologists usually part from philosophers on the issue of the purity or absolute nature of that freedom. Kenneth Roberts offers a brief definition of leisure as 'relatively self-determined nonwork activity'.[6] Freedom from role expectations, environmental constraints and resource limitations is seldom total. Leisure as activity is usually socially situated with impinging role expectations and implicit structural elements.

Aristotle combined intrinsic meaning with freedom in his later definition in book VIII of the *Politics*. Leisure is not only time free from obligations and therefore not realized for slaves, but is done for its own sake with the outcome of 'intrinsic pleasure, intrinsic happiness, intrinsic felicity'. While such a classic approach may presuppose freedom for choice, leisure cannot be limited to activity chosen and carried out totally without constraint. Rather, on a freedom–constraint continuum leisure would be located at the freedom side. If something 'has to be done', then it isn't leisure. On the other hand, leisure is more than choosing between tending the garden and washing the dishes. Choice alone does not define leisure, but leisure is existential in requiring choice and catching up that quality of choice in its outcomes.

According to Joffre Dumazedier, when it challenges constraint, 'Leisure assumes the character of an existential reality'.[7] Leisure is not residual, but is a social space in which we not only retain, but insist on some freedom to choose. That choice may culminate in various parameters that constrain and limit the activity. We may well choose a setting laden with both rules and conventions for behavior. We may choose a social context in which there are strong sets of expectations placed on our interaction. However, the selection of those parameters is still existential, a choice of an environment that has the potential for satisfying leisure as well as some limitations.

Leisure as a Social Reality

Leisure, however, is social as well as existential. It takes *place* not in the mind alone, but in the social world. The most thoroughgoing analysis of the social nature of leisure was presented by Neil Cheek and William Burch[8] in *The Social Organization of Leisure in Human Society*. They argue that leisure is embedded in the biosocial nature of humankind. In modern social systems leisure has the particular purpose of providing the interaction context for tying together primary groups. Leisure is a social space in which the social bonding of intimates, family and friends is developed. As such, leisure not only has a social function, but is in turn shaped by that purpose. The freedom of leisure is often expressed in precisely those situations in which important relationships have their face-to-face reality.

There are other ways in which leisure is social. Stanley Parker[9] and others point out that leisure has been different since the development of an industrial and urbanized society. The very shape of leisure ecology is now determined by the modern megopolis or conurbation that exacts high time costs for most leisure outside the residence.[10] In the interrelated press of institutional schedules even time takes on a social reality that structures the timing of leisure.[11] Some have suggested that an emerging 'postindustrial' society eventually will relax temporal rigidities based on bygone industrial timetables. However, at present, ours remain social systems with constraint symbolized by maps and clocks.

A less obvious dimension of the social reality of leisure is found in the regularity of leisure episodes. Even in the seemingly discrete episode there are all kinds of social rules, conventions, definitions and expectations. These are so taken-for-granted that they pass without notice. For example, the sexual designation of participants in any social interaction directs the expectations of all actors so thoroughly that only a sharp violation will reveal the underlying structure. This aspect of leisure will be explored more fully in Chapter 6. Here it is important only to recognize the implicit as well as explicit frameworks of leisure interaction.

Models of Leisure

Beginning with the assumption that leisure is a complex rather than simple phenomenon, multidimensional rather than monothematic, three approaches to displaying its components seem to have gained recognition in leisure studies. One factor in the emerging acceptance of the complexity of leisure is the development of research and theory-building from more than one disciplinary perspective. While the various social science disciplines may be complementary rather than competing, each does tend to focus on somewhat different dimensions of leisure.

One line of research has employed a series of scales to attempt to measure the dimensions of leisure satisfaction. Referring to leisure in general rather than to particular activities Beard and Ragheb have identified six components of perceived satisfaction as follows:[12]

(1) Psychological: a sense of freedom, enjoyment, involvement and challenge.
(2) Educational: intellectual challenge and knowledge gains.

(3) Social: rewarding relationships with other people.
(4) Relaxation: relief from strain and stress.
(5) Physiological: fitness, health, weight control and wellbeing.
(6) Aesthetic: response to pleasing design and beauty of environments.

However, this approach is limited by its focus on leisure in general rather than on an identified set of behaviors and by its assumption of a common understanding of the parameters of leisure. Other approaches tend to be more grounded in actual behaviors and environments.

Psychological Models
One approach is to examine the perceived experiences of those who engage in leisure activity. Leisure may then be defined in terms of the experience rather than the activity. This approach has the advantage of incorporating the now-evident fact that the same meanings may be found in a variety of activities. Three psychologists have been most identified with contributions to this perspective on leisure.

John Neulinger has developed a systematic model of leisure based on the definitions of the experience by the participant.[13] The primary dimension is 'perceived freedom' – the feeling that an activity has been chosen because the actor wants to do it. This is the essential condition of leisure. However, he adds two other similar elements to the model. The first is motivational and the second that of goals. Leisure is motivated by intrinsic factors and tends to have final rather than instrumental goal orientations. The motivational and goal factors can be combined in the statement that leisure tends to be done for its own sake rather than as a means to another end. Again it is the experience that is crucial – the perception of freedom and intrinsic satisfaction.

The intrinsic satisfaction element is highlighted by the work of Mihaly Csikszentmihalyi, who has investigated a variety of activities and contexts to discover more of the nature of the intensity of experience. He has proposed a model of 'flow' or autotelic activity in which its meaning is the intense experience itself.[14] 'Flow' is experienced in an optimum condition between boredom in which the challenge is less than the actor's ability and anxiety in which the challenge is perceived as too great for self-defined competence. When the task matches ability, then the result may be 'flow' in which elements of the external world recede from consciousness and *doing* the action becomes fully engrossing. Nothing exists, at least for the moment, except matching competence to challenge, skill to task. Such an experience may be found in settings labeled work as well as leisure. Csikszentmihalyi suggests that such totally intrinsic meaning may be the experience that gives primary meaning to an activity and brings participants back for more.

A third psychological approach is based on the work of B. L. Driver of the US Forest Service and employs a series of scales developed to measure the outcomes of the use of natural resources for outdoor recreation. Such outcomes are labeled 'experience opportunity' and may vary from activity to activity and from setting to setting.[15] Benefits of stress reduction, family solidarity, health, or commitment to environmental conservation vary depending on the experience and outcomes sought. Further, the behavioral intentions that guide decisions about future activity are related to past experiences as well as future outcomes sought. In one research exploration Michigan recreationists were tested on their expected outcomes for four kinds of activity.[16] Social camping was scored highest on experiencing nature, family togetherness, being with others, escape, mental change and avoiding the expectations of others. Back-country camping was expected to yield experience of nature and escape; trail biking, being with others and exploration; and tennis, physical fitness, exercise and achievement. None of the four outdoor activities scored high on dominance control, social recognition, tension release, or risktaking. The limitation to outdoor recreation, usually resource-based, precludes generalization of this research to all of leisure. However, the method is sure to be expanded to a full range of activities and environments.

Leisure psychologists are employing their research tools to investigate the meanings of leisure as *experience*. The affective and cognitive components of leisure experiences are being differentiated and measured in ways that are complementary and frequently cumulative. While psychological models do not encompass every element of leisure, they do reveal the diverse set of experiences that may be found and the significance of the activity and the context for those meanings.

Sociological Models

Sociologists have, predictably, focused more on factors related to the social system than the nature of leisure experiences. Perhaps the largest number have employed some version of that tried-and-true sociological variable, social class, to attempt to understand leisure behavior. The *class determination model* takes some aspects of social position as indices of social class (life chances) or social status (life style). Factors such as financial resources, introduction to skills and interests, role expectations related to work and community status, cultural values and access to opportunities are assumed to vary according to social position and consequently to determine leisure choices and orientations. The less-than-definitive results of this approach will be summarized in Chapter 2.

More recently the *immediate community model* has concentrated on stable and close associations, particularly family and friendship groups, as the mediating agents in leisure socialization. These immediate communities, while class-situated, change through the life course as both resources and goals also change. The family, although limited by social position and resource history, is seen as an opportunity for leisure learning as well as a set of constraints.

In the *social role model* leisure is understood to be related to but not determined by economic, familial and community roles. These roles change in both context and content through the life course. Leisure is not always secondary to other roles, but exists in the confluence of work and immediate community roles. Role changes add and subtract both opportunities and constraints to leisure as well as lead to new anticipated outcomes.[17] This approach is processual and includes how roles are defined and redefined through the life course as well as how they are classified in the social system.

While psychological models point to the perception of freedom, sociological models imply that freedom is more than a feeling or attitude. Rather, in the social context, relative freedom and constraint are not the same for all people since a number of social factors limit or expand the real options for leisure-related decisions. Leisure may not be as determined as implied by the class determination model, but it is also not entirely a matter of personal definition.

One model was developed from a review of both historical and contemporary approaches to leisure. In general, it was found that the constant dimension defining leisure is relative freedom.[18] The second dimension that is common but not universal is differentiation from work. Leisure is generally understood as 'chosen activity that is not work'. A diagram displaying this model includes four cells: (1) unconditional or pure leisure that is chosen in relative freedom and clearly distinguished from the required activity of work; (2) coordinated leisure that is similar to work but still freely chosen; (3) complementary leisure including social activity constrained by role expectations with the possibility of being a compensation for work constraints; and (4) required activity that is *not* leisure and may include various kinds of maintenance and preparation for or recovery from work (Figure 1.1).

Note that the dimensions of this approach are traditional sociological variables: work and family roles, social class and status, and differentiation within the social system. The more recent shift among leisure sociologists has been away from assumptions of the economic determination of leisure to a recognition of family and other immediate communities as at least intervening variables between social structure and leisure. Leisure is more and more viewed as part of the

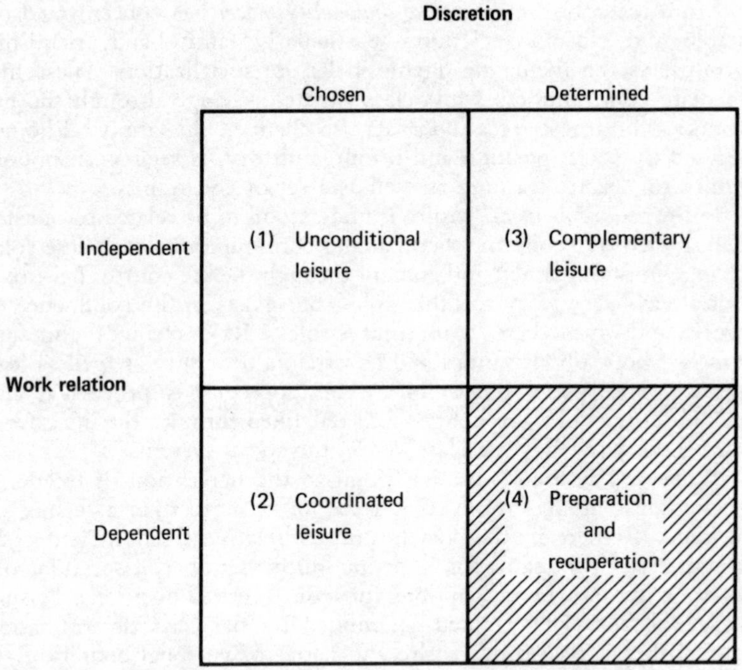

Discretion

	Chosen	Determined
Independent	(1) Unconditional leisure	(3) Complementary leisure
Dependent	(2) Coordinated leisure	(4) Preparation and recuperation

Work relation

Figure 1.1   Leisure: a simplified paradigm.

social space of family and community rather than the derived half of a 'work and leisure' pairing.

Social-Psychology Models
If there are values in both the approaches introduced – the psychological and the sociological, then it would appear that some union of the two would be even more productive. Beginning in the latter part of the 1970s such combined perspectives have been presented. The proponents are not all designated 'social-psychologists' as a distinct scholarly species, but tend to be eclectic sociologists who have followed the tradition of Max Weber in recognizing the necessity of incorporating the definitions of the social actor into explanatory theory.[19] More and more, such sociologists are beginning to join with psychologists who accept that attitudes are learned and altered in social contexts and that behavior is situated in social structures.

In one such united approach B. G. and Nancy Gunter have proposed a model that incorporates the psychological involvement of the person in activities or life styles and the structuring of time and

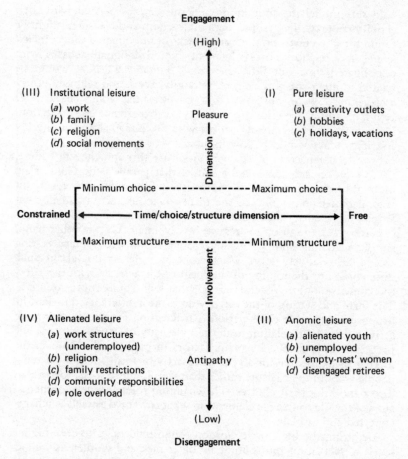

Figure 1.2   Involvement and choice in leisure.

events.[20] The degree of freedom of choice is found to be situated in the structure of time that is sociological in its embeddedness in social institutions such as work, family and religion. Social institutions regulate a rhythm of time in which the choices of leisure must be made. The more psychological *involvement* dimension includes the positive affectivity of enjoyment or self-fulfillment at one end and antipathy at the other. Choice within the time structure, then, may be either relatively free or constrained. Involvement may be positive or negative in affect or psychological outcome. They present a diagram that employs these two dimensions to distinguish four modes of leisure (Figure 1.2).

In this model the four kinds of leisure are associated with their activity contexts. *Pure leisure*, high on freedom and pleasure, might be found most in creative outlets and blocks of unobligated time. *Anomic leisure*, free but low on involvement, would designate activity with unobligated time but little direction. *Institutional leisure* would be related to other social roles such as family, work and religion. *Alienated leisure*, low on both freedom and pleasure, would characterize activity with little choice, opportunity, or experience of satisfaction. In general, the engagement of those who fill time in anomic or highly restricted ways would be low in intensity or satisfaction.

From a perspective of changes in leisure through the life course, Chad Gordon has developed a model that parallels the Gunters' in highlighting the intensity of expressive involvement. However, his second dimension is that of the forms of leisure activity.[21] For example, he proposes that games, sports and intense dance or religious experiences are high on expressive involvement. On the other hand, simply watching sports, reading, conversation and solitary resting would be relatively low. Whether he is right or not about such differentiation, the joining of the form of the activity with the affective dimension of involvement is one that will require more attention. The form and setting of the activity do make a difference. Further, he proposes that in life cycle periods participation in different forms of activities varies in relation to desired intensity of expressivity. While participation is shaped by many factors through the life course, the linking of expressive involvement to activity form focuses on what people want in their leisure rather than simply those social forces that direct and limit their choices. The changing roles and developmental aims of the life course are elements in what is wanted as well as what is expected and available.

Analyzing the life course Gordon found tendencies to seek higher levels of relaxation and solitude by older men and women as well as lower levels of diversion and sensual expression. However, developmental and creative leisure are only moderately related to lifespan stages. His analysis not only reports the decline in sport and entertainment types of leisure known to be associated with youth, but follows the 'career' of other forms of leisure in relation to developmental changes. Leisure as the expression of self through symbolic and pleasurable encounter with the environment is not just a feeling state, but is embedded in particular forms of activity.

In a sequence of studies of leisure roles in three communities Kelly has revised the dimensions of the work relation and relative freedom model to incorporate a dimension of meaning.[22] After discovering that adults seemed to value most their leisure that was defined as least free from role constraints, he designed his research to differentiate between positive values and the meeting of role expectations in social leisure involving intimates and friends. In general, the leisure that is embedded in primary roles and therefore robbed of the purity of being unconditionally for its own sake is also the leisure most adults would be least willing to give up.

By distinguishing between positive 'relational' satisfactions such as 'I enjoy the companionship', 'I feel I belong' and 'it strengthens relationships' from those that are role-determined such as 'expected to by family' and 'it's a duty', leisure interaction that is valued primarily for the experience can be distinguished from activity that first of all meets role expectations. Compensatory and recuperative outcomes were also found to be primary for some leisure choices. As a result, a revised model was developed that retains relative freedom as one dimension and distinguishes intrinsic from social leisure as dimensions of meaning. When types of activities were classified according to a ranking of perceived satisfactions by the participant, all four types of non-work activity were found significant. While activity that is highly role-determined might not be considered leisure at all by some definitions, it is an important kind of activity that is closely related to leisure in many forms and environments (Figure 1.3).

In this model not only is freedom retained as a central defining element, but the social meaning of leisure is stressed to recognize the reality of recuperation from the constraints of other roles and the centrality of primary-group interaction as a kind of leisure. Relational leisure is chosen first because of the interaction rather than the form of the activity or the locale. A closer examination of family leisure will be

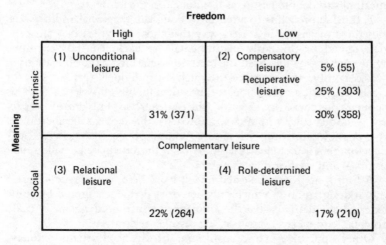

Figure 1.3 Percentages of activities in the revised paradigm.

introduced in Chapter 5. It is important to note at this point that an inclusion of positive social meanings of leisure choices unites the psychological findings that expressing and developing relationships are major desired outcomes from leisure with the sociological perspective of the contribution of leisure in building intimate communities within the larger social system.

The models that incorporate elements of meaning from psychology and of social context from sociology seem best equipped to deal with the fullness of a phenomenon that is both expressive and learned, done for its own sake and in response to social expectations, always an experience of the actor and more often that not an episode of social interaction.

Definitions of Leisure

What are the defining elements of leisure that differentiate it from other related phenomena? Certainly, the first is some element of freedom. Freedom may take the form of choice, discretion in the use of resources, perception of alternatives, or relative lack of coercion. In any case, at a minimum for an activity to be leisure, it must be chosen in a definition of the situation that it did not have to be done.

A second defining element would seem to be that at least in part the engagement is for its own sake. This has been expressed in a number of ways. The Aristotelian approach of intrinsic motivation has been held central by DeGrazia,[23] Neulinger,[24] Csikszentmihalyi[25] and Kelly.[26] Gordon offers the distinction between expressive and instrumental meanings to denote leisure as not done for 'greater ends'.[27]

A third approach is to attempt to designate the social and personal functions of leisure in such a way that those activities that are role-determined or primarily instrumental are excluded. For example, Dumazedier[28] defines leisure as 'activity – apart from the obligations of work, family, and society – to which the individual turns at will for either relaxation, diversion, or broadening his knowledge and his spontaneous social participation, the free exercise of his creative capacity'. One difficulty with such an approach is that it opens the question of the possible functions of leisure without being exhaustive. Self-development is included as legitimate but the anticipated development of first-hand relationships is not.

A fourth approach, rejected out of hand here, is to make leisure a moral designation in which only activities defined as 'good' by some external standard receive the accolade. Leisure need not be socially acceptable to be free, intrinsic, expressive, or creative.

Other approaches, once common, hardly need attention today. Leisure is known to be activity or experience chosen in the midst of a time framework, not time that is left over or residual. Also no list of activities however lengthy or precise – can encompass everything that can be leisure or exclude that which cannot. However, while some precision is necessary to further investigation and communication, the best definitions are those that make sense in a general cultural context. They should not be so esoteric or precious as to be meaningful only to a few self-selected scholars.

Among the current definitions combining simplicity with the inclusion of elements that provide at least fuzzy boundaries between leisure and other non-work are the following:

> Gordon: 'Leisure may therefore be conceptualized from the action perspective as discretionary personal activity in which expressive meanings have primacy over instrumental themes.'[29]

> Roberts: Leisure is 'relatively self-determined non-work activity'.[30]

> Kelly: 'Leisure is activity that is chosen primarily for its own sake.'[31]

Each of these definitions is based on the social-psychological perspective in incorporating both experiential and social dimensions. Each insists that leisure is 'doing something' in the sense of being chosen rather that being purely a state-of-mind. However, none limits the kind of activity, time, or space location, or the experience to something rarefied and elite. Also each at least comes close to what most people seem to mean by the term 'leisure is what I don't have to do'.

Varieties of Leisure

There has been a tendency to think of leisure in terms of activities that are aligned with the particular interests of the investigator or commentator. Those in community public recreation have stressed organized programs; physical education professionals have focused on sport; those in the arts on cultural enterprises; in the commercial world on activity requiring special locales or equipment; and resource managers on forest and water-based activity. In fact, none of these are the major kinds of leisure as measured by either time or value in North America or the United Kingdom.

Kenneth Roberts reports that the 'big five' in Britain today are not sports, the countryside and the arts, but rather TV, alcohol, tobacco, sex and gambling.[32] With a quarter of 'free time' devoted to watching TV, all else must follow when measured by frequency and duration of participation. Certainly, all kinds of locales of alcohol consumption along with all activity in which sexual interaction broadly defined is a major element encompass much of the social leisure not occupied by watching TV with others. However, Roberts still includes only activity that can be designated by form or use of a particular product or resource.

More comprehensively, leisure begins with all the informal interactions that take place throughout the day of those who live amid families, neighbors, friends and workmates. In the three North American communities adults were asked which kinds of leisure they valued most or would least want to give up. When a wide range of possibilities were presented, the results suggested that what is relatively informal and accessible takes precedence in importance as well as frequency. In rank order the kinds of activities were as in Table 1.1

Table 1.1   *Rank Order of 'Important Activities' in Three Communities*

(1) Marital affection and intimacy	(12) Short car trips
(2) Reading for pleasure	(13) Gardening and yard care
(3) Family conversation	(14) Home and shop projects
(4) Activity as a couple	(15) Arts or crafts
(5) Family outings	(16) Entertaining at home
(6) Visiting family and friends	(17) Hunting and/or fishing
(7) Play with children	(18) Child-centered events
(8) Watching TV	(19) Informal conversations
(9) Outdoor sports: individual or	including telephone
pair	(20) Hobbies: collecting, etc.
(10) Eating out	(21) Companionship on the job
(11) Religious worship	

Source: Kelly, 1982.

There were differences from community to community related to resources, climate and cultural interests. In the Pacific northwest camping ranked fifteenth; indoor activities were more important in a mill town with a long winter; and concerts, theatre and listening to music more valued among eastern suburb-dwellers with higher education levels. Further, in the eastern new town with its planned walkways and forest access, walking and jogging were ranked ninth. However, the overall consistency reinforces the summary that the leisure most important to most adults is social, familial, easily accessible and requires little special preparation or resources.

When this research was replicated with a small sample of forty adults in the British West Midlands new town of Telford in 1980, the rankings were not strikingly different. The rank order was: marital affection and intimacy; visiting family and friends; reading for pleasure; play with children; listening to music;* outdoor sports; short car trips; activity as a couple; family outings; vacation trips; watching TV; going to pubs or clubs;* and gardening. Family and social inter-action at home and using a car dominated the list.

Another approach is to examine national surveys for evidence that glamorous and media-promoted activities are unjustly neglected by conventional people reporting their routines and commonplace lives. However, the results yield the other side of the same coin. For example, in a National Household Survey completed in the United States in 1977, only 11 percent reported sailing during the previous year, 7 percent trying downhill skiing and 2 percent engaging in cross-country skiing. Activities such as scuba diving, hang gliding, surfing and other attention-getting risk sports were tried even once by less than one-half of 1 percent of the adult population.[33] Another approach to the question of what people do as leisure is to differentiate according to the scale of the social context. Leisure may be solitary, intimate, group, or mass in social setting.

Solitary Leisure
Considerable leisure is solitary in nature. Most reading is done alone or attempting to ignore others who may be present. Some walking, running, driving and other movement is also solitary. Contemplation is facilitated by being alone as are some forms of religious practice. At least one form of sexual activity may be solitary as is some engage-ment with hobbies and the arts. And then there is the phenomenon of being 'alone in a crowd' with the possibilities of daydreaming and fantasizing in which the environment is suspended or bracketed for a time. While TV may usually be watched in company and even in communication with others,[34] on some occasions it is a solitary activ-ity. Unfortunately, there has been little research into the special mean-ings of solitary leisure.

Intimate Leisure
Leisure with regular primary-group associates such as family and close friends may well be the major single category of activity. For those who are married, dyadic interaction – whatever its quality – is a major use of non-work time. Further, the satisfactions of such companion-ship are significant to the relationship itself. In much the same way both the nuclear and extended family provide the major social context of leisure. Cheek and Burch have presented evidence that outdoor recreation is familial roughly half the time with the exception of

*Asterisked activities were not on all US lists.

sports.[35] When family and friends are combined as 'intimates', then most outdoor recreation falls into this category. The same is true of entertaining, eating out, going to pubs and clubs, driving, vacations, outings to shopping centers and markets and going to church. In fact, far and away the most common social scale for leisure is that of primary groups, persons with whom we have quite regular interaction. This fact is of more than statistical interest. It suggests that a major basis of social solidarity as defined by Emile Durkheim may well be grounded in leisure interaction, that leisure makes a major contribution to social identification and cohesion.

Group Leisure

Leisure in social groups other than intimates may be less common but still important. When motivational and experiential dimensions of leisure are given attention, then group interaction is more than a context for leisure. Rather, it is frequently the central aim and content of the episode. While frequency and salience of group leisure that is not primarily familial or otherwise 'intimate' may decrease through the life course, there remain a number of social occasions and settings in which there is interaction with those outside the immediate circle of intimates. In some cases the party, institutional event, or setting is designed to facilitate interaction that remains essentially impersonal.

Mass Leisure

Some leisure is engagement with the mass culture, especially TV, motion pictures, music and other such media. In the case of concerts in major halls or stadiums such engagement may be termed mass leisure. As such, mass leisure is restricted to leisure that brings together so many people in one time and place that their relationships are essentially as well as functionally anonymous. Further, the very anonymity of the rock concert or football crowd is a part of its character. That mass quality may engender responses and meanings that would be quite out of place in a smaller group where identity may be quickly known. An analysis of one such setting, the skating 'roller derby', argues that the popularity enabling it to outdraw major sports in some cities despite being ignored by the media is based on its structure.[36] Affective participation by the mass of spectators is induced by the drama of violence, speed and physical encounter played out on the track. Both men and women are demonstrating skill in a familiar working-class activity with a highly charged competitive structure that permits identification with both teams and individual skaters. The emotional outbursts of 'spectators' are an intensification of that found in other sport and cultural mass events. This form of marketed and even contrived spectacle contrasts with the intimate context in its structural impersonality and mass response.

Investment and Intensity in Leisure

Reference to mass media immediately raises the question of the relative intensity of engagement. Not only is much TV watched in a state of fatigue, but often it is combined with conversation, eating and drinking, and even reading. TV may not have the cultural impact that its hours imply due to the low intensity of much watching. On the other hand, the intensity of engagement in some dyadic interaction including sexual intercourse, in a performance of music or theatre, or a peak experience in a sport, may be all out of proportion with the time elapsed. Just as flying has been character-ized as 'hours of boredom punctuated by a few moments of stark terror', so other activities may have the core of their meaning to the participant in a few moments of intense involvement. Leisure ac-tivity requires some qualitative analysis to be understood. It is more than a quantitative use of time or resources. Leisure is 'affective' in emotional involvement and investment.

Kenneth Roberts has suggested that leisure is essentially 'anomic' in its lack of clear and compelling social norms directing behavior.[37] The possibilities of innovation and invention are maxi-mized in leisure as they are minimized in a bureaucratic organiz-ation. However, Roberts goes on to recognize that such anomie is only relative and that leisure is influenced by the role norms of the various family, work and community positions occupied by indi-viduals.

A pluralistic approach suggests that leisure may be relatively anomic, alienated, role-determined, affective, or residual. Leisure may be central to self-definitions or peripheral. It may lead to self-actualization or be so inauthentic as to perpetuate alienation from human development. It may be freedom or a political instrument of repression, anomic or an element of social solidarity. And at some times in history leisure has been all these and more.[38] Although the orientation of this book is toward the *experience* of leisure and its manifestations in face-to-face groups and the more intimate social worlds, leisure has to be recognized as an element in a social milieu at once related to social institutions and yet not fully determined by them, responsive to social norms and ideologies and yet with an element of openness and indeterminancy, a social reality and yet resting on the premise of the existential reality of decision. The variety of leisure styles and settings together with its learned behav-iors and ethnic forms lead to the conclusion that leisure is a pluralistic phenomenon in the complexity and change of modern societies.

Sociologies of Leisure

Despite the previous plea for a combined sociological and psychological approach to leisure, incorporating both its social context and experiential quality, sociology remains the disciplinary base for the approach offered here. However, there is more than one way to do sociology. The most familiar begins with the institutions of the society and their integration into a mutually reinforcing and functioning system. This approach is called 'systemic' or 'structure functional' sociology. A second approach stresses the conflict potential of the society due to social divisions and differential power. It is based on the analysis of Karl Marx and is labeled 'conflict' or 'neo-Marxist' sociology. A third perspective begins not with the institutions of the social system, whether in conflict or equilibrium, but with the social actors who interpret their social environments and develop lines of action and interaction based on those interpretations. This approach is called 'interpretive' or 'symbolic interactionist' sociology.

In the past most Western sociology of leisure has tacitly or openly been of the systemic variety.[39] The terminology, selection of researchable questions, and theoretical strategies, have been based on the premisses of that variety of structural analysis. More recently there have been several proposals that the existential nature of leisure may require some research and theory development that begins with the more person-oriented interpretive model. The possibilities of contribution to sociological theory from an existential approach to the study of leisure are explored in Chapter 8. However, a number of key concepts that will be useful during our exploration of leisure identities and interactions needs to be introduced in a non-technical way here.

The Social System

From a systemic or structural perspective, the society is made up of a limited number of social institutions that are integrated in such a way as to provide for the maintenance and stability of the system. These institutions include the economy, government, education, family and church. The *function* of each is its contribution to the system. The functions of the family in Western societies, for example, are said to include reproduction, child nurture, sexual regulation and continuity of propertyholding. One debate is whether leisure is also an institution in modern society with the functions of 'intimate social bonding' and restoration for productive enterprise ('work') or is simply a social space secondary to the fundamental institutions.[40]

Within the social institutions individuals take their positions in the *roles* that together make up the institution. These roles are behavioral expectations associated with positions, are learned in the process known as *socialization* and together make up the basic social structure of the institution. For example, in the school students not only learn what is expected of them in their student role, but also the reciprocal behavior that can be expected of those in the role of teacher. Further, we learn that although individuals may define and enact roles somewhat differently, there are limits to those role definitions that we may cross only at the risk of penalty or sanctions.

From this perspective, the potential problem of the disintegration of the system is rendered unlikely by the general agreement on value orientations engendered through the nurturing, socialization and education processes of the system's institutions. Change in the system tends to be gradual as a response to inconsistencies created by innovations or external pressures.

Social Interaction

However, from an interpretive perspective, the social system is not quite that machinelike or integrated. To begin with, society is seen as more of a process in continual flux than a system. Any attempt to understand social interaction must incorporate that change or processual nature. Further, the regularities of the society are built up out of the learned interpretations of the social actors and are, therefore, subject to change as those definitions change. Social actors are continually defining and redefining not only those with whom they interact, but also themselves. They have *social identities* based on their positions in institutions but also *personal identities* as they define themselves. In social interaction the presentation of personal identities comes together with the social identities perceived by others in a process of identity-building and revision. Our personal identities are always subject to revision in the interaction process where all actors define the situation and each other and act in accordance with those definitions.

Roles, then, involve an interpretation of how the role will be enacted as well as of the general expectations associated with it.[41] Self-concepts, definitions of the self, or identities are developed in our essaying various roles and reading the feedback of others on our performances. Socialization is not only learning generalized role expectations, but also how we can use communicative symbol systems to comprehend the particular expectations of a situated role and to present how we intend to take the role. Social interaction, then, is a negotiated process employing a variety of symbols and signs rather than a mechanical occupation of predefined positions. In society we not only try out identities ourselves, but also 'cast' others in our expectations of how they will enact their roles.

In this negotiation social identities are developed in a reciprocal process of self-definition, presentation within a role context and interpretation of the responses of others. The concept of *role identity* has been formulated to refer to how we define ourselves in the roles that we essay.[42] Further, as we move through the course of our lives, we add and drop a variety of roles. The *life course* consists of the succession of roles taken through a lifetime, a succession that is related to age and to the opportunities and expectations of the society. In general, persons move from a *preparation* period (largely childhood and youth) through the *establishment* of family and economic positions and investments to an *integrative* period in which the limits of the lifespan are recognized and met.

The perspective of this book, then, is that of the interpretive sociologist or social psychologist concerned with leisure interaction as a context of identity development through the life course. Its presuppositions are those of a social existentialism that defines social interaction as the negotiation of interpreting actors who seek both continuity and change in their development of satisfying identities.

A Note on Conflict Sociology

The choice of the interpretive perspective is not intended to suggest that there is little or no value in either systemic or conflict models. Systemic sociology, the consensus approach of most Western sociologists, has already contributed much to the understanding of leisure in relation to social structures and institutions. Unfortunately, there has been relatively little research and theory-building from a conflict perspective.[43]

Perhaps the basic issue concerning leisure from a neo-Marxist set of assumptions is that of 'authenticity'. When the society is viewed as deeply divided with a minority establishing and maintaining power through their ownership and control of the means of economic production and power exercised through its institutions, then leisure may be one instrument of social control rather than a social space for the expression of the freedom essential for human development. Such use of leisure for social control is made possible by the 'false consciousness' of the exploited that renders them unable to recognize that they are being alienated from their own humanity. Through the mass media leisure comes to be identified not with freedom and creative expression, but with the possession and use of marketed products of the economy. This 'commodity fetishism' seduces the relatively powerless non-elites into believing that their work is adequately rewarded if they are able to purchase the packages of leisure that are sold and leased by both business and government. As a consequence, leisure becomes one more social space in which freedom is surrendered and authentic human development and interaction are lost to an acceptance of what the market offers.

The possibilities of inauthenticity and exploitation are certainly real in leisure as well as in work. Nor is the analysis of those possibilities in any way in conflict with an interpretive approach that concentrates on the social actor and the quality of leisure experience. In fact, precisely such analysis may be necessary if conflict analysis is to progress from assertions based on impressions and ideologies to an argument that is based on an understanding of what is happening to people in their leisure.

The Centrality of Leisure

One persistent theme of this presentation will also serve to introduce the following chapters. That is the theme of the centrality of leisure. If it were ever true in the early days of the Industrial Revolution that leisure was what was done only after all work was finished, it is not the case now. Partly because leisure, at least in the sense of daydreaming and interspersed moments of spontaneous interaction, takes place in almost every work situation, and partly because for many people the task and obligations of social roles are never fully met, leisure is chosen out of and in the midst of constraints. It is not leftover.

However, from the perspective of this book, leisure is central even more because it may be a crucial life space for the expression and development of selfhood, for the working out of identities that are important to the individual. Adolescence is only one life course period in which leisure settings and interactions may be most salient in the building of self-definitions of social and physical competence, exploring other-sex relationships and seeking social support for emerging independence. Right or wrong, for many youth it may be school and work that are leftover or at least secondary in personal investment.

Finally, leisure has increasingly been found to be central to the maintenance of the society itself as a social space for the development of intimacy. While a social system requires cohesion and solidarity on the larger scales of localized, national and international communities, there is still the question of primary or face-to-face community. Leisure not only contributes times and places for exploring relationships that may lead to familial commitment, but also the varied times and places in which marriage and family cohesion and affection are enhanced and expressed. Leisure is the social space of friendship, of much parenting and nurture, of community interaction and of the family itself. The affective and expressive elements not only of personal identities, but of the stable and reliable interaction groups around and through which our lives are built, are to a considerable extent those of leisure.

This is why sociologists may have been off-target when looking first at work and leisure rather than at leisure and the family, at social position rather than immediate communities and at status and class rather than taste and culture. Leisure is expressive culture, inter-actional more than organizational, and a matter of choice as well as determination.

In the chapters that follow we will re-examine leisure from this perspective. Certainly, a persistent theme will be that of the centrality of leisure to identities and to social interaction. The first section, consisting of Chapters 2–4, begins in Chapter 2 with a review of leisure styles in relation to social factors such as ethnicity, age, sex, work and social position. In the same chapter, the significance of access to resources for leisure choices will precede a review of the leisure socialization processes.

Chapter 3 examines changes in leisure through the life course. The focus will be on the meanings of leisure in relation to life course role transitions rather than on changes in what people do.

In Chapter 4 attention will be more on the self as developed and expressed in leisure. Who we are is a matter of nurture as well as nature, of both intent and feedback. Leisure as a critical social space in which identities are tried out, modified and confirmed may lead us into major investments in leisure. These investments of identity sali-ence rather than money can place a very heavy affective load on leisure action and interaction.

Part Two moves more to the social contexts of leisure. Chapter 5 concentrates on that primary context, the family. Leisure as family interaction as well as the significance of leisure to the quality of marriage and family life through the life course leads to an examination of leisure and intimacy. Issues of family-related social trends are also outlined and their implications for leisure suggested.

Chapter 6 probably contains the most material new to leisure stud-ies literature. Here face-to-face interaction is the focus of analysis. Leisure settings, occurrences and events are examined in the process of interaction and in the meanings of such interaction processes for actors and for social roles and institutions.

In Chapter 7 some of the implications of the preceding analysis for leisure planning and provisions, especially for the public sector, are drawn out. A general model for developing priorities for planning is presented.

Chapter 8 is an attempt to develop a framework in which leisure sociology can begin to contribute to sociological theory. The social model of a dialectic between existential and structural elements is introduced as the basis for an analysis of the significance of leisure identities and interactions.

References: Chapter 1

1   Robert J. Havighurst, 'The nature and values of meaningful free time activity', in *Aging and Leisure*, ed. R. W. Kleemeier (New York: Oxford University Press, 1961), p. 317.

2   John R. Kelly, 'Leisure styles and choices in three environments', *Pacific Sociological Review*, no. 21, 1978, pp. 187–207.

3   R. Crandall, 'Motivations for leisure', *Journal of Leisure Research*, no. 12, 1980, pp. 45–54.

4   J. R. Kelly, 'Leisure: a simplified paradigm', *Journal of Leisure Research*, no. 4, 1972, pp. 50–62.

5   Sebastian DeGrazia, *Of Time, Work, and Leisure* (Garden City, NY: Doubleday/Anchor, 1964).

6   Kenneth Roberts, *Contemporary Society and the Growth of Leisure* (London: Longman, 1978).

7   Joffre Dumazedier, Foreword to *Leisure and Popular Culture in Transition*, 2nd edn, ed. Thomas M. Kando (St Louis, Mi: Mosby, 1980), p. ix.

8   Neil H. Cheek and William R. Burch, *The Social Organization of Leisure in Human Society* (New York: Harper & Row, 1976).

9   Stanley J. Parker, *The Future of Work and Leisure* (New York: Praeger, 1971).

10   J. R. Kelly, *Leisure*: Englewood Cliffs, NJ: Prentice-Hall, 1982).

11   B. G. Gunter, and Nancy C. Gunter, 'Leisure styles: a conceptual framework for modern leisure', *Sociological Quarterly*, no. 21, 1980, pp. 361–74.

12   J. G. Beard and Ragheb Mounir, 'Measuring leisure satisfaction', *Journal of Leisure Research*, no. 12, 1980, pp. 20–33.

13   John Neulinger, *The Psychology of Leisure* (Springfield, Ill.: Charles C. Thomas, 1974).

14   M. Csikszentmihalyi, *Beyond Boredom and Anxiety* (San Francisco: Jossey-Bass, 1975).

15   B. L. Driver and Perry J. Brown, *The Opportunity Spectrum Concept and Behavioral Information in Outdoor Recreation Resource Supply Inventories*, Rocky Mountain Forest and Experiment Station, Fort Collins, Colorado, USA, 1978.

16   B. L. Driver, *Quantification of Outdoor Recreationists' Preferences*, Proceedings of Penn State HPER Symposium on 'Research, Camping, and Environmental Education', 1976.

17   Rhona Rapoport and Robert L. Rapoport, *Leisure and the Family Life Cycle* (London: Routledge & Kegan Paul, 1975).

18   Kelly, 1972, op. cit., n. 4.

19   J. R. Kelly, 'Sociological perspectives and leisure research', *Current Sociology*, no. 22, 1974, pp. 127–58.

20   Gunter and Gunter, op. cit.

21   Chad Gordon, 'Development of evaluated role identities', in *Annual Review of Sociology* (Calif.: Annual Reviews, Inc., 1980), pp. 405–33.

22   J. R. Kelly, 'A revised paradigm of leisure choices', *Leisure Sciences*, no. 1, 1978, pp. 345–63.

23   DeGrazia, op. cit.

24   Neulinger, op. cit.

25   Csikszentmihalyi, op. cit.

26   Kelly, 1972, op. cit., n. 4.
27   Gordon, op. cit.
28   Joffre Dumazedier, *Toward a Society of Leisure* (New York: The Free Press, 1967),
     pp. 16–17.
29   Chad, Gordon, C. Gaitz and J. Scott, 'Leisure and lives: personal expressivity
     across the life span, in *Handbook of Aging and the Social Sciences*, eds. R. Binstock
     and E. Shanas (New York: Van Nostrand Reinhard. 1976).
30   Roberts, 1978, op. cit., p. 3.
31   Kelly, 1982, op. cit., n. 10.
32   Roberts, op. cit., p. 28.
33   Kelly, 1982, op. cit.
34   Roberts, op. cit., p. 96.
35   Cheek and Burch, op. cit., p. 16.
36   George H. Lewis, *Side-Saddle on the Golden Calf* (Pacific Palisades, Calif.:
     Goodyear, 1972), pp. 42–9.
37   Roberts, op. cit., p. 89.
38   Kelly, 1982, op. cit., 3–6.
39   Kelly, 1974, op. cit.
40   Cheek and Burch, op. cit., ch. 6.
41   Gordon *et al.*, op. cit.
42   George McCall, J. Simmons and J. L. Simmons, *Identities and Interactions*, rev. ed
     (New York: The Free Press, 1978), p. 65.
43   Kelly, 1974, op. cit.

Part One

Styles of Leisure: Variety and Meaning

The wide spectrum of activities and environments that can be chosen for leisure is only the beginning. Leisure ranges from intensely personal experience to the development of role relationships and from momentary dallying to sustained investment. Individuals vary in both what they do as leisure and how they do it. The crucial question is 'why?'

In the three chapters that follow, we will examine ways of approaching answers to that question. The first approach is essentially structural. The social contexts of leisure may include many dimensions, but together they are offered as the primary factors that shape leisure decisions and styles. However, two sources of doubt are implicit in the structural model of explanation. The first is the generally low correlation between such factors and participation differences. The second is based on the observation that the variety in how leisure is undertaken, in styles, may be more significant than the variation in what is done.

Nevertheless, leisure is not unrelated to its social and environmental contexts, totally idiosyncratic and esoteric. One approach that allows for both variation in styles and some explanation of regularities is based on the life course. As we make our way through the journey of life, we encounter a number of rather predictable role changes. Those role changes alter both the opportunity contexts and the expectations for leisure behavior and attitudes. Styles and orientations of leisure change as we move through the life course.

Related to life course changes is the development of our identities, who we are to ourselves and to others. Leisure is one life space in which we may develop our self-definitions and present them to others. Leisure, then, is not just a product of social forces exterior to the self, but is at least in part a consequence of our definitions and decisions. Part One explores such social and psychological elements in contemporary leisure styles.

2

Variations in Leisure styles

In Chapter 1 something of the variety in leisure activity, social environments and meanings has been introduced. Now we begin to turn to the question of 'why?' concerning the demonstrated variety. One approach proposes that leisure is a segmented element of life, essentially an experience that has its own meanings. This separatist view of leisure may even suggest that the experience of leisure is very special and reserved to a few persons whose life conditions transcend the ordinary constraints and values of a culture.[1] Leisure becomes a precious and rare condition of the 'soul' when an elitist perspective is adopted. Less exclusively leisure may be viewed as simply a set of emotions or 'state-of-mind'. This segmentalist view may deal with environmental constraints tangentially, but is more likely to concentrate on psychological constructs as the main limiting factors.

At the other extreme, a deterministic approach takes leisure as the dependent variable. Models are constructed that attempt to explain leisure totally in terms of other factors, usually economic or social. Leisure in this view is usually defined as activity that takes up time and is constrained by and contributes to the presumed central institutions of the social system work, family and the state, or for students, the school.

However, there is a third possibility. It is that leisure is neither determined by social and environmental factors nor fully independent of them. The social context of leisure does influence what is seen as possible, desirable and enjoyable. Leisure is, after all, learned behavior and the learning takes place in our social relationships. Leisure is viewed as neither wholly enmeshed in prior elements nor separate from them. Rather, the most realistic model is 'pluralistic'.[2,3] Leisure does vary according to its social context. Not only what people do, but how they engage in leisure is differentiated by a number of social and cultural factors. Styles vary, perhaps even more than the choice of the activities themselves. With whom we have learned the activity generally shapes how we go about it. There are so many ways to eat, drink, play, converse, travel and entertain that styles differ widely.

On the other hand, leisure is not wholly determined by any external factor or set of factors. Leisure retains an existential dimension, a reality of freedom. We do choose – at least within a range of perceived possibilities – what we will do, how we will do it, and with whom we participate. Leisure is a pluralistic phenomenon, related to its contexts and yet not fully determined. Social rules and expectations have influence, but are interpreted by the actor to preserve a latitude of behavioral responses.

From this perspective, we can go on to examine the external influences on leisure without adopting a deterministic model. The issue is more than how particular activities are selected. Styles of participation may be more significant than the activity itself. Cultural factors, position in the social structure, opportunities and barriers, and particularities of socialization through the life course are combined in the lifelong process of leisure development.[4]

Only an introduction to the external influences on leisure can be attempted here. What follows is an outline of cultural and historical, social and opportunity dimensions of leisure socialization. In a suggestive rather than exhaustive analysis this chapter is preparation for the more intensive examination of life course role and identity changes.

Cultural and Historical Factors

Culture, the learned and transmitted elements of life, is woven through everything we do. For example, the meanings of eating together in some cultures prescribe sets of responsibilities and privileges that extend past meal times and places. One who breaks bread becomes a guest rather than a stranger. On the other hand, in urban fast-food settings, norms of anonymity apply among people literally brushing elbows while eating. Eating is more than taking nourishment; it is laden with expectations and customs that prescribe its styles and its meanings. Not only such social norms of culture, but also technological use, interaction styles and complex sets of rules must be learned in order to participate in most leisure.

The Ethnicity of Leisure

All interaction is ethnic in the sense of having content made up of the learned particularities of the culture. Again just how one carries out the behaviors expected in a specific situation involves more than a general acceptance of a role. To be a waiter at an expensive restaurant with a clientele expecting a high degree of attentiveness and deference is quite different from serving in a truck-stop. And the differences are reciprocal. Being served in one such situation in a style appropriate to the other could lead to expulsion in a way also culture-determined.

How is the game played? The degree of overt competitiveness acceptable in a sport such as tennis has changed, especially since its professionalization. How are overtures of interest essayed at a party? Behavior quite acceptable at an American college 'mixer' would elicit swift retribution by a male family member in many oriental cultures. The point is that leisure is ethnic, learned in the particularities of a culture.

In a comparison of leisure in two new towns, one in the United States and the other in the British Midlands, the kinds of leisure important to adults were remarkably similar. Despite marked education and occupational differences between the samples, both valued immediate community interaction most highly as their leisure.[5] Marital interaction, play with children, visiting family or friends and family outings ranked with reading, listening to music and outdoor sports as the favored types of leisure. However, differences of style were observed. For example, meeting friends in the pub was common in the UK social pattern while in the USA entertaining at home was usual. Family roles seemed different with the expectations for direct conversational interaction and sharing higher in the American families.

In an analysis of racial differences in outdoor recreation participation in the United States a 'cumulative deprivation' explanation of differences was advanced.[6] When financial resources and access to hotels, swimming-pools and beaches, and socializing institutions such as universities, were systematically denied one racial group, then the consequences are not immediately altered just by changes in law and social acceptance. The range of opportunities perceived as viable have produced sets of interests that will change only over a period of new socialization possibilities. Evidence that black people are now increasing their rates of participation in natural-resource-based recreation attests to changes both in personal resources and perceived access. However, learning to value what had been denied is a change process with differential rates among cohorts. The cumulative deprivation explanation partly accounts for the current increase in forest and water activities particularly among younger blacks.

The ethnicity of leisure does not deny environmental influences on participation styles. Rather, the styles learned are specific to the groups in which we find our social identity. The ways we play, converse, eat and drink, and otherwise interact are those we have learned among those who are 'our people'. Further, those styles serve to preserve and strengthen the identity of the group and give members a sense of being part of a collectivity that is real. Something of who we are is found in the ethnicity of our leisure associations.

Technological Change

Nevertheless, culture is more than the learned behavioral styles of our ethnic groups. There are technological innovations that may cross cultural barriers when they are diffused by the world markets or other means. Modes of adoption may be ethnic, but the impacts transcend even language differences.

Certainly, the two technological developments that have had the greatest impact on leisure in Western nations in this century are the car and TV. The car has revolutionized the mobility of populations across age and ethnic barriers. In fact, the leisure provisions of both public and market sectors generally presuppose the mobility of such private motorized transportation. Especially in North America the entire ecology of everyday leisure is auto-dependent.[7] With similarly striking impacts, the diffusion of TV in North America and Western Europe has made every time-use study prior to 1960 of only historical interest. Whatever the variations in intensity of use, the availability of low-cost inhome entertainment has done more than replace older technologies. TV has become the primary medium transmitting sport, the arts, language and social information to almost every household.

A more recent innovation has been the transistor and its miniaturized radio. At extremely low cost the musical offerings of the world are now at hand (and at ear) for those who wish to move through the world accompanied by such sound. As a result, one of the first impressions gained in multinational travel is that the music accompanying the life of teens sounds much the same. The common language is English and the musical aggregations are similar from California to Oslo and from Stockholm to Naples. Reproduction by video and audio means has permitted adoption of musical modalities across cultures by age cohorts until cultural definitions are blurred.

Interaction Styles

The varieties of ways in which different groups perform much the same social functions suggest the shaping power of culture on leisure. Examples are as numerous as studies of leisure settings. Again bars and pubs vary in their constituencies and consequent behavioral expectations. The stories of those who have stumbled unaware into public houses with quite specific clienteles reinforce the significance of such cultures. In North America there are bars with behavioral patterns 'developed to expedite the social styles and goals of unmarried adults seeking new contacts, male or female homosexual groups, married adults seeking temporary liaisons, teens in groups rather than couples, family groups, and so on. Some such establishments have backrooms with restricted admission and quite rigorous rules for exchange. In societies characterized by considerable cultural plural-ism leisure may exhibit segregated locales that facilitate different interaction styles. Again the rigor and pervasiveness of the dif-ferentiated norms and customs are illustrated by the potential of embarrassment, humor and even danger when applied in the wrong setting.

Despite such differences, styles of interaction in leisure settings also tend in some ways to reflect the general culture. For example, there are many ways in which the same set of fifty-two cards are employed in games. The variations of rules from one game to another may be no greater than the differences in second-level rules or conventions specific to the style expected in the specific setting. However, the games themselves at least in part mirror the type of society in which they are developed.

The card game of contract bridge has been analyzed not only as a middle-class but as a bourgeois game, a derivation of the capitalist social system in which it was created.[8] Contract bridge, a variation on the older game of whist, was created by a capitalist (a Vander-bilt, no less) on an ocean cruise to add excitement to the older game. However, it was an entrepreneur, Ely Culbertson, who refined and marketed the new system. Including a series of terms connoting sexual encounter – 'forcing bid', 'covering my honor' and 'trick' are examples – Culbertson promoted a game that is based on the risks of contracting and the penalities of failure. While the attributes of good bridge-playing – cool and restrained calcula-tion – are those assumed to be possessed by successful males in bourgeois society, up to 75 percent of bridge-players are women. Thus, the game offers middle-class women an opportunity to play at a market surrogate and even play aggressively. In the play world that does not have consequences in the real world of business the game episode provides an opportunity for calculated risktaking that has non-serious but measured results. It thus reflects the capitalist cultural ethos, permits the sexual encounter until recently largely excluded in the real world of business, and still does not threaten sex role exclusions and divisions. It is, then, a distinctively capitalist game.

Without belaboring the point, there are ample indications that forms of leisure are partly shaped by the cultural ethos in which they are developed. This would seem to be the case on a microlevel that differentiates styles of playing the same game as well as macro-levels distinguishing the forms of the games themselves.

Culture, then, is one dimension in the content of leisure. What is consumed, played, encountered and observed in leisure events is of the culture. Culture is a resource of leisure. Further, what is defined as a viable opportunity for leisure is culturally shaped. Activities and resources that are central to the perceived opportunity contexts of one group may not even be defined as leisure by another.

Just as important, the styles of engagement with opportunities and resources are shaped by cultural definitions. As new technologies are made available, the mode of their adoption or rejection differs according to the norms that develop within a culture. Just how we come and go, act and react, speak and listen, vary according to what we have learned in our socialization histories.

Social Factors

The initial approach to accounting for variations in leisure behavior reflected the simplest research mode of the sociologists studying the issue. Correlational analysis of types of leisure participation with social aggregate variables was followed by a series of somewhat more sophisticated models. All along, there was an underlying question: when differences were found, what did they mean? For example, can greater bar and pub visiting by working males in blue-collar neighborhoods be attributed to alienation from satisfying work, segregated family roles, lack of space in the residence, a desire for peer interaction and acceptance, or some combination of such factors?

The following discussion is intended as an introduction to the life course approach to leisure identities and interactions. However, an institutional approach to leisure requires more than assessing the magnitude and significance of correlations. Always there is the question: *what does it mean?*

The Social Aggregate Trap

All of us tend to deal with problems in some familiar framework and attack them with familiar tools. It is no surprise that when sociologists were drawn to the investigation of leisure, the first line of attack would be to employ survey methods to seek relationships between social position variables and leisure participation. Further, when the approach could be sold to government agencies as the most probable way to predict participation and serve as a basis for planning, then such surveys were given at least occasional financial support.

The premise was that social aggregates – segments of the population who did not interact, but could be identified by common characteristics such as age or type of occupation – would be found to have distinctive leisure patterns. Especially when some of the early research compared quite different occupational groups such as professors and laborers on such status-related items as membership in community voluntary organizations, significant differences were discovered.

Compounding the problem was the now-evident artefact that statistical significance is often found in large samples when the substantive variation is rather small. Nevertheless, the common wisdom was that social status variables were able to 'predict' important differences in leisure behavior.

In time, the common wisdom was found to be less than adequate. Although certain relationships remained – the bourgeoisie disproportionately join community organizations, youth play team sports, men go to bars and the poor do not take up downhill skiing or sailing – people seemed to have more in common than previously suspected. Further, there appears to be much in common in the leisure of those in an age cohort that crosses social status lines.[9] Also Roberts suggests that there may have been some changes since the earlier research efforts in the 1950s and 1960s.[10] A greater diffusion of interests and opportunities may have reduced stratification differences in leisure, at least on the simple level of the types of activities engaged in. Money, transportation, smaller families and housing disperson have all had impacts on leisure.

However, a more fundamental problem also threatened the model. The level of analysis was seen as inappropriate for the study of the phenomenon. The independent variables aggregated, on the basis of one or more shared characteristics, individuals who did not share items much more important to understanding leisure behavior. Especially when it was found that face-to-face communities of families and friends seemed to be the primary leisure socialization influences,[11,12] the aggregation approach seemed theoretically tangential.

At the same time, the dependent variable was also being questioned. 'Participation' was often measured simply as having done an activity once during the previous month or year. Sometimes multiple occurrences were measured. In any case, the failure to differentiate the varieties of locales for 'swimming', styles of 'parties' or 'entertaining', or playing ball with one's children from a competitive adult league, raised questions about what was being measured. Especially common activities such as reading, walking, or even fishing were seen to encompass such a spectrum of behaviors to render simple participation categories substantively vague.

Refocusing the Analysis
A number of suggestions were offered by those beginning to question the aggregate correlational approach. All in some way replace the statistical aggregate with groupings of individuals who do in fact interact. One version of the shift was proposed by Field and O'Leary, who proposed that leisure be analyzed in terms of 'social action systems' that identify the type of social group that joins in learning

and doing the activity.[13] Reinforcing this approach was the increasing evidence that a high proportion of regular leisure is closely related to family interaction.[14] While family and peer social action systems may vary according to their social placement and socialization opportunities, the immediate communities are both the agents of leisure learning and the usual companions for participation.

The kinds of independent variables employed in surveys – income, occupation, education level, age, sex, race and indices of social status were now understood as indicators of socialization probabilities. Rather than referring to social status as a direct 'determinant' of leisure, status was defined as an indication of the kind of interests and opportunities likely to be a part of a person's experience. Leisure socialization was then viewed as a process carried on in company with a series of intimate others through the life course.

Nevertheless, the continued stratification of the social system was still held as an essential element in the social context of leisure. While there might be more differences than uniformity in activities chosen within a status category such as 'middle-income white-collar suburban parents', there remain as well some important differences in resources and opportunities. At the very least, being poor fundamentally restricts the range of leisure that is possible, especially that which requires costly travel or private space. Yet, even for the poor, the varieties of leisure choices and styles and the overlap in activities with the more affluent made clearcut differentiation difficult.

The Multivariate Model
At the same time, the increased sophistication of computer statistical programs permitted new kinds of examination of the same kinds of data. It became possible to enter a number of variables into equations in ways that could assess both their relative and combined power to account for differences. Such methods were less subject to sample size bias and more precise in measuring just how much statistical variation is present.

The results, combined with the new focus on groups rather than aggregates, places the previous common wisdom in jeopardy. In the United Kingdom Kenneth Roberts adds technological innovation, mobility given by the car, new awareness of what is possible and desirable, and relatively undifferentiated amusements of the mass media and common entertainments to the demographic and income changes to account for the blurring of presumed class differences.[15] William Bacon has analyzed both national surveys and Sheffield-area workers to conclude that the weight of the evidence would seem to be that sharp divisions among social strata cannot now be located.[16] The evidence of broadening of opportunities may be intensified by less clearcut divisions in the class system of British society. The manual workers studied were affluent enough to own cars, defined their work in terms of extrinsic rewards, pursued a relatively home- and family-centered life and were influenced by the responsibilities of parenthood.

In North America a variety of analyses has led to much the same conclusions. Analysis of a 1973 national survey in the United States began with finding that the most common leisure activities are those that are not status-differentiated: reading newspapers, watching TV, visiting friends and relatives, other reading, listening to music, driving and walking for pleasure, and dining out.[17] An analysis by the author of a 1977 household survey of outdoor recreation participation employed several multivariate methods that separated out the contribution of each demographic and social position variable from the others. Especially with multiple regression analysis, the results reinforced the growing consensus that leisure choices are not sharply differentiated.[18] Sex, age, family life cycle period, race, family income, occupation and education level together accounted for only 7–9 percent of the variance in combined forest, water-based and sport participation, and 0–3 percent for single activities such as hiking, picnicking, sailing, swimming, tennis, skiing, camping, golf and waterskiing. Sex did account for 6 percent of the variation in fishing and 10 percent for hunting. With the dependent variables still the old ones of participation frequency, the results are that similarities outweigh differences.

Jiri Zuzanek has studied similar data for Canada and concluded that an egalitarian pattern characterizes leisure when measured by participation rates.[19] However, there are differences by income for expenditures and of total time for leisure related to certain status and occupation variables. Differences are most pronounced when the dependent variables are resource-specific or costly activities, related to the amount of discretionary income available or to factors that shape personal timetables. In the same way, in the United States differences in activities that are highly age- or sex-differentiated show significant variation. However, in general, when these specifics are controlled, the remaining variance accounted for by traditional social categories is minor.

As a consequence, the once-casual generalizations about prediction and determination have become less and less global. There remain important differences. However, they are either less dramatic than was the case in 1960, were not measured as accurately as now, or both. As will be examined next, when participation is the dependent variable, the significant relationships to background factors tend to be rather specific. Also there may remain quite important differences in *how* the same activity is undertaken.

Age and Leisure Participation

Even beyond the obvious changes in leisure or play through child-hood development, there are significant shifts in leisure participation related to age. Some of the changes reflect altered opportunities such as the loss of a number of team sport and arts opportunities on leaving school. Others are related to diminishing physical prowess in later years, reduced income at retirement, or the responsibilities of parenting for those with young children. The effects of age and family life cycle change cannot be easily disengaged, so that multi-variate analysis controlling one variable generally has only minor variation remaining for the other to explain.

Some of the age-related changes are essentially self-explanatory. For example, team sport participation drops off sharply in school-leaving years, individual and pair sport engagement dips at the same time and then drops even more sharply in the forties, and resource-based outdoor recreation such as fishing, camping, or hiking shows a steady decrease with age.[20] On the other hand, a sport such as golf indicates no real drop in participation until the sixties. Nevertheless, age is associated with a shift away from physical activity and toward home-based activity and social interaction.

The family life cycle affects not only what is done, but why and with whom. While courting and marriage do not radically change the activities themselves, in the process the primary companion more and more becomes the 'intimate other'. Especially for the parents of young children, not only do home-based familial activities tend to replace leisure that requires travel and blocks of time, but the orientations of leisure change.[21] For parents of young children, nurturing responsibilities not only constrain leisure, but become a primary satisfaction. Being with spouse and children, developing patterns of satisfying interaction and supporting and joining older children in their developing recreational and educational interests are central elements of leisure. Family interaction is itself a major leisure activity that is carried out in a variety of contexts including home, car, outdoor resources and shopping centers.

There has been considerable attention given to the differential impacts of aging and family responsibilities on men and women. A British survey found that family responsibilities have a more marked impact on the sport participation of mothers than fathers.[22] Further, men seem more likely to return to some sport engagement in middle years than do women. However, all research that compares different age cohorts at the same time rather than the same cohorts at succeeding times may reflect social change more than age-related differences. It may well be that men and women who are in their twenties today will be rather different in twenty years from those who are in their forties now.

Further, there may be age-related changes in the meanings of leisure as well as in the activity choices themselves. For example, Chad Gordon and associates found a number of age-related leisure changes.[23] Among them were the following:

- The older the respondent, the lower the general level of leisure activity, the narrower the range of activities, the less 'intense' its forms, the less physically demanding, and the more likely to be at home.
- However, in this nonlongitudinal study, the proportion of those seeking developmental goals was not strongly related to life course period and for men creativity aims actually increased in the later years.

It would seem that a number of factors are indexed by age. Not only physical ability, but access to resources, age-appropriate expectations, non-leisure responsibilities and orientations, and psychological development are all factors in leisure. In time, improved resources and new definitions of what is appropriate for older people to do may alter many of the declines found today in cross-sectional research.

Sex and Leisure Participation
Differences in participation in most leisure activities between men and women in the United States are negligible or non-existent. Women swim, walk, bowl, play tennis, attend movies and concerts, garden, give parties, watch TV and drive at essentially the same rates as men.[24] They read and shop for pleasure somewhat more. Only hunting, fishing, team sports, golf and drinking in bars have significantly more male participants. These are activities in which the sex role norms are quite different and from which, to a large extent, females have been systematically excluded. The large differences in hunting and drinking rates reflect the particularly masculine aura of those activities.

However, such figures only begin to distinguish sex role differences in leisure. Women, in most leisure settings, are expected to behave rather differently from men. The behavioral expectations at a party, at the racket club or even the racetrack, and at the swimming-pool or beach, call for self-presentations, clothing, walking, approaching persons of the other sex, display of skills and same-sex modes of interaction that are sex-specific. While the range of acceptable behaviors for females is widening to include demonstrations of competence and initiative formerly labeled as unfeminine, for the most part we are able to assign sexual identification to styles of interaction.

Further, the societal roles of women have impacts on their leisure far beyond opportunities structures and behavioral norms in leisure settings. Particular attention has been given to women whose life chances are limited by their family background and current resources. Women of working-class backgrounds who are the mothers of young children in families supported by the modest and often uncertain wages of an unskilled or semi-skilled worker seem to have little of the freedom characteristic of true leisure. In a British study the regular visiting of kin was less than liberating. However, family and friend interaction was the main dimension of leisure for such wives, especially when they were not employed and had ongoing responsibility for young children.[25] On the other hand, the stereotype of the husband who is always off with his 'mates' was not supported. In fact, the working-class husbands were less likely to go out without their wives than the middle-class men. Nevertheless, the general picture of leisure constrained by role responsibilities, uncertainties in relationships, limited resources and a generally narrow view of life's possibilities is found in both British and American studies.

A North American study of working-class families in California stresses the limiting of leisure and self-development due to the interweaving of factors of sex role socialization, failures in marital communication, uncertain incomes from working husbands and a lack of independent income, pressures to care for children and a general atmosphere that the task of life is just to get through the hassles of the day.[26] Leisure is set in the context of the entire history and contemporary environments of the women who have to settle for less than expressive and enriching experiences of self-development and fulfillment.

It is no accident of methodologies that age and sex are more strongly correlated with participation in some leisure activities than any other variables. Our societies are stratified by both age and sex with opportunities and expectations that are highly differentiated in some areas. Further, age and the family life cycle are intertwined in their combined effects. However, the influences of age and sex are not independent from social class or status differences. What is open to and expected of males and females, the young and the aging, are partly shaped by the social contexts and chances related to social position. Leisure in contemporary societies is multivariate as the particular situational elements in leisure vary by occupation, income, residential setting, ethnicity and educational experience in ways that are combined with age and sex. However, such social factors appear to be more related to style than which activities are chosen.

Social Position and Leisure

As suggested above, the indices of social position taken together do not account for much of the variance in what people do as leisure.[27] Perhaps the older descriptions of the industrial city with its dramatic constriction of the lives of workers and incredibly lavish leisure styles of the affluent elites are now dated. Social change may have brought about not only increases in the financial resources of 80–90 percent of the society to a level permitting some discretionary spending for leisure, but also a democratization and diffusion of leisure interest and styles.[28] Changes in working-class life include a five-day work week, higher incomes, the car, private residence, TV and a measure of relative security that permits some planning.[29] Together with smaller families, a shorter childrearing period, longer lives with better health, general basic education and the development of a variety of commercial and public leisure resources has come a greater awareness of both the opportunities and legitimacy of some leisure enjoyment. Therefore, the sharp cleavages of leisure once based on social class have become softened and blurred by technologies, the availability of resources, and perhaps altered attitudes as well.[30]

It might then be more accurate to investigate social position as a single complex variable rather than a series of discrete items entered into a marginally revised equation. Max Weber defined social status as a matter of style. Leisure styles are interwoven with other elements of life style. While styles are not rigidly determined, social position does often index different modes of camping, drinking, entertaining, travel and theater-going. Supporters of the symphony and Shakespearean theater are disproportionately those with higher education, who in turn are most likely to have been reared in homes of higher social position.[31] In the United States styles of forest use are partly differentiated by the pickup truck and hunting-fishing orientation of the non-elites vs the backpacking or sports-car style of light camping of younger persons with at least a college education. In both the United Kingdom and North America types of public houses and styles of drinking appear to be increasingly social-status-differentiated. The first sign of such clientele specialization is in the type of music that can be heard through the conversation. What is suggested here is that the particularities of how and with whom we engage in our leisure remains influenced by our educational and social histories even when national surveys indicate little variation in the generic activities themselves. Further, social position – usually indicated best in relation to leisure by education – is a complex variable that represents the probabilities of a socialization history coupled with considerable chance idiosyncratic experience.

Also some differences are worth noting even when it remains true that variation within a social category is almost always greater than differences between categories. In Britain the amount of TV-watching falls off somewhat as education level increases and tends to be replaced by social interaction.[32] In Canada education was also found to be the best social predictor of participation in outdoor recreation.[33] A somewhat different approach employed factor analysis to distinguish orientations of leisure among an affluent California sample.[34] Significant relationships were found between intellectual styles of leisure and higher social position, again best indicated by education, and a more modest relationship with a group of costly 'glamour sports'.

One suggestion is that diffusion is a process constantly altering this relationship of status and leisure. For example, activities such as tennis and camping are now widely diffused but once were more elite. That same diffusion, through a process that may include mass media introduction, usually requires social group mediation. Such diffusion may in time transform the now-elite sport of trailskiing into one engaged in by many attracted to its low cost and availability in climates with snow.

Work and Leisure

Sociologists have probably given the most attention to the relationship between work and leisure. The old model – based on either institutional or Marxist premisses – assumed that leisure was determined by work. Again in the early days of industrialization with work scheduled six days of twelve hours or more for factory workers, evidence was not hard to find. Further, the connections between bourgeois entrepreneurial work and participation in certain status-confirming organizations were clear.

All such 'self-evident' data led sociologists into an unfortunate dead-end. Without question, industrialization has shaped the time and space of our societies. The employment schedule, the time required to get to and from work, and the increasing geographical separation of employment and residence all have their power to influence the context of leisure. However, it is quite another matter to assert that the conditions and constraints of employment determine leisure choices. Rather, this bias obscured for a period what ought to have been at least as self-evident: that leisure is actually closely related to the social world of family, home and community.

The structural arrangements of the economic institutions of a society do have their influence on leisure. Employment schedules constrain leisure for all who are employed or in a household with others who are employed just as home chores and parenting responsibilities are continually impinging factors for parents of younger children. However, in a 1977 employment study in the USA, workers gave the greatest priority to their family and marriage with the 'spillover' in roles most consistently found between family and leisure rather than work and leisure.[35] Despite a generally instrumental view of employment, the work schedule most impacts leisure when it varies due to shift assignments.[36] With the increase in service-retailing employment of men and women, such varied schedules will be a major element in timetables of leisure participation in the future.

However, the real issue is the extent to which work and leisure are related in meaning and style. Are there clear and consistent correlations between type of work and types of leisure? Do the theoretical models stand the test of research? With a variety of terms and diagrams, proposed relationships between work and leisure are as follows:[37,38]

- Segmentation: no consistent relationship.
- Positive influence: a 'spillover' from work to leisure in skill, association and/or meanings.
- Negative influence: leisure becomes a contrast to or escape from work constraints, a compensation that many reflect alienation from the productive process and community.
- Reverse or reciprocal influence: leisure may have some impact on employment in skill acquisition or preferred environments as well as being impacted by the work relationship.

Probably the most accurate summary of past research is that the relationships are complex and varied. Further, a number of intervening variables have to be taken into account. Among them are:

- The salience of work: leisure is more likely to be treated as secondary and instrumental when the worker has a strong career orientation.[39] On the other hand, when employment is defined primarily as a means to greater ends,[40] then work schedules and relationships may even be adapted to leisure ends. The central reward of employment then becomes the enabling income.
- Work satisfaction: disillusionment with the personal outcomes of employment, which generally increases over the years[41] and may reach a crisis stage with managers and office workers,[42] may turn some toward the alternatives of leisure and non-work communities.
- Situational analysis: while the relationship seems generally weak in both the United Kingdom[43] and North America,[44] there are

specific situations in which the work–leisure tie is significant or in which a particular element is salient. Those who engage in physically exhausting work or who commute long distances are likely to choose relaxing and recuperative leisure on workday evenings. Some particular occupational settings, such as being on a small college faculty, produce considerable leisure association with work colleagues. And some who listen to other people's problems all day may well prefer to be alone in some of their leisure.

- Resource variables: employment has important impacts on time and income as leisure resources. Some workers have considerable discretion over their schedules while others have none. It would appear that such resource differences may reinforce variation related to employment associations and produce complex effects.

In general, it would appear that no simple model is sufficient. Even including personality variables, Johan Pennings found weak or no support for either spillover or compensation explanations of leisure determination.[45] The author found that compensation/contrast reasons for selecting leisure were secondary in up to 25 percent of adult choices, but were the primary goal in only 5 percent.[46] What is suggested is that the relationship varies through the life course, is somewhat dependent on the salience and satisfactions of the work relationship and may be highly situational. No simple model is either adequate or accurate. The safest generalization appears to be that work and leisure are more and more independent rather than interdependent. Leisure is part of the non-work world.

Nevertheless, there is one issue that should not be bypassed too quickly. There is considerable evidence that most employment, while providing some satisfactions and feeling of having a place in the society, yields little in the way of knowing oneself to be a contributing part of a socially necessary productive process. Such alienation from work denies a person the self-definition of meaningful engagement that thinkers as diverse as Martin Luther and Karl Marx have proposed as essential to human development. In case studies of 200 blue-collar workers William Torbert was able to discern ways in which those who were cut off from possibilities of self-fulfillment in regimented work were not only likely to seek it in the family–community–leisure social spaces, but might be less able to exercise freedom and spontaneity than those with more autonomy at work.[47] Alienation at the job may have effects that reduce a person's capacity to reach out for expressive freedom and relationships with others. We are, after all, whole beings who learn and change in all our social situations. However, the proposition that those most limited or alienated on the job are most likely to find their leisure identities in their leisure is suggested only by limited research.[48]

The value of case studies that can take into account situational items is illustrated by a study of Tyneside shipbuilders.[49] In hours away from the workplace, home and family activities dominated leisure. Even the schedule of the working-man's club featured regular events for the family or couple. The most common activities were visiting friends and relatives, shopping, gardening, family outings away from home, watching TV, reading, listening to the radio, jobs around the house, entertaining, playing with children and working on the car at home. Visiting the pub or club for a drink was a common event for over half with wives going along frequently. However, on-the-job interaction with fellow-workers in both informal conversation and interspersed games was also an important element of the overall meaning of work, the most important for 25 percent of the shipbuilders. On the other hand, although 75 percent had 'good friends' in the yard, just over half met such friends regularly away from work and very few said they prefer other shipbuilders as friends. The general picture is one in which informal interaction is a regular and important part of the work experience, but leisure tends to be largely separated – a matter of family, home and pub or club. Among these relatively skilled workers, their employment has satisfactions that render suspect any easy analysis of alienation, but their leisure remains neither an extension nor an antithesis of work. Yet even in this traditional set of crafts, most leisure is found in the non-work spaces of life.

Summary of Social Factors

No clearcut and pure model, ideological or not, 'explains' the relationship between leisure and social position. This includes both simple models of direct determination and those implying that leisure is a totally separate and segmented experience. At the very least, items such as education, family life cycle period, occupation, income and race are indicators of the social action contexts in which leisure is learned and carried out. The failure to find sharp and dramatic differences based on social position does not imply that there is no relationship at all.

Leisure must be understood in social contexts that are quite similar for a variety of people. The separation of the workplace and residence, stress on the nuclear family, availability of mass media such as TV and private transportation via the car, wider sets of perceived opportunities in the countryside and community, and a level of income permitting some expenditure on leisure, are all common to most of the population. Further, expectations for childrearing, marital companionship, home care and maintenance, and the impacts of school and work schedules do not clearly differentiate those who work in factories, offices, or schools. As a consequence, similarities of both time use and leisure orientations seem to outweigh differences.

This 'pluralistic' condition of leisure may not satisfy those who prefer a statistically viable causal model, demonstration of a relationship between work and leisure that fits an ideology, or a view of leisure as an exotic and rarefied affective experience or 'condition of the soul'. Leisure is interspersed among all the role relationships, schedules and artefacts of our social and cultural system. It is characterized by a particular measure of freedom and yet is responsive to pervasive sets of cultural definitions and social expectations. Leisure is in the real world, even when there are moments or events of transcendence in human intercourse or creative activity.

And while leisure may not be 'determined' by social position, age, or sex, its choices and environments still exist within social systems that differentiate rewards, opportunities and customs. Most societies still contain the very poor and the very rich, however the proportions may have changed. Ethnic and subcultural identification and communities remain powerful influences.[50] The similarities in leisure among different occupational or religious groups should not be allowed to obscure significant varieties in leisure styles.

Opportunity Factors

To a great extent, leisure opportunities and the resources to overcome resource limitations are dependent on the social factors just outlined. Geographical limitations may be overcome by travel which usually costs money. Cultural limitations are generally lessened through education which remains related to family income and social position. Nevertheless, there are dimensions of opportunity factors that have their own power to shape leisure. The basic premiss is that most leisure *takes place*. That is, even informal interaction requires a physical setting for meeting and talking. Many kinds of leisure require special spaces, indoors or out. And access to space is not equal for all in a society.

Personal Resources

'Leisure opportunity begins at home' might be a slogan for leisure sociologists. The first resources of leisure are those of the household. They include not only the residence itself, but also combinations of financial and cultural resources. Even more important, the household provides in some measure the intimate community of leisure companions, catalysts, instructors and decisionmakers as well as a set of responsibilities that may limit opportunities.

The first resource other than space and a social community is probably income. Those below certain margins of maintenance are in a condition of scarcity that radically impacts every element of life. The degree to which persons or households are above marginality is significant in societies in which many leisure opportunities, facilities, implements and required transportation are chiefly provided by the market at a price. It is hardly a surprise that a sport such as downhill skiing calling for both travel and equipment attracts participants who are measurably above economic survival levels. Income at least provides a filter even for consideration of many kinds of leisure. Priorities can be exercised only when there is some discretionary income to allocate.

For many of those with employment-related income, there is a tradeoff between income that may be used for leisure and the time that is also required. Past research in North America had found that workers generally would choose income in preference to time when faced with overtime or second-job possibilities. A more recent study indicates that time may be given a greater salience than previously, especially when it can be obtained in a block long enough to permit some special kind of activity.[51] Many workers desire periods of time free for chosen activity even at the price of forgone income. However, longitudinal analysis indicates that this choice of time decreases in periods of economic recession.

Another approach to the relationship of leisure to discretionary income is found in a case study of families who are marginal economically with little stability in either economic or social support.[52] Their leisure for the most part does not seem to be a matter of choice at all. Some family interaction even though frequently conflict-ridden, drinking, neighboring, fixing something that is broken (most often the car) and just getting through the day occupies most time and attention. These urban immigrants are caught in marginality rather than achieving any freedom to choose and weigh relative values. Kevin Lynch's study of children in several cities suggests that many are victims of 'experiential starvation' that is likely to place severe limitations on their ability in later years to perceive a range of opportunities for enrichment or to define themselves as able to enter into a fuller life.[53] Income combines with other familial and environmental factors to stunt the perceptions of what is possible as well as the opportunities themselves.

Income is only one element in thresholds of leisure development, but especially in a capitalist economy it is a basic one. However, related to poverty in many societies is racial or ethnic identification. When the history of a society has incorporated the designation of a racial or ethnic group as perpetual servants or even unfit for regular employment and full social participation, then the consequences build up over generations of deprivation. In the midwest of the United States interviews of older black adults revealed that racial discrimination in their childhood had prevented their even considering many kinds of water sports, travel, or commercial entertainment as possibilities. Now they remain more involved in activities and institutions that were open to them in their earlier years. Analysis of a national survey supported this view since black participation in resource-based outdoor recreation, although increasing, is clearly differentiated by former racial barriers to opportunities as well as by costs.

Just as important a personal resource is the self-definition of competence. In Chapter 4 we will examine the development of skills and social competence in relation to leisure identities. However, it is important here to note that the cumulative deprivation resulting from a lack of resources and opportunities has consequences that may be internalized in self-definitions. When we define ourselves as *able* to learn or do something as leisure, then it may be an opportunity. However, if we have a perception of inability, then we may cut it out of our range of possibilities as though the activity existed only in another world.

Finally, despite many descriptions of work environments that provide little or no opportunity for free interaction, even a few moments at a time,[54] in most work situations there are times of social exchange, periods of idleness at least for daydreaming and even episodes that mix enjoyable experiences with an economic purpose. Leisure may be found interstitially at the workplace and in worktimes as well as on weekends. In a study of the leisure of upper-level managers the difficulty of distinguishing work and leisure came not only from the long hours and heavy responsibilities, but also from the pleasant environments and variety of exchanges in the executive suite, the business lunch and the company trip.[55] Even employment settings and timetables can provide an important leisure resource for some. In somewhat different ways a young mother who fully recognizes the constraints associated with caring for an infant also finds great satisfaction in various responses related to feeding, clothing and otherwise caring for the child.

Space and Distance Factors
The space available for leisure at home is the primary but not the only significant space factor in leisure opportunity structures. The ecology of contemporary leisure encompasses space inside and around the residence, the neighborhood, community interaction locales such as retailing centers, public indoor and outdoor space in the community, time and distance intensification due to the decentralization of the

modern metropolis and the distance of special natural resources from population centers with the assumption of private transportation. Not only are most National Parks in the USA or the Lake District or Dales in the UK some distance from the cities, but public transportation is either non-existent or extremely time-inefficient.

Beginning with the home and immediate environments both activities and interaction modes are influenced by the amount and design of the available space. When possible, families choose housing appropriate for their life cycle period and life style requirements.[56] However, many do not have such options. As housing costs escalate, more and more households may find themselves with little designated 'leisure space' at home and less private space of yard and garden. Multiple-unit housing restricts both the amount and privacy of outdoor space and is usually smaller inside as well. The density of use affects informal interaction, quiet and solitary leisure, mutual tasks and play, and the possibilities of entertaining. It may well be that meeting others in the pub in Britain is as much an adaptation to the size of residences as a cultural value. Also the significance of the TV set in a flat with no private space except a shared bedroom may be in its attraction of individual attention that avoids density-caused conflicts as as well as its availability.

The neighborhood is also a part of the ecology of leisure. As walking has decreased and the parking-surrounded shopping center replaced many neighborhood shops, one of the main opportunities for informal interaction outside the household has become rare. Neighborhoods require a number of interaction exchange points or locations. They may be shops, street intersections, a small-town post office, or a tea or coffee establishment. For some, neighborhood parks may provide such a leisure locale, especially if they are within a quarter-mile or less of the residence.

It is possible to argue that parks are not so much places for designated activity as they are environments for social interaction. By and large, in the urban neighborhood square or the suburban playground, people come to parks together and meet others there. Parks then tend to develop regularities of the timed use of space by various groups. A set of benches may day after day attract young mothers in the morning, workers eating lunch at noon, a retired set until 3 and an age-specific gang of teens in the early evening.

Not enough attention has been given the impacts of immediate space on leisure. The traffic flows in the home as well as the neighborhood, opportunities for privacy as well as group activity, the interaction of varying family styles with residential design, the loss of neighborhood identity due to the failure to develop places of social intersection and the multiple effects of high-rise living environments are all issues important for leisure in today's society.

Rather more attention has been given to the issue of the financial and time costs of travel to outdoor recreation resources. An analysis of national participation data indicates that regional differences in resources and climate as well as the kinds of resources for outdoor recreation likely to be available in cities vs rural areas are factors in outdoor recreation participation.[57] Access as measured by distance is a major element in even considering the possibility of forest hiking, stream fishing, or lakeside camping.

Further, travel itself is not only a cost in time and money, but also a part of the recreational experience.[58] In fact, that prerequisite of so much away-from-home leisure, the car, is often a leisure environment itself. In a world often circumscribed by the authority of others the car offers at least an occasional opportunity to set one's own direction and destination. The car is freedom as well as transportation and, as such, an instrument of self-direction and decision.

Financial costs are one factor distinguishing styles of vacation travel.[59] Some travel little or not at all. Some take only occasional vacation trips in rather routine ways. Others plan their budgets carefully and travel in moderation. However, there are also adventurers who seek new experiences and locales. Leisure travel is undertaken by some for the experience as well as to get to a particular destination.

Nevertheless, distance is a deterrent to many kinds of leisure. The time involved, cost and the general requirement of reliable private transportation rules many out of styles, frequency, or length of travel. As a result, most leisure tends to be close to home even when there are free or low-cost beaches, forests and mountains an hour or two away.[60] Especially for low-income households, personal resource limitations and costly distance are compounded to limit leisure opportunities.

Leisure Socialization

There is a dialectic in leisure socialization.[61] The first pole is the simple issue of how leisure is learned. Not only interests and skills related to specific activities, but how do we acquire attitudes that lead us into a variety of leisure experiences as we move through the life course? Research has demonstrated that childhood experiences, especially in the family, are crucial, but that we may gain new interests and develop new skills throughout the life course.[62] Leisure socialization is a social process that takes place in the context of institutional roles, but is most directly developed in interaction with our immediate communities of family and friends.

This first element in leisure socialization is not simply one in which the individual is acted upon. Rather, tracing of the process of entering, maintaining, or withdrawing from sport participation has identified the critical self-defining factor.[63] When young men and women assess their competence and skill-acquisition as inadequate or below group norms, they are most likely to withdraw. In much the same way, throughout the life course, we evaluate not only the satisfactions being received from participation, but also the extent to which the investment of ourselves promises long-term benefits. Further, the perceived fit between the activity, environment, associations and our own personality orientations permits judgement as to the congruence of the choice with our aims and identities. Not only the activities and attitudes, but the decision process itself is learned and subject to change through the life course.

The other pole of the leisure socialization dialectic is that of development *in* leisure. What happens to us in our leisure as we move through the life course? We may make our decisions based on perceived opportunities, resources and out of what we have learned in a developmental process closely tied to our social placement. Further, our opportunity structures and our self-definitions are specific to our age and sex. Particular decisions about what to do at a specific time are also shaped by a number of situational factors such as schedule, the availability of companions, weather and the requirements of designated space.[64] However, there is also a more persistent element in the dialectic of leisure choices. It is our understanding of what has happened to us in similar leisure contexts. In so far as we seek to grow and develop as well as to just have fun, then leisure is one social context in which we develop in the journey from birth to death. Leisure socialization, then, is lifelong rather than subject to total childhood determination, contextual rather than segmented, dialectical rather than the result of external factors. We are socialized both in and into leisure, yet retain an element of existential freedom to decide.

References: Chapter 2

1   S. deGrazia, *Of Time, Work, and Leisure* (Garden City, NY: Doubleday/Anchor, 1964).
2   J. Kelly, *Leisure* (Englewood Cliffs, NJ: Prentice-Hall, 1982), p. 129.
3   K. Roberts, *Contemporary Society and the Growth of Leisure* (London: Longman, 1978).
4   J. Kelly, 'Socialization into leisure: a developmental approach', *Journal of Leisure Research*, vol. 6, 1974, pp. 181–93.
5   J. Kelly, 'Recreation and leisure in a British new town', paper presented at the Research Symposium of the National Recreation and Park Association, Las Vegas, 1980.
6   J. Kelly, *Race, Resources and Outdoor Recreation* (Champaign, Ill.: University of Illinois Leisure Research Laboratory, 1980).
7   J. Kelly, 1982, op. cit., ch. 14.

8   H. Gardner, 'Bureaucracy at the bridge table', in *Side-Saddle on the Golden Calf*, ed., G. Lewis (Pacific Palisades, Calif.: Goodyear, 1972), pp. 138–53.

9   N. H. Cheek and W. R. Burch, *The Social Organization of Leisure in Human Society* (New York: Harper & Row, 1976), pp. 106–7.

10 Roberts, op. cit., p. 19.

11 D. Field and J. O'Leary, 'Assessing participation in leisure activities,' in *Leisure and Recreation Places*, eds, N. Cheek, D. Field and R. Burdge (Ann Arbor, Mich.: Ann Arbor Science, 1976), ch. 5.

12 Kelly, 1974, op. cit.

13 Field and O'Leary, op. cit.

14 J. Kelly, 'Family leisure in three communities,' *Journal of Leisure Research*, vol. 10, 1978, pp. 47–60.

15 Roberts, op. cit., 2 and 3.

16 W. Bacon, 'Leisure and the craftworkers', in *Leisure and Urban Society*, ed., M. Smith (London Leisure Studies Association, n.d.), pp. 7, 2–7, 19.

17 Cheek and Burch, op. cit., p. 26.

18 J. Kelly, 'Outdoor recreation participation: a comparative analysis', *Leisure Sciences*, vol. 3, 1980, pp. 129–54.

19 J. Zuzanek, 'Social differences in leisure behavior: measurement and interpretation', *Leisure Sciences*, vol. 1, 1978, pp. 271–93.

20 Kelly, 1980, op. cit.

21 Kelly, 1978, op. cit.

22 B. J. Rees and M. Collins, 'The family and sport: a review', in *Leisure and Family Diversity*, ed., Z. Strelitz (London: Leisure Studies Association, 1980).

23 C. Gorden, C. Gaitz and J. Scott, 'Leisure and lives: personal expressivity across the life span', *Handbook of Aging and the Social Sciences*, eds, R. Binstock and E. Shanas (New York: Van Nostrand Reinhold, 1976).

24 Kelly, 1982, op. cit.

25 H. Gavron, *The Captive Wife* (Harmondsworth: Penguin, 1968).

26 L. Rubin, *Worlds of Pain* (New York: Basic, 1976).

27 J. Wilson, 'Sociology of leisure', *Annual Review of Sociology*, no. 6, pp. 21–40, 1980, pp. 21–40.

28 T. Kando, *Leisure and Popular Culture in Transition*, 2nd edn (St Louis, Mi: Mosby, 1980).

29 M. Smith, S. Parker and C. Smith, eds, *Leisure and Society in Britain* (London: Allen Lane, 1973), pp. 35–6.

30 Kelly, 1982, op. cit., ch. 6.

31 ibid., ch. 19.

32 Roberts, op. cit., p. 103.

33 T. White, 'The relative importance of education and income as predictors in outdoor recreation participation', *Journal of Leisure Research*, vol. 6, 1974, pp. 191–9.

34 G. McKechnie, 'The psychological structure of leisure: past behavior', *Journal of Leisure Research*, vol. 6, 1974, pp. 27–44.

35 G. Staines, and P. O'Conner, *The Relationship between Work and Leisure* (Ann Arbor, Mich.: University of Michigan Survey Research Center, 1979).

36 Roberts, op. cit., p. 16.

37 S. Parker, *The Future of Work and Leisure* (New York: Praeger, 1971).

38 Kelly, 1982, op. cit., ch. 7.

39 D. Goldman, 'Managerial mobility and central life interests', *American Sociological Review*, vol. 79, 1973, pp. 119–25.

40 S. Levitan and W. Johnston, *Work is Here to Stay, Alas* (Salt Lake City, Utah: Olympus, 1973).

41 R. Cohn, 'Age and satisfaction from work', *Journal of Gerontology*, no. 1 vol. 34, 1979, pp. 264–72.

42   R. M. Kanter, *Men and Women of the Corporation* (New York: Basic, 1977).

43   Roberts, op. cit., p. 113.

44   Cheek and Burch, op. cit.

45   J. Pennings, 'Work and leisure: an empirical reassessment', paper presented at American Sociological Association, New York, USA, 1976.

46   J. Kelly, 'Leisure as a compensation for work constraint', *Society and Leisure*, vol. 8, 1976, pp. 73–82.

47   W. Torbert, *Being for the Most Part Puppets* (Cambridge, Mass.: Schenkman, 1973).

48   E. Spreitzer and E. Snyder, 'Work orientation, meaning of leisure, and mental health,' *Journal of Leisure Research*, no. 6, 1974, pp. 207–19.

49   R. Brown, P. Brannen, J. Cousins and M. Samphier, 'Leisure in work: the occupational culture of shipbuilding workers', in *Leisure and Society in Britain*, eds, M. Smith *et al.*, op. cit.

50   Kelly, 1982, op. cit., 14.

51   F. Best, P. Bosserman and B. Stern, 'Income-free time tradeoff preferences of US workers', *Leisure Sciences*, vol. 2, 1979, pp. 119–41.

52   J. Howell, *Hard Living on Clay Street* (New York: Anchor, 1973).

53   K. Lynch, *Growing Up in Cities* (Cambridge, Mass.: MIT Press, 1979).

54   H. Braverman, *Labor and Monopoly Capital* (New York: Monthly Review Press, 1974).

55   F. P. Noe, 'Autonomous spheres of leisure activity for the industrial executive and the blue-collarite, *Journal of Leisure Research*, vol. 3, 1971, pp. 220–49.

56   W. Michelson, 'Discretionary and nondiscretionary aspects of activity and social contact in residential selection', *Society and Leisure*, vol. 5, 1973, pp. 29–54.

57   J. Kelly, 'Because it's there: a re-examination of the opportunity theory in outdoor recreation', paper presented at Midwest Sociological Society Minneapolis, Minnesota, USA, 1979.

58   Kelly, 1982, op. cit., ch. 16.

59   W. Perrault, D. Darden and, W. Darden, 'A psychographic classification of vacation life styles', *Journal of Leisure Research*, vol. 9, 1977, pp. 208–24.

60   W. Emrie, *Recreation Problems in Urban Impacted Areas of California* (Sacramento, Calif.: State Department of Parks and Recreation, 1970).

61   D. Kleiber and J. Kelly, 'Leisure, socialization, and the life cycle', in *Social Psychological Perspectives on Leisure and Recreation*, ed., S. Iso-Ahola (Springfield, Ill.: Charles C. Thomas, 1980), ch. 5.

62   J. Kelly, 'Leisure socialization: replication and extension,' *Journal of Leisure Research*, vol. 11, 1979, pp. 121–32.

63   E. Snyder and E. Spreitzer, *Social Aspects of Sport* (Englewood Cliffs, NJ: Prentice-Hall, 1978), pp. 57–62.

64   J. Kelly, 'Situational and social factors in leisure decisions', *Pacific Sociological Review*, vol. 21, 1978, pp. 313–30.

3

Life Course Changes

The concept of the 'life course' views the individual life as a journey from birth to death. This journey, while not exactly like that of any other person, is made in company with a cohort of others who were born at about the same time in the same culture and who experience the same set of macrosocial events – the same wars, recessions, technological innovations, and national tragedies and successes. On a microsocial level the journey is made with a series of other persons who form a succession of intimate communities.

One element of the life course approach is that of the family life cycle. The normal progression is from the childhood family of orientation to the adult family of productivity, from the family that nurtures the self to the new nuclear unit in which one becomes the partner and nurturer. The adult sequence includes preparental, parental and postparental periods. These family roles and their expectations have considerable impact on leisure resources and constraints. The life course includes parallel 'careers' of which the familial and work are most commonly defined as central to understanding life's meanings and contexts.

The life course model assumes some continuity as well as disruption in various strands of life's investments and contexts. Further, major elements of life such as work, family, other immediate communities, leisure and the larger political-social context are seen as mutually influential. The family life cycle approach tends to view as inevitable the progression from one period to another and now must be adjusted for the larger proportion of the population that zigzags through the sequence with a number of irregularities and interruptions. The 'career' metaphor suggests a regularity of progress with continuity that may or may not characterize work, leisure, or family life courses.

Typical Leisure Transitions

Without going into detail, some of the implications of this approach will introduce the chapter. For example, we know that one major leisure transition comes at the time of leaving school when the organized context of team sport participation, especially for males, is left

behind. As a result, such participation drops off sharply for the cohort of school-leavers and graduates. The main reason is not some age-related physical debilitation that prevents such activity, but rather a loss of the facilitating context of the school and the taking on of new sets of schedules and expectations related to employment, marriage and family. There are many such common life course transitions in leisure:

- For teens in school, leisure consists not only of school-related games, sports, parties, organizations and associations, but also a fair amount of just 'hanging around' and informal meeting of peers with no specific aim or activity context.
- For those who are embarking on the beginnings of employment and family careers, there are evident shifts to more home-centered leisure, activity with the 'intimate other' of the period, in time the complex set of opportunities and responsibilities related to parenthood, and the beginning of 'adult' community participation. The transitions may come easily for some whose anticipatory socialization is thorough and with considerable difficulty for others whose commitment to such an institutional role is ambiguous.
- For parents of older children, considerable leisure investment may come to revolve around the various leisure involvements of those who are active in school and summer sports leagues, arts enterprises and age-group organizations. In fact, interaction with other parents similarly engaged in support activities may become a major social context of leisure as new friendships are gained.

The life course model does not account for all variations in leisure participation or meaning any more than do oversimplistic work or social status determination models. However, significant changes in leisure are related to work, changing resources, opportunities, role expectations, and self-definitions through this age-related sequence. The basis is the family life cycle not because almost everyone has the same set of roles and relationships, but because of the close ties between leisure and the family.

The family life cycle model is based on the statistical probability of a 'normal' family career. It is assumed that courtship, marriage, parenthood, launching, retirement and widowhood will continue to be the sequence for most adults. In the days when 95 percent would marry, 90 percent of those have children, and so on, the framework seemed adequate for general analysis. The existence of a less stable 'underclass' and the small proportion of those with less orderly life styles did not divert attention from the great consuming, stable, middle and working classes who followed the pattern with statistical fidelity. Even those experiencing the breaks of a divorce or early widowhood usually got back on the cycle with another marriage.

Further, the approach has been found to be quite useful in examining issues such as marriage satisfaction, housing preferences, community involvement and even leisure. In the 1980s increased attention is being given to the greater variety in patterns: more married women who are employed especially during the childrearing period, more childless marriages, higher divorce rates and a greater number of singles in the population.[1] At any given time, most children are being raised in two-parent families, but the likelihood is greater that during childhood there may be some disruption of the biological parental dyad. There will be more single-parent households at any one time as well as more irregular marriage careers. Therefore, any use of the family life cycle as a basis for analyzing leisure must recognize the significance of change that in the USA and UK now includes a majority of adult women being employed, the greater amount of adult life being without children living at home, longer periods in early adult life prior to marriage and prior to childbearing, single adults comprising up to 40 percent of households, and more individuals who experience serious changes and disruptions through their family careers.

Nevertheless, the family career basis of studying leisure has been demonstrated to be quite valuable, especially when the other careers of the life course are taken into account.[2] The intersecting career lines of family, work and education, community roles and leisure are seen as mutually influential. At certain periods in the life course one career may appear to dominate the others in matters of resource allocation, scheduling and personal priorities. Interrelationships may be complementary or conflicting. In any case, any one career is best understood by taking account of the others.

In addition to the role changes of family, work and leisure, this life course approach has increasingly incorporated a developmental orientation. It is assumed that a person does more than go from one role to another impervious to the succeeding experiences. Rather, in every role through the life course, we are learning and changing. Development does not take place only in childhood and in adult-directed institutions. We change in our definitions of ourselves and the world, in our modes of response and adaptation, and in our orientations and values. Sometimes particular transitions require radical adaptation in behavior and in our role identities. Other change is gradual. But we do change – not only our role contexts, but our selves.

For example, the leisure identities that are appropriate at one age may be quite out of place at another. What is expected of a university student varies from an age-stratified campus bar to a multifamily

Christmas party. At that same party the heterosexual expressions of affection acceptable from a child or a grandfather may be quite unacceptable when offered by a single male to females of about the same age or by a wife to someone else's husband. Age, sex and role relationship all enter into the range of appropriate behavior. As we move through the life course, we not only learn what are the expected behaviors, but we also learn *in* the series of relationships. We change in how we define ourselves and others as well as maintain considerable continuity of identity. As a consequence, a study of leisure through the life course includes how we learn in our leisure as well as how our leisure changes.

The role identity approach assumes both continuity and change through the life course. Chad Gordon has proposed that our concepts of self vary in a number of dimensions that include affective styles, physical attributes and capacities, life goals, immediate satisfactions, both social roles and personal identities, sense of competence and worth, definitions of autonomy and control, social opportunities and contextual styles and global value orientations.[3] The meanings and implications of our sexual identities, ethnicity, occupational identities, and so on, change as we move from one role to another and as different roles gain periodic ascendancy. Leisure is neither fixed nor separate from all these developmental changes. Rather, leisure is part of the weave of roles and identities that are extended into the fabric of life.

Change in Meanings and Expectations

Change in roles are accompanied by shifts in leisure expectations. When leisure is defined in relation to social networks rather than as some leftover period of time, then every major shift of roles would be expected to impact leisure.[4] Changes in family roles, the increasing independence expected of students, the shift to full-time employment, unemployment, parenthood, a variety of community roles and statuses, grandparenthood, retirement, and so on, all alter the leisure engagement expected of us by those whose lives are most closely intertwined with ours. However, the more generalized expectations of others also shift. Leisure behavior acceptable or even expected for students in the spring is condemned as is responsible and childish for the same group of new graduates in the fall.

Especially leisure complementary to other social roles changes through the life course. In fact, the proportion of role-related leisure increases for those who have become parents and continues through that phase of the life cycle. Such leisure that involves parents and their children is not only a response to expectations (role-determined), but is also chosen because of the values placed on such interaction (relational).

Further, both resources and external opportunities change as we widen our geographical world in childhood, are expected to participate in a series of school programs, gain the further mobility and freedom of a car and an independent income, and have both the responsibility and space of a residence for ourselves or our new nuclear family.

While we retain some aspects of our identities, such as gender, through the life course, even our self-definitions of the meanings and expressions of our gender-differentiated sexuality may change. There is for most persons a core of continuity, but also a sequence of altered role identities. We would find ourselves in difficult straits socially were we to present ourselves to interesting members of the other sex in precisely the same ways at ages 14, 18, 28 and 48. We would be in an even worse condition if we did not understand ourselves and our sexual identities in new ways as we progress through those years. Nevertheless, what we have experienced and learned in every preceding period becomes part of us as we enter new contexts and essay appropriate identities.

Theoretical Frameworks

The approach to be employed in this chapter combines three models of analyzing leisure roles and identities through the life course. The first was developed and demonstrated by Rhona and Robert Rapoport in their report on *Leisure and the Family Life Cycle*.[5] This model takes the intersecting roles of work, family and leisure through the life course. They add a developmental perspective that age-related growth requires a series of tasks be undertaken and accomplished for successful adaptation to the succeeding periods of life. For example, the adolescent – however close to his or her parents - has to develop independence in order to undertake the social roles expected in the early establishment period. Leisure related to school and peer groups facilitates such independence through the formation of activity-based groups that assume some autonomy of decision by participants. The Rapoports propose that the developmental tasks of each life period are the basis for life-basic 'preoccupations' that produce 'interests' in types of expression and interaction that take the form of particular 'activities'.

The second framework is that of Douglas Kleiber and the author who outlined leisure through the life course by differentiating socialization into leisure from the socialization that takes place in leisure.[6] Again there is the insertion of the developmental process into the more traditional life course periods. They have divided the life course into six periods of preschool, younger childhood, adolescence and youth, young adulthood, middle years and later years including retirement. In this analysis there is considerable stress on the contribution of children's leisure or play to the learning required to deal with the adult social world.

The third approach is that of McCall and Simmons, already introduced, that brings together structured expectations of social roles with the modes of enacting those roles through role identities.[7] Here the context of work/school, family and leisure roles will be augmented by analysis of the sexual, productive, social and intimate identities developed and expressed in leisure. In general, the sociological work –family–leisure role framework will be reoriented to incorporate the social-psychological dimension of the personal definitions of social identities.

Three Life Course Periods

There are innumerable ways of dividing up the life course. Each takes a particular sequence of roles as primary and fits other elements to that sequence. In this analysis the life course is divided into only three periods. Although each might be profitably subdivided several times, in this introductory outline the three suggest most clearly the main periods of life in modern society.

The first period, *preparation*, includes preschool and school years. During those years some begin their first encounter with employment and some even make their final decisions about life partners. Parenthood does not follow school for all and the practice of returning to educational programs later in life is becoming more and more common. However, those early years are designed to lay the basis for later productivity in the society. Not only school, but also family and leisure, cannot be understood apart from those future orientations.

The second period, *establishment*, is difficult to define in years but in general begins with school-leaving and full-time employment. Establishment does not end with a clearcut event for most, but draws to a close when life events begin to bring about different definitions of life and the meaning of its roles. Establishment is defined by the centrality of production and performance in most roles and by the preoccupation with making a place in the society and its various institutions.

The third period, *culmination*, is one in which a new time orientation becomes salient. Life is now seen as limited, more than 'half-over'. Meanings become more important than accomplishment. Culmination is ideally a period in which the themes of the past are drawn together into a satisfying pattern of meaning. However, it may also be a time of relinquishment of roles and relationships and the experience of loss.

In each of these periods certain life events are crucial in requiring entrance into new institutional roles and the redefinition of the self in roles that are continued. The place of leisure roles and identities in this process can only be suggested on the basis of contemporary research. However, both the complementarity of roles that reinforce significant identities and the conflict resulting from radical identity shifts from one role to another may be found in leisure as well as more institutionalized roles.

The Preparation Period

Childhood and youth are not a simple and trauma-free progression to adulthood. Rather, the requirements of preparing to assume adult roles together with age-related sets of expectations as member of families, peer groups, school institutions and economic enterprises make any but the highest-level generalizations difficult. Nevertheless, those first sixteen to twenty-four years cannot be understood apart from the societal expectations that the child *become* something different in time. It is a time with future-oriented meanings.

Chad Gordon has analyzed the dilemmas of development as an ongoing dialectic between security and challenge.[8] In each of life's sequential periods the struggle between security and challenge takes different forms. For the young child, 1–2 years old, it is a relatively simple compliance vs self-control dilemma related to parents. With the social world expanding beyond parents for the 3–5-year-old, the dilemma becomes expressivity vs instrumentality. Social acceptance and competence become developmental tasks with play and school as central contexts in later childhood, ages 6–11. Acceptance vs achievement themes carry on the same struggle in early teen years, but with greater specificity of evaluation of abilities. Then in later adolescence, ages 16–18 or 20, the acceptance theme turns to intimacy and evaluated competence in the working out of independence. In the transition to early establishment the social theme widens its context and the independence theme merges with that of evaluation in striving for self-determination in the institutional world. While security and social acceptance on the one hand, and response to challenge on the other, remain significant not only do their social or role contexts change, but the existential thrusts also change in relation to developmental needs. In every period, including that of preparation, life involves dilemmas and conflicting goals related to social acceptance and individual expression. Our persistent issue revolves around the meaning of leisure in that developmental process.

Preparatory Roles
This complex period of preparation can be subdivided into any number of differentiated stages. For our purposes, we will bypass infancy and deal only with childhood and youth as the two major segments of preparation. The transition from childhood is marked not only by physical changes of adolescence and more focused sexuality, but also a mobility that gives greater salience to peer relationships and the thrust toward independence.

(1)   *Childhood roles*: Children in Western culture live thoroughly in the context of their family of origin, especially in their preschool years. However, their social world is a constantly expanding one in which a variety of leisure or play contexts also take a central place. By the age of 5 or 6 the family member and playmate also becomes a schoolmate and is subjected to the schedules and role expectations of that institution.

School roles: the social world of the child who enters the regularity of a school changes in many significant ways. Geographically the neighborhood expands to include on a regular basis new schoolmates. In some cases the school schedule involves considerable travel and the anxiety of 'making the bus'. Life becomes tied to an impersonal timetable in a radically new way. In the school often there are a variety of ages, ethnic backgrounds and abilities in a density heretofor unimagined. The initial anxieties in time turn to more focused tasks: gaining social acceptance and demonstrating competence to handle the new expectations. In this institutional world different kinds of games and enterprises are mixed in their provision and freedom of choice. Some are required in the school program. However, the same activity – be it a game, sport, or music – can also become a recess or after-school activity. At that time the major issue of inclusion is paramount. 'Significant others' include or exclude one from participation. With a broader range of potential participants, the old neighborhood inclusion is left behind and a developing social organization deals in evaluation of skills to determine whether or not one may play. Being *there* is no longer enough; now it is important to be *good*, to do it relatively well. Social acceptance is related to those evaluations not only of social acceptability based on perceptions of 'fit', but also on activity-specific competence. And the main realm is play – especially the game with roles, rules and outcomes.

Family roles: the prior role of child in the family would appear to be the basis for learning the new roles in neighborhood play and the school-related activity. Among these developing roles is that of play companion. Very young children are as much the objects of play episodes as they are reciprocal participants. Nevertheless, with a sequence of toys and activities that reflect the learning readiness of the child as well as the aims of the parents and siblings, the child is involved in familial leisure roles. Research indicating that not only the schedules of adults, but also their leisure orientations, are altered by taking on the parent roles[9] suggests that the child, too, is expected to join in a variety of leisure interactions. The crucial relationships with parents are developed in play as well as in maintenance. In this play the child is a reciprocal if subordinate actor who gives and receives affection, displays and develops motor control and communication skills, and learns the affective responses and displays appropriate to the interaction. The more structured episodes involve the role-learning of formal and informal games[10,11] that become more and more elaborate through childhood. In such play the child is constructing a view of himself and of his/her 'fit' with others in a world that gradually expands outward from the family of origin.[12] Leisure roles are not only expressive and pleasure-seeking, but also require demonstrated competence to learn, move, interact and communicate. In play settings the child begins to have not only a sense of self, but of self-esteem. Learning involves not only the sense of 'who', but also of 'what kind of who' in relation to others, especially parents and other immediate family.

Play roles: play for children is a response to the environment, including the social environment, that varies with the immediacy and complexity of stimulation.[13] Childhood leisure roles also vary by sex, age and cultural definitions. In Telford New Town boys were found to engage in more physical activity and girls more in play that anticipated nurturing roles.[14] The same kind of observations of schoolyard leisure in the United States included more complex and competitive interaction for boys and less organized play in small groups for girls.[15] Such differences are suggested as one factor preparing males better for adult roles in complex organizations of business and government. By the time children are playing with peers, especially at school, they have already been subjected to considerable socialization in families and are quite aware of gender-related expectations. Play roles, in family and neighborhood, are not only a means of gaining affective gratification, but also are significant settings in which modes of interaction are learned and styles of coping with the world developed. In play roles, the child not only moves and interacts with significant others, but comes to have a particular view of the self who is able to do these things.

(2) *Youth roles*: School roles: the school context becomes more and more important to development as children move into adolescence. However, 'school' encompasses not only classroom settings, but also

the myriad activities and interactions that surround and permeate the institutional schedules. In the more fluid social context outside the classroom, and even outside the gym and playing-field, leisure provides a social space for the development of roles of friend, intimate and even lover. However, the school itself, with its central mission of evaluation and social sorting,[16] is an institutional context for a number of competence-testing roles. Student, athlete, organizational leader and arts practitioner are continually evaluated roles in the institutional system while more informal roles receive regular feedback in a 'peer review' process of selection. Acceptance and self-definitions of competency not only for that time, but also for the future, are developed in the school roles. In fact, there are continual reminders by adults that performance in school is directly related to both performance and opportunities to perform in later establishment roles.

Family roles: while the family may seem to move out of its previously central place in leisure as children become adolescents, there is considerable evidence that family interaction remains important. One indirect way is in the support of many activity roles by parents who not only pay the costs, but provide transportation and the schedule accommodation required for participation. The family tensions arising from external schedule requirements related to school, leisure and employment roles of teens may have considerable impact on the quality of informal interaction within the home.[17] Adjustment of expectations for leisure interaction by parents and siblings is required if the residual time spent with other family members is not to continually reflect the developmental urge toward independence. Conflicting needs for autonomy and acceptance may make familial leisure interaction less than harmonious during much of adolescence.

Play roles: what is most important to recognize is that leisure roles may well be most central to working out the intimacy, peer acceptance, cohort identification, self-definitional and independence tasks of adolescent development. It is precisely in the leisure settings including those places of informal 'fooling around' that central issues are attacked. Anticipatory socialization includes not only the competitive roles of sports and the expressive roles of the arts, but also the intimacy roles of deep relationships with others of the same and the other sex. Defining oneself as competent physically and intellectually is important enough, but a self-concept of ability to be a friend, confidant and lover may be even more crucial for development. Further, life is not just a set of unrelated roles. Erik Erikson has pointed out the need to maintain some sense of continuity in both self-definitions and in the perceived definitions of others.[18] With the increased mobility and resources granted most teens, their leisure roles become those that allow for the most experimentation and seeking of reinforcement and affirmation. It is the variety of leisure for youth that provides a context for trying out both abilities and identities.[19]

Preparatory Identities

The roles are the context in which identities are developed and expressed. Among the identities central to this period are the sexual, productive, social and intimate.

Sexual identities: From earliest memory, we have known ourselves to be identified by gender we are boys or girls, male or female. And soon we learn that one day we will be men or women. In childhood in most cultures clear distinctions are made in what is expected of male and female children. Further, identification with the same-sex parent as well as with siblings and significant others is a powerful element in shaping our self-concepts.[20] As a consequence, the evaluations of competence received from family and others in childhood are tied not only to age, but gender expectations. We are good or not-so-good at things as a 7-year-old *girl* or 2-year-old *boy*. We learn to perform in relation to those expectations. This is far more profound in human development than which games and toys are encouraged. It means that there is no identity apart from gender identification and no set of role expectations that are not in some ways sex-differentiated.

In adolescence this gender identification has a new series of specific meanings as our sexual identities and role expectations take on the dimension of sexual interaction. A common sequence includes a drawing back from heterosexual interaction into one or more same-sex friendships that have an element of sexuality that is less than fully understood or expressed.[21,22] Much leisure becomes a sharing of music, reading, games and intimate communication in settings set apart from larger groups. However, for most teens this same-sex intimacy evolves into an exploration of a wider world of other-sex relationships. Again, leisure settings and activities become the main social space for this development that may move from group interaction to a narrowing to one other-sex intimate. At the same time, such intimacy becomes a context for the expression of both security and challenge themes in development. In research on this sexual identity formation perhaps too much attention has been given to formal events and to explicitly sexual interaction and not enough to more tentative and less structured leisure interaction.

Productive identities: In the preparation period there are only limited opportunities to engage in the 'real world' of productivity. Nevertheless, children and youth are expected to prepare for production roles not only in school, but also in leisure. Intellectual preparation in school and home often involves various games. One difference between a child's relatively autonomous play and adult-directed activity is often the insertion of the learning component by the adult. In much the same way, various adult-directed sport activities are intended to develop capacities for decision, role-taking, teamwork, competition, negotiation and leadership that will prepare for later productive roles. The concept of achievement is introduced early into the lives of many children, as much in the context of play as of school. Further, differential rewards – material and psychic – early become a part of the experience of 'playing' in ways that have evaluated outcomes.

For teens, the structures are more complex but the aims often more explicit. Not only are social rewards of status and prestige related to performance by productivity measures such as scoring the most points in a sport contest, but the youth is encouraged to define the meaning and value of many activities in terms of achievement.[23] In the temporary and limited context of the game, identities are formed that internalize learned evaluations of ability to compete, produce and 'score'. The leisure of youth reflects the values of the culture in such stress on measurement of production not only in school, but on the playground. It is no wonder that much of the self-selected play of adolescents seems to involve a rejection of such measurement and an embrace of less differentiated expressivity.

Social Identities: First in the family and then in neighborhood and other peer contexts, basic social skills of regular interaction are learned in play.[24] How to interpret and respond to the expectations of others, deal with not only structured roles, but problematic situations, and develop lines of interaction that may lead to outcomes preselected with goals in mind are all learned in play settings by the child. A child learns not only the regularities of roles, but also how to take on those roles in satisfying ways and how to develop strategies to shape the course of the interaction. In the play/leisure episodes there is the opportunity for testing self-presentations and finding which identities meet with validating responses from others.[25] Such identities are sex- and age-related, but also are the beginning of self-definitions that have some persistence through the life course. Such identities of leadership, humor, physical strength or skill, and organizing and negotiating ability are built up in countless episodes of validation. On the other hand, self-definitions of inabilities may also be learned from play sequences. One may be 'last chosen' as well as 'captain' or 'star'. One evident difference in adult-dominated games is that generally all are included while in the child-organized episodes exclusion and explicit judgements as to competence are common. As a result, the identity-learning potential both positive and negative – may be greater in relatively free play.

For youth, the widening circles of social interaction also involve structured institutions that are designed to reflect the 'adult' world and its roles. Youth are caught in most critical dilemmas of development with independence tasks pulling outward from former intimacy contexts and yet with a continued need for basic belonging. As a result, identities that are as valued in peer groups, including self-presentation elements of cohort-identifying music, apparel, vocabulary and other symbols may come into conflict with identities valued in the family or school. Youth learn both the necessity of multiple identities and shifting presentations in different contexts, but also the subtleties of presenting an identity in one leisure event that is in tune with expectations slightly different from the past one. Solidarity with peers not only calls for identity shifts from home and classroom, but requires delicate alterations depending on just who else is in the interaction episode and what the 'game' of the moment is. The problematic nature of much teen leisure provides the widest latitude for both identity development and strategic self-presentations.

Intimate identities: In childhood, play and intimacy are most closely joined. Earliest play experiences are generally with parents and others in the nuclear family. Play not only involves responses to signs of increasing complexity from 'peek-a-boo' on – but also expressions of affection. As the play world widens, the complexity of both the play and the relationships increases. However, the uniting of play as response and activity with acceptance, warmth, love and inclusion leads to development of the fundamental meaning of play in the identity of the self as one who is accepted and loved in demonstrating the ability of join in the interaction. Leisure is more than a context of intimacy; in a child's leisure, assurance of intimacy is affirmed and demonstrated.

During teen years this union of leisure and intimacy takes on the wider spheres of peer acceptance and of sexual interaction. From the basis of learning, a self-definition of the self as one who is able to give and receive signs and demonstrations of intimacy, the new and often threatening possibilities of sexuality and intimacy outside the family are explored and developed. Again leisure not only provides the most common setting for such development, but is joined in our expectations with building relationships of closeness, communication and trust. The dance, party, concert, game, walk, swim, picnic, trip, or evening at home are the activity setting for which the real meaning is the building of a relationship. The social skills and identities that have been learned in less intense leisure are brought into play in more focused relationships. In time, even the fateful enterprise of courting is done in leisure contexts.[26]

Themes of the Preparation Period

Although childhood and youth are diverse and complex periods of the life course, there are a number of themes that run through the period. All are based on the social definition of the period as one that has its culminating meaning in the succeeding years and roles. The first eighteen or more years of life are defined largely in terms of what they will lead to in the next major period. With family and school future-oriented, one dimension of leisure that should not be ignored is that at least in some episodes, events and setting the meaning may be most self-contained. Play/leisure, with all its developmental implications, is the most contemporary part of the life of the child with most or all of its conscious meaning focused on the present. It may also be that partly because of such investment in the present the consequences for identity development are most crucial.

Expressivity vs role socialization: Play and leisure are contexts of learning. Not only the processes of learning to interpret role expectations and fit oneself within their parameters, but also coming to grasp the regularities – the structures – of social institutions may take place in games and social occasions as well as in school. Further, in the family, play and learning how to interact with others are continual and simultaneous. In institutional settings, especially the school, a variety of 'play' activities are actually designed with role socialization as the covert purpose. Latent functions abound, especially when events are designed and controlled by socializing adults. However, a child's play and a youth's leisure are also expressive demonstrations and even outbursts of personal identities in interaction with others. With all the constraints and expectations pervading the life of even the youngest child, there are moments and times of expressivity of a playing out of emotions and a reaching out for the pleasure of the episode. Play and leisure may also be self-contained in their meaning for the moment. In such expressivity some of the most authentic expressions of developmental reaching and striving may be manifest.

Automony vs community: Child and adolescent development not only incorporates new and more inclusive social relationships, but also requires changes in old relationships. While family and other immediate intimates of infancy and the preschool years are not abandoned, they lose some of their all-encompassing primacy with each year of growth. This sequence of shifts in salience requires that greater autonomy be developed. While play and leisure may be integrally joined with the building and expression of all levels of social relationships from the family outward, they are also opportunities for gaining self-direction and trying out new decision processes of self-determination. In the expanding social world it is often the least institutionalized spaces in life that allow for the crucial expression of independence as well as of chosen relatedness.

Intimacy and sexuality: As previously suggested, the union between play and intimacy begins literally with the first infant responses to being held and stimulated. Not only for adolescents exploring the meaning of their sexuality and of what it means to be a sexually identified being with others of the same and the other sex, but for all stages of development, leisure is a central social space for trying out, refining and consolidating sexual identities. However we may analyze the links between intimacy and sexuality, they are joined in all kinds of leisure settings and interactions. The presentation and interpretation of sexual identities as well as the development of intimacy takes place in the multifaceted areas of child and adult play.

Competence: Underlying the learning of roles and the development of identities is the theme of evaluation. In the interpreted evaluations of significant others we come to have conceptions of our own abilities in different aspects of life. How we learned physical and mental skills, how we appear to others, how we deal with different kinds of social situations and how we measure up to others in the varied situations of social interaction are all learned. For example, as the basis for a later readiness to attempt to develop a new leisure or work skill, our self-definition of ability to learn similar skills may be more salient than previous experience with the specific task. Self-definitions of competence are learned in all the contexts of development and especially in the responses of significant others. Individuals who strive unsuccessfully to overcome early parental expressions of incompetence are only one negative example of the importance of such self-definitions. When particular games or interaction events are defined as central for that time in life, then they may have persistent consequences for self-concepts.

The Transition to Early Establishment
There are many significant transitions within each of the three periods of the life course. However, transitions from one to the other might be expected to have the greatest impacts on leisure. Major changes in roles seldom leave identities unaffected.

The transition from preparation to establishment, like others in a social system, is not just a sudden shift of roles. Rather, considerable anticipatory socialization has taken place, especially in a period with the central motif of such anticipation. Nevertheless, the changes are profound – from student to worker, from family of origin to a new family of intimacy and production, from relative dependence to relative independence. For most in contemporary Western societies, this transition also involves a new residence, some different friends, geographical shifts for many and, most of all, a new time definition that 'this is it!'

A survey of recent graduates of the University of Illinois was followed by intensive case studies of eight individuals – four of each sex – in a variety of life circumstances.[27] A series of collaborative interviews was employed to investigate how the major role transitions had affected leisure and the place of leisure in making the role and identity transition. Changes in activities were essentially as predicted and reflected opportunity shifts away from the campus to the residence and to interaction and individual activity there. More significant shifts were found related to new family roles, especially for those who had become parents. Both schedule and resource constraints and orientations toward intrafamilial activity changed the timetables, locales and styles of leisure. Despite considerable variation among the eight, several themes emerged:

- The sexual exploration and sexual identity-development orientations of student leisure were altered by marriage, and the commercial meeting places of student leisure for the most part gave way to home interaction and entertaining.
- The two who were single differed in their basic life orientations with one concentrating on establishment of the work role, and the other building a life style around her recreation commitments.
- The role of parent required a number of adjustments which were managed by most in ways that still incorporated significant leisure elements, now most often familial, at home, or carefully scheduled and planned.
- For those who were now married, the spouse became the central leisure companion except for one dual-career couple who maintained a major set of segregated activities and associations.
- Establishing a *place* in the community through leisure associations such as church and status-yielding voluntary organizations was important to most of the couples.
- Surprisingly, leisure was not set aside during this transition to establishment roles as much as adapted to contribute to the change. For all but three, one of whom was unemployed and one married to a student and therefore not really into the transition, leisure remained an important element of life. Despite changes in locales, associations and orientations, leisure still had a place of importance in overall life patterns. However, leisure was expected to contribute to other roles, especially the familial. In marriage,

leisure companionship is a goal and role expectation as well as a convenience. The productivity preoccupations of the period reorient leisure, but do not push it aside.

The Establishment Period

The period of establishment begins when a person takes on central roles of family and economic production. Preparation for work roles may continue part-time or intermittently, but education becomes a complement to work rather than work to education. While many do not enter marriage at this time, a majority still either enter a commitment for marriage or seek one while completing school or in the first year thereafter. Further, although postponing childbearing is also increasing, the actuality or potential of parenthood becomes part of the lives of most adults within a few years.

One evident theme of the period is *productivity*. Fundamental orientations change, so that the period becomes one of determining and inaugurating investments intended to provide the basis of the remainder of life. Productivity in home and family as well as in work are central value orientations. Decisions are made that are designed to lead to possibilities of measured, recognized and rewarded accomplishment. In a 'career' view that anticipates many reward and status goals, what is done is expected to lay the necessary groundwork for future fulfillment.

However, a second theme is that of securing a place in the social system. The preparatory institutions of the school and family of orientation now give way to the economy and new family of adult establishment. Not only a job, but a position in the workforce is sought that yields both a current identity and the possibilities of future status and security. In Western societies the new nuclear family is recognized not only as fundamental to social placement in this period, but also as the basic social unit of residence, maintenance and social interaction. For most people, the establishment of a family unit is essential for finding and gaining a place in the society.

One way of viewing life in the establishment period is as a set of nesting roles. The familial roles are the foundation of intimate acceptance, maintenance support, economic consumption, social position, community interaction and gender-role investment. From the family come the parenting roles, leisure roles that change significantly with family life cycle progression, and the work roles that have their meaning for most primarily in their contribution to the family-home investment. The residence itself is more than shelter, especially in North America. The home becomes a symbol of being properly rooted and established. It is the location of the home that most determines social circles in the modern metropolis, not employment identification. As a result, rising housing costs and increasing shortages in some areas threaten self-concepts of achievement and security as well as alter contexts of both privacy and interaction.

The Rapoports divide the period into three parts:[28] the first, early establishment, has as its focal preoccupation the choices and plans for productivity and as a problem the allocation of limited resources into various roles. The second, mid-establishment, is the period of the rearing of school-age children. The central concern is for performance. Obligations and loyalties become a source of conflict. The late establishment period, when children are out of school, turns preoccupations to the broader issue of evaluation with the potential problem of negative judgements about commitments made years before. Late establishment is a bridge to the taking stock of the culmination period, but includes the risks of crisis and radical change.

Until recently, we could assume a 'normal' sequence of roles and identities that would be based on work and family progression. The changes brought by parenthood and employment rise and decline, and related assumptions of roles and responsibilities were predictable and navigable enough to be termed 'passages'.[29] Most lives were assumed to make the journey pretty much on time and along the charted routes. Now, however, there is increasing evidence that most persons experience some traumatic change during the journey. Many are confronted with loss of employment or at least diversion of presumed career lines, disappointment or loss related to their children, crises of marriage that may result in divorce and associated traumas, and possibilities of health and other attacks on the security and regularity of life. While the analysis that follows will deal with more regular assumption of establishment roles and identities, we must recognize that most people have to deal with unanticipated changes as well as the predictable role transitions of the life course. For some, the crises are caused by external events – wars, depressions, or the loss of intimates. For others, the crises become part of personal development when inconsistencies and contradictions reach a climax that precipitates life course changes in family, work, or other roles.

Establishment Roles
Work, family and leisure roles are related not only in the allocation of resources of time, money and energy, but also in that identities and styles of coping developed in one social space may be carried over into the others. Further, changes that are inaugurated in one set of roles have consequences for the others. In general, persons who are conventional in one life space are unlikely to assume markedly distinct

identities in other roles. Further, aims of establishment – of making a place in life for oneself – are carried out in leisure and family as well as in work.

Work roles: Assumption of a central work role is for most early establishment adults a necessity of maintenance. Most men and women seek employment, and an increasing proportion of adult women retain such a role through most of their adult lives. However, we should not presume that employment is the same as a work career. Most people have 'jobs', not well-developed careers. They may have goals, either within their employment setting or for transfer to another. However, the primary meaning of such work is its contribution to the more immediate productive areas of life, home and family. It is not incidental that so many men invest themselves in the maintenance of homes, cars and other items that provide something of an experience of producing, of setting work tasks and completing them. Even when the job provides some social identification and enjoyable associations with workmates, its meaning is more likely to be extrinsic than self-fulfilling.[30, 31, 32, 33] The main aim of such employment is – or at least becomes the provision of economic security and resources of life's central interests.

While such an orientation toward work is most evident in the factory and mill and among those who are employed in mass shops and offices where each worker simply fills a slot and is always replaceable, there is evidence of a disillusionment process for those with more variety and autonomy in their employment. Social workers and school teachers often lose some of their initial goals and enthusiasm and even experience an extreme disenchantment called 'burn out'. Corporation employees, either in a gradual process or in a crisis of evaluation, may define their investment in their management or technical roles as without deep and satisfying meaning.[34] One analysis of work and leisure salience for British managers suggests that their values are increasingly home-centered.[35] As a result, there is tension between the expectations of devotion to the firm and the job and the reality of instrumental definitions of work. A study in Liverpool found that blue-collar workers are somewhat more likely than white-collar to have friendships with workmates, but that the stereotype of an occupational culture that dominates non-work life is not supported.[36] While some professionals may continue to blend their work and non-work associations so that work colleagues become primary family friends, such integration is not the dominant pattern for most workers, especially in large urban areas.

Work roles have their impacts on other roles. Family and leisure timetables must give way to employment priorities. Community status and social access remains related to employment status, but in multifaceted rather than monotonic ways. Certainly, the security of resources based on employment is tied to the cycle of value in the employment market. No aspect of life is unaffected when economic shifts or health problems close off opportunity for workers, and not only reduce income, but threaten future employment.

Family roles: Nevertheless, for most establishment adults, the family comes first. Not only are family roles generally considered the most important in life, but investments of self and resources are turned toward a familial kind of productivity – toward children and the home. It is not enough to view role expectations and requirements as constraints on leisure or as norms directing the allocation of resources. The family is more than the central unit of consumption, sexual regulation, or reproduction and childrearing. It is the focus of meaning for most adults.

We will examine the relationship of leisure and the family in more detail in Chapter 5. Here only an outline of family roles and identities will serve to hold its place in the life course analysis. First, family roles are those most closely related to leisure. As a result, no transition in the life course so affects leisure as those of the family, especially for those assuming the role of parents. Studies in Britain[37] and in the United States[38] are consistent in their finding that leisure becomes familial for parents in time allocation, locales, associations and meanings. Further, this orientation applies – if not exactly equally across class and status classifications in the societies. Whatever the labels – 'bourgeois', 'home-centered', or 'privatized' – the family becomes the central institution in its role expectations as well as opportunities for investment and interaction. For so many, just maintaining the home, family relationships, the viability of the family context and 'paying the bills' is the task of establishment that takes up most of life's energies and efforts.

Leisure, then, is defined in terms of its contributions to the family as well as a social space of freedom. Parents invest time in supporting activities for their children that are intended as contributions to development. Time together for couples is to be found in leisure, in informal more than formal events.

However, there is also the possibility of disenchantment in family roles. In her study of working-class wives Lillian Rubin sketches the disillusionment of many of the women who have not found the intimate communication and sharing in their marriages that they had hoped for.[39] The limitations in scope related to social integration, work and leisure seem to be particularly acute for these women whose self-investments in education and leisure turned to homemaking and motherhood while they were young. They still define their lives primarily in terms of family roles, but without a clear sense of personal return on the investment.

Leisure roles: While the case studies of young men and women entering early establishment found that leisure continued to be important to most, there was also a clear shift toward leisure roles that complemented family and community roles. The preoccupations with productivity and securing a place in life carried over into some leisure.[40] While personal choice and expressivity were not abandoned, the new sets of roles and requirements had powerful impacts. In general, research on adult leisure has found this element of complementarity to be pervasive. While the particular expectations and opportunities for leisure change as children move through their preparation period and eventually leave home, attempts to develop leisure that builds the intimate relationship of the family unit continue, sometimes past the preferences of the children. The family schedule revolves around the multiple roles of members with the leisure of children given a measure of salience. For a time, personal expression and idiosyncratic interests may give way to leisure that contributes to family solidarity and to developing social identities through community organizations such as churches and youth-serving clubs. Yet to be studied in detail is the possibility of shifts in leisure roles in the later establishment period when children have become more independent in their leisure and parents are free to redevelop leisure investments that are personally fulfilling.

Establishment Identities
Satisfaction in this period is closely related to taking work, family and leisure roles *well*. Performance is evaluated and meaning derived from positive definitions of effectiveness. Especially in the middle years of establishment, family roles peak in their salience, so that results are a source of meaning. Not only mothers, but also fathers, may define themselves first of all in terms of their parental investments and the results.

Work identities: In this period there is a developing sense of meaning that provides some integration to life or a sense of deprivation without it. In the cultural ideology such integration is provided centrally by a relationship to the economy. According to traditional views, a man answers questions about his identity with some announcement of his work: 'I am a welder' or 'I'm with the railroad'. This is not only his public social identification, but also his personal identity, his definition of himself. Women, on the other hand, have been expected to find their identities in supporting and nurturing roles, primarily in the family. Their employment has been defined as financial support or supplement rather than a career. Now there are changes for both men and women. A realistic appraisal of a high proportion of jobs is that they are not likely to yield a satisfying identity. Not only is there likely to be mid-life disenchantment, but even for early establishment men there are few captivating goals clearly set out in a career model. The second change is that more women are seeking social identity that is based on work roles of economic productivity.

Certainly, for some with considerable autonomy in their work and with a career orientation that retains goals and related rewards, the work role may provide a central and satisfying identity for most of adult life. For some, work roles are only intermittently satisfying in personal and social identification. The process of coming to terms with the meaning of work may involve a redefinition of its potential, a gradual loss of centrality and meaning, or a change in occupation sometime during mid-establishment.

Now we recognize that the corporation, the human services agency and even the school may not provide fulfilling opportunities for work investment and identity through an entire work career.[41] Even those in professions may experience mid-career crises that throw into question goals and identity investments carefully constructed for up to two decades.[42] And for the worker who is always defined as replaceable, a unit whose skills can be learned by another and whose routines change little from year to year, it is hardly a surprise that employment is defined instrumentally and that income is the central element of job satisfaction.[43]

While some may find compensatory identities in their leisure,[44] for most the central realm of investment and meaning becomes home and family. Even the man or woman who continues to make the self-introduction of 'I'm a high-school teacher' or 'I work at General Electric' finds much of the meaning of that role in maintaining a home, supporting a family and seeking the validation of being important to an intimate set of people who have never seen the inside of the factory or office.

Family identities: The establishment period is one in which the centrality of the family encompasses the changes of parenting. Although fewer men and women are ready to accept the responsibilities of parenting uncritically, perhaps recalling that they were less than wholly fulfilling as products of the investments of their own parents, the high-impact changes of establishment for most are those beginning with the birth of the first child.[45] Not only is the schedule drastically altered, especially for most mothers, but the entire shape of life becomes different. Some work roles have strong future orientations, but many do not. However, parenthood has a clear set of future expectations, requirements, constraints and opportunities. Further, the future is recognizably one that changes each year as children are born, develop and eventually become more or less independent. Parenting has a career, whether work does or not.

In that career, the identification of child and parent is reciprocal. The child is a product, one that requires care and nurture and who responds in ways not wholly predictable. There is uncertainty as well as anticipation, reward as well as cost, and an identity that develops along with the child.

At the same time, parents usually find that the roles in their marriage are changed by becoming parents with mutual dependence and communication requirements balanced by a diffusion of attention that may lessen the intensity of the dyadic relationship. Further, many mothers give up the financial and social resources of employment during the early phases of childrearing. This may have consequences for leisure opportunities, self-definitions of worth and independence, relative power balances within the nuclear family, meeting old and new budget obligations, and a sense of freedom and autonomy. Almost by default, the mother turns to that role for her revised identity and to the child for validation of her performance.

There is a tendency to define the roles of the never-married and the formerly married in terms of their lack of nuclear family identities. In many cases the intention of retaining a leisure or work identity that is central may be a major factor in not marrying or becoming a parent. Other identities tend to become central for establishment adults who are not invested in the family production roles. However, an analysis of the leisure, life satisfaction and self-concepts of those in a transition *from* marriage, the currently separated, indicates that the replacement of such a central identity requires a difficult process of adaptation.[46]

Even for those who have taken a particular leisure association as central to their schedules, identities and life styles, coordination with the expectations and role requirements of other family members is critical.[47] The previously introduced mataphor of nesting roles would seem to apply as well to identities in the establishment period. It is in the context of familial roles and identities that other self-concepts find their place. It is no wonder, then, that as parenting roles change from the extreme demands of the preschool period through the various stages that precede launching, all other roles are altered. Parents not only invest time and money in their children, but a great deal of themselves – in a self-definitional sense – as well.

Leisure identities: Does this imply that leisure during the establishment period tends to be secondary and residual? For some, it is. However, the more common pattern is that the meanings of leisure are, like schedules, meshed with family roles and identities. Further, the themes of productivity and performance, carried out through parenting as well as in work, are also integrated with family and home engagement. The residence as context for family productivity and as a product itself is significant in establishment life styles. Children are not only leisure companions who provide some of the structure for non-work time, but are also the purpose of much leisure as activities and settings are chosen for their potential contribution to the children's development. In fact, the eventual performance of the children in school, games, sport, or social enterprise may be employed as the measure of effective performance by the parents. As a result, the pressures on children to perform at an expected level become a central element in the familial investment in child-centered recreation.

During the establishment period leisure may change from dyadic relation-building during courting and early marriage, to home-centered and unscheduled interaction when children are quite young, to a redevelopment of a balance of leisure activities still closely related to the development of children and then to a re-evaluation of meanings and satisfactions as children gain independence and, in time, leave the parental home. Leisure identities become more and more disengaged from the parental roles during later establishment.[48] During the thirty years or more the changes are dramatic – from being single to the intense dyad of early marriage through the parenting cycle to a return to the marital dyad. And that is assuming no major disruption of the cycle – through illness, loss of employment, divorce, remarriage, relocation, or death in the nuclear family.

Amid those changes, leisure identities may rise and fall in salience. As personal and social resources change, role expectations wax and wane in centrality and self-definitions are subjected to question and even attack from without and within, leisure identities also change in salience, orientation and context. Major components of expressivity and freedom may be in quite different balance with social components of intimacy and status. What we expect of ourselves may change more radically than what others expect of us, and leisure may become the social space that allows for the fullest expression of such change.

Themes of the Establishment Period

The overall theme of the period is the investment in productive roles and consequent self-definition in terms of evaluated performance. When family or work roles are central to this process, then leisure may be chosen to complement whichever identities and investments are central. However, in the period there may also be times and processes of disillusionment and dissolution. The family and work roles may not provide the continuity, satisfaction, or validation commensurate with the investment. For some, leisure investments may be developed that provide opportunity for the expression of identities and the involvement in face-to-face communities that support those identities.

Especially when traumas disrupt the anticipated course of life in this mid-period, leisure may gain in salience. For those who either never are able to inaugurate a work career at all or who find that what begins as a career becomes in time just a job, leisure may become a social space in which competence is developed, expressed and appreciated. For those increasing numbers who have to adapt to disruption of the family life cycle, leisure may become a means of coping with the change, re-establishing intimacy, or rebuilding the fragmented nuclear family. This does not mean that leisure is always secondary and shaped by work and family roles. However, decisions to make significant investments in leisure roles and identities require either a rejection of the pervasive determination of work and family or the development of an integrated life style that defines leisure as a contributing and complementary part of the whole.

A second theme is that of social integration. For those in the most demanding periods of the family life cycle, merely the integration of schedules and the allocation of scarce resources may be difficult enough. However, from a developmental perspective, there is more. The considerable requirements of family interaction and support during childrearing call for a reorientation of patterns within the nuclear family and in relationships to other social units. In leisure parents may withdraw from such engagements and radically adjust their interface with others. Social integration becomes for many the relating of the nuclear family to other families more than a matter of personal interaction. Social integration is through the family to the larger society in significant ways. Leisure, then, becomes so integrated with family roles and identities that the independence and launching of teens requires a redevelopment of the social contexts of leisure for many.

The third theme is that of satisfaction. Leisure is not separated from the developmental dimensions of productivity and performance. Rather, in leisure these aims may be carried out in ways that are related to the family and especially children as well as to the home and personal achievement. A major element in leisure satisfaction becomes the demonstration of having performed roles well, whether the particularities involve the house and garden, a sport or craft, or simply being a 'good' father or mother.

The Second Transition

The transition from establishment to culmination cannot be dated with any precision. It may be associated with certain role changes – the launching of children, a re-evaluation of the career possibilities in work, or even the anticipation or actuality of retirement. For most people, these are processes rather than fixed and dated events. However, the 'third age' of the life course is different. It involves an evaluation of meaning that may have been buried under the everyday requirements of establishment roles. It is a time in which the limits of life are recognized – not only the temporal limit defined by death, but limits as to what is possible in the meantime.

The transition may be traumatic for some, especially when associated with a limit-notifying event such as a heart attack, the failure to gain an anticipated promotion, or recognition of the loss of some functional ability. Whether or not a re-evaluation of life necessarily must involve some pain and disruption remains a question to be investigated. Nevertheless, at least in an achievement-oriented culture, some recognition of limits would seem inevitable. In a society in which we shield ourselves from death, its impending reality may come as a shock to some.

In this transition – however processual or traumatic – leisure may serve as a kind of 'bridge'. In leisure, continuity may be found when other roles are changing. On the other hand, leisure may also be an opportunity to explore new possibilities of meaning and expression in the face of the failure of others. Leisure may become more and more a set of 'evaluated roles' in which we find satisfaction through developing and carrying out their tasks and relationships.[49]

The Culmination Period

Labels for the third period of life vary in connotations. Some are neutral: 'third age' or 'later life'. Some are tied to one role: 'retirement' or 'postparental'. Some are intended to be upbeat and positive: 'golden age' or 'the fullness of time'. In any case, there is a recognition that life is different when most of it is past and the future is recognizably limited. One central element is that recognition coupled with an attempt to make sense of the whole matter. It is a time of coming to terms with a life that has come to a particular place and isn't going to go on forever.

Such recognition may be painful and frightening. On the other hand, it may involve acceptance, appreciation and integration – a drawing together of the various strands of the life course into a whole with meaning and coherence. In any case, there is a shift in time orientation. In this third age people look back for meaning and also look ahead in a new way: 'what is it all about now that productivity and performance are mostly past?' 'What does it mean when I accept a certain if unpredictable end?'

At the same time that meanings are being questioned, there is a diminution of involvement in some roles. Although most adults retire voluntarily in the United States, there are many pressures that may decrease the rewards of employment. Further, technological unemployment is displacing more workers at the same time that growth in public sector services is slowing. As a result, ceilings in income and uncertainties in stability of employment will increase the proportion of workers who do not work steadily up to a fixed retirement date. The work role, like the parental, will be one of gradual diminution for many.

One problem in dealing with the later years in the life course is that those now in their forties and fifties are not likely to become just like those now in their seventies and eighties. Cohorts differ, and the culmination period can be expected to be different by the year 2000. Those entering their sixties and seventies will be better educated, have had higher incomes, have fewer adult children and a relatively long postparental life cycle phase, have higher expectations for health and physical activity, and be part of a cohort that is a much larger proportion of the total population. Whether later cohorts will retire earlier or later and the measure of public support for health and housing remains to be decided. The point is that we cannot assume that future cohorts of culmination adults will be essentially like those of today.

Nevertheless, there are some well-documented developmental tasks that are not likely to disappear. Older adults will continue to have to come to terms with death – their own and that of intimates. They will continue to need to make sense of their lives, to seek a measure of personal and social integration.[50] Whether or not older persons are granted a special level of respect in a culture, they need to come to respect and accept themselves. No longer is it possible to assume that real fulfillment will come at some period in the future. The future is limited

Gordon analyzes the development dilemmas of the later years as follows:

Maturity: age 45 to retirement – dignity vs control.
Retirement: to onset of disability – meaningful integration vs autonomy.
Disability: to death – survival vs acceptance of death.

The central set of tasks centers on the maintenance of independence and self-direction in life. Prerequisites are reasonable health and financial resources, however provided. 'Meaningful integration' has at least two dimensions. The first is interior: the integration of meanings, accomplishments and failures into an acceptance of life with meaning and worth. Such integration of meaning has been termed interiority or integrity. The second dimension is social. Social integration seeks to achieve stability of relationships among a set of intimates, family and friends, who accept and value one another's identities. In the later part of this period the gradual loss of such intimates requires the adaptation of survivors.

It should also be stressed that by the time individuals reach the culmination period, they have been learning for a long time and have developed characteristic ways of coping and adapting to change. The developmental approach that stresses change and continued learning should not be emphasized to the extent that continuities and even rigidities are ignored. Well-learned and practiced modes of defining the self and relating to others are not laid aside because integration becomes a developmental need. Rather, old patterns and habits are retained to the extent that they may seriously inhibit adaptive culmination.

Culmination Roles

At least to the point that severe impairment turns life into mere existence, older persons continue to have sets of roles with related expectations. However, changes in those roles may be severe and to a large extent externally imposed. This is especially true with work roles.

Work roles: The fact that retirement is more of a process than an event for most adults does not imply that the change is trivial. Not only are incomes altered, but the schedule and rhythm imposed on life by regular employment is lost. Nevertheless, there seems to be considerable continuity in the process. On the job, older workers come to be defined as relatively fixed in their present positions rather than on a career ladder. For many, their anticipation of retirement is accepted by others and may be envied by some. For those in positions requiring physical strength and stamina, injury and illness may reduce consistency of employment years before any retirement age. Various forms of functional disability contribute to what is more often already an instrumental view of employment. Robert Atchley suggests that the job history of most workers evolves in ways that set the stage for retirement.[51] Further, retirement itself has its productive roles related to residential maintenance, family support and the possibility of a variety of helping or crafting roles.

Atchley further proposes that retirement itself is a process with anticipation and continuity elements easing the transitions.[52] The approach of retirement is followed by a honeymoon phase of inaugurating anticipated enterprises, a disenchantment phase in which loss is experienced, and then periods of reorientation, stability and termination. The point is that the final phase of work roles is processual with transitions and reintegration of self-definitions that match the role shifts. In that process, varied as it is for persons of different histories, several issues are emerging. One is the impact of the increasing number of women who have had their own work careers and who experience retirement for themselves as well as for husbands. A second concern is the likelihood that work role changes may be combined with the lack of a familial social context for many who come to this period unmarried and/or childless. A third issue is that of social support – all the problems of housing, health care costs, maintenance and fulfilling leisure that are compounded by the loss of employment income and retirement incomes that do not rise with inflation.

Family roles: Cross-sectional studies have indicated that the later integrative years prior to retirement may be a period of higher marital satisfaction than the preceding establishment.[53] There are a number of factors including less pressure and conflict from childrearing, more discretionary resources of time and money, an abatement of work career pressures and, perhaps most of all, the 'drawing together' process itself. Nevertheless, there are major transitions in family roles during these later years. The first encompasses the shift in parenting expectations due to the 'launching' of children from their parental home. However, it is important to recognize that the support functions and interaction contexts of parents and their adult children are altered but do not disappear.

A second transition for many is that they assume responsibility for their own aging parents. Just at the time that some adults experience reduced constraints as parents, they may take on new ones related to their own parents.

A third transition in family roles is the loss of a spouse to death. Widows, usually women, have to cope with the loss of the most immediate companion, usual leisure associate, main helper in maintenance, coparent and generally most significant other. Again the process of adaptation to this radical change – however anticipated in many cases by gradual health decline – requires acceptance and readjustment facilitated by the presence of intimate others.[54] Social networks of companionship and support, in which leisure and helping functions may overlap, are critical. Loneliness is a multifaceted condition that has its own timetables related to the past as well as to the social schedules of potential companions. One possibility is that a primary function of leisure for widows is the provision of social integration through contexts for regular interaction.[55]

Another issue is derived from changes in the stability of marriage in contemporary society. Although in North America most older persons are involved in social networks, live with a spouse, enjoy satisfying contact with their adult children, and participate in a set of friendship and activity networks,[56] an increasing proportion may not have the support of a single intimate companion. More persons may enter culmination with more education and a greater variety of leisure experiences, but without the continuity of a life partner who is the coparent of one's children.

Leisure roles: Leisure, understood as more than activity, is not just a way to fill time at any age. Approaching leisure in later life as a way to fill time left over from the diminution of other roles misses the significance of leisure in human development. However, the overwhelming evidence of a general constriction of the range of leisure activities associated with aging suggests that some constraints and inhibiting factors are operative.

A study of leisure in the Highlands and islands of Scotland reinforced other research in finding regular participation in home-centered leisure including reading and gardening.[57] However, there was also considerable interest indicated in arts, crafts and a variety of group social events. Research on constraining factors among older persons in the United States does not suggest they are sitting around with nothing to do. Nor were attitudes about what was expected of people their age a major factor in not participating in desired activities. Cost and transportation were factors, but the main one was a lack of time.[58] Even in retirement, time is a scarce resource for most. In a study employingthe family life cycle as the independent variable, in later years family obligations became less of a barrier but stress and a lack of clear expectations and opportunities became more of a factor.[59] Greater freedom and reduced expectations require a transition for many adults who have had reduced latitude for leisure during the central parenting years.

In this third age the reduced familial expectations produce a transition in leisure with a re-evaluation process similar to that related to work and family roles. Now there is more choice, but that discretion may find some unprepared to exercise it until they redefine their identities with significant leisure expressions and relationships outside the nuclear family. Further, a re-establishment of the marital dyad in leisure styles may call for considerable adaptation.

Leisure demonstrates more continuity than discontinuity in the culmination period. In general, older people are no more interested in special clubs and age-segregated events than they were in earlier adult stages.[60] On the other hand, old activities and relationships may gain new meaning and salience through this period of integration. When new decisions are made as to what is important, fulfilling and worth the investment of resources including finite time, then leisure roles may be readjusted. Some may be given much greater priority, while others are placed in the background. The contribution of some kinds of leisure to social integration, personal expressivity and desired development coinciding with the reduction of family and work-related expectations and demands opens the possibility of revised sets of leisure investments with increased salience for life's meaning.

Culmination Identities
The altered role contexts in work, family and leisure suggest that how we take those roles and define ourselves within them may also change. Continuity in social contexts and activity choices can obscure shifts in what they mean.

Work identities: Already cited are studies indicating that the presumed centrality of work may have been overdrawn. Robert Atchley's research has yielded findings of relatively minor identity loss in the retirement process because employment was not that central before.[61] In fact, he finds that self-concepts remain relatively stable in later years despite changes in health and participation. One reason is that persons have already adapted to considerable role change and have developed identities that can persist through change. In relation to work identities, in Britain few retired workers – white-collar or blue – reported missing work itself, although a quarter missed the income.[62] Employment gives a time framework to life that may require replacement, but the social identity of being a retired worker who *did* a certain job is acceptable to most. While the nature of one's occupation is a factor in satisfaction and in attitudes toward retirement, the major resources in coping with later life change are income, health and social integration.[63]

It is important to retain a self-definition of being a person of value and worth at any time in the life course and especially in the culmination period. However, the contribution of work to a viable identity is based on the complex interaction of factors such as commitment to the work role, work history, economic resources, level and satisfaction of social competence and integration, the perceived cultural evaluation of older persons and satisfaction in leisure involvement.[64] In one interview study of retirees all these factors were found to be important to adaptation to postemployment roles.[65] However, the styles of occupation did seem to have some carryover to leisure styles in retirement. The continuity is more than from pre- to postretirement leisure, but from the entire set of earlier role identities and styles to the new ones.

Family identities: There are a number of interrelated dimensions in family identities including a renewed expectation of leisure companionship from the marriage partner. Family, both nuclear and extended, provides for most older persons a primary helping network, one that is usually reciprocal rather than simply giving or receiving. Family identities are a source of satisfaction and meaning in the process of drawing together and coming to terms with life in the culminating process of integration. Not only the sharing of stable and loving relationships with one or a few others, but the centrality of being an accepted person in the intimate community is crucial to later-life adaptation.[66] Who we are begins with those intimate identities. It would be rare that occupational or leisure identities, however wide the recognition of competence, could substitute for such intimacy. Family is for most the hub around which social integration, timetables and priorities are constructed.

As a result, when an older person is left alone, the support and interaction security of intimacy must be recovered in some way in order to maintain viable life. For example, widows may develop such support networks with other widows that supplement or even replace the loss of the nuclear family when the spouse dies and adult children have established their own families.[67] A variety of relationships may become quasi-families with mutual support that is mingled with scheduled and informal social interaction. However, even with such support, the identity of parent and former spouse remains central to self-definitions of having lived a life of worth that deserves respect.

During the reappraisal phase of this third age marriage and parenthood may come under critical evaluation.[68,69] In some cases a marriage may be dissolved and in others a new contract negotiated, usually with considerable conflict. For many parents, earlier dreams must be revised to meet the reality of the development of children who by now have begun their own establishment period and given evidence of their own role performances. Coming to terms with realities may require redefining one's identity as parent, marriage partner and family member just as work identities call for reappraisal that often entails some disenchantment. Life seldom turns out to be all that one might hope in family roles as well as occupational.

Leisure identities: For a few, leisure becomes the central identity that gives meaning and coherence to the rest of life. Not only satisfaction, but also schedules, stable communities of intimacy, goals and priorities, and continued personal development, may be found in major investments in a consuming leisure enterprise.[70] However, for most, leisure is one aspect of life and closely tied to family engagement. It is an activity context in which identities are expressed and relationships worked out rather than activity with its own self-contained meaning. However, in later years the relative freedom of leisure may more and more offer opportunity for the development of role identities that yield satisfying self-concepts of competence, mastery, learning, growth, and personal investment and expression.[71]

Gordon's analysis of the place of leisure in identity development is grounded in life course research with a social-psychology basis.[72] He brings together many of the diverse themes of leisure in later life that illustrate the multiple but interrelated identities salient to continued satisfaction and growth. Leisure may provide continuity in associations as well as in activities in which there is already a foundation of skill and satisfaction. However, in the re-evaluation of culmination, leisure also offers chances to begin things that are new or have been neglected due to establishment constraints or priorities. While the costs and other requirements of some later-life leisure may restrict participation, leisure can be a special space for some reconstruction of life's styles and patterns when other roles remain relatively locked in. At least as important is the close tie between leisure and social integration. As already suggested, leisure is the social space in which a range of relationships is inaugurated, developed and expressed. Family, informal and activity-based associations are the most common, with the attention given to formal voluntary organizations other than churches probably misplaced in terms of their salience to most culmination adults.

One important leisure issue is that of variety in leisure activities. The former assumption that doing many different things as leisure would contribute to satisfaction has been found invalid.[73] Rather, a more intense involvement in fewer activities may well be more satisfying. As a result, research on older people that primarily measures range of participation rather than intensity may be off-target. In fact, in this period's integration and evaluation, peripheral or unsatisfying leisure may be laid aside to give priority to what is more enriching. Voluntary organization memberships, for example, may be dropped in favor of one expressive or creative engagement. In support, Gordon did find indications of such a possibility as well as of lessening satisfaction for many.

One issue that remains to be investigated is whether or not leisure identities can replace those related to other roles in providing meaning and integration to life in the third age. Can leisure become, for some, a central set of role identities around which life can be reoriented?

Themes of the Culmination Period

The persistent theme of this period is that of re-evaluation and the attempt to develop a new integration of life. Looking back is from the perspective that life has limits, time framed by death and one's own possibilities. The question becomes, 'now, in a recognition of those limits, what does it all mean and how can it be completed with dignity?' Whether the questioning and evaluation comes in an intense and traumatic event or over several years, development requires some sorting out and reweaving of the various strands of life.

Work, family and leisure roles change during this third period of life; and the identities developed and expressed in those roles change as well. In bringing coherence into this final period there is the desire to develop a new integration. For most, this integration centers around home investments and family roles. For some, leisure may provide the most satisfying life space in which to seek an integrity of meaning and fulfillment. In any case, there is a reassessment of values and investments and their potential for the remainder of life.

For some, there is a turn toward 'interiority' and a new stress on the self. After years in which preparation and then performance have been turned to social roles and productivity, the self may be defined more as an end. As a result, a greater priority may be given to outcomes that enrich the self and to continued growth and development.

At the same time, social integration is crucial. Intimate communities, including marriage and the family, may be re-evaluated to try to measure just what they contribute to a satisfying life. In some cases major changes or adjustments are found necessary. In others relationships that do not meet original expectations are accepted and maintained despite their inadequacies. However, a major function of leisure in this period is to provide a context for the maintenance of valued intimate communities and an opportunity for the development of new ones.

Amid this process of assessment and reorientation, in contemporary societies there are certain prerequisites for coping. They are adequate levels of health and economic resources. It must be recognized that for many without those levels, life in this period continues to be or becomes just a struggle to get through each day. Renewal and growth fostered by re-evaluation and a new integrity of life are hardly possible when the resources to cope with constraints and limitations are missing. Freedom to develop identities and interaction relationships is not a universal possibility in this time of culmination.

The aim of culmination is life with integrity and authenticity. The opportunity is to establish enough freedom from former role expectations and requirements to rebuild identities and their contexts. However, the third age may also be a time of disintegration for those who lack the resources – internal or external – to take stock and draw life back together. It is an opportunity that entails risk. Further, we come into the period as persons with histories that shape and limit just how deeply we may reassess, how radically we may change, how courageously we may explore and how fully we may love.

Models of Change

The dimensions of change through the life course involve both roles and identities, both how we are related to the institutions of the social system and the personal style of our actions. In attempting to analyze the place of leisure in life course changes most approaches have adopted some variation of an activity model.

The Activity Model

In general, most research on leisure in relation to the life course has detailed the addition and subtraction of activities in relation to age. Chronological age has been presumed to indicate a number of factors of role, physical, resource, opportunity and interest change. As a result, the summary graph has usually been one that displayed a downward-sloping line representing the number of activities engaged in and sometimes a measure of frequency. From this perspective, socialization research has concentrated on starting activities and either continuing or dropping them. The social and opportunity contexts of inauguration and continuation have been offered as explanations of the process.

Various modes of analysis have suggested that participation in activities or in types of activity can be understood in terms of styles of leisure. For example, active leisure is found to decrease with age and passive leisure to become more common. Or home-centered leisure is said to characterize the leisure of working-class wage workers more than that of bourgeois entrepreneurs or professionals who are more likely to have a component of community involvement. A series of factor analyses of various participation surveys have been employed to suggest that individuals adopt styles of leisure that may change through the life course.[74]

The author has offered two amendments to the leisure styles model based on activity patterns. The first proposes that most adults cannot be stereotyped in terms of a particular kind of leisure.[75] Rather, according to research in three North American communities, leisure participation is more likely to be *balanced*, with a variety of activities and settings chosen to satisfy a variety of meanings. Some leisure is more social in its orientation and some more personal, some relaxing and some intense, some informal and available and some involving special events, and so on. The balance hypothesis allows for individuals who are more monothematic or singleminded in their leisure, but finds that variety in activity and meaning is characteristic of the leisure styles of most adults.

The second amendment adds the concepts of a *core of activities* common to most persons. These activities were found in a factor analysis of a national survey to be left out of the factors because they did not differentiate among those in the sample.[76] Rather, activities such as reading for pleasure, watching TV, visiting family and friends, outings in the car and informal interaction with family at home were common to almost all in the sample. What is indicated is that there exists in a culture such a common core of activities that are generally available. They form a consistent set of both solitary and social kinds of leisure. Beyond this core, individuals develop a balance of activities that changes through the life course as both opportunities and aims are altered. Further, even those who pursue one kind of leisure single-mindedly usually engage in this common core of leisure.

The Role Identity Model
However, any activity model omits important dimensions of both the developmental and social contexts of leisure. To begin with, the meanings of leisure are at least as significant as the activities themselves. Further, understanding those meanings requires taking into account the role commitments of a person. Both the roles and expectations for enactment of the roles change in different life course periods. As a consequence, the role identity model begins with the meaning of activities and their contexts in relation to social roles and the identities that are developed and presented in those roles.

Leisure, then, is found to provide a context in which identities may be expressed in settings allowing for particular freedom, for choice and expressivity often much more limited in other contexts. Leisure, further, partly because of that freedom and openness, is a social space in which the fullness of relationships can be explored and developed. It is a context for intimacy, for social integration that may be especially salient through critical life course transitions. Leisure not only changes form through the life course as activities are added and subtracted, but it changes orientations. Changes in expressivity and social integration alter the fundamental meanings of leisure even when activities themselves are retained.

References: Chapter 3

1   George Masnick, and Mary Jo Bane. *The Nation's Families: 1960–1990* (Cambridge, Mass.: MIT-Harvard Joint Center for Urban Studies, 1980).
2   Rhona Rapoport, and Robert N. Rapoport, *Leisure and the Family Life Cycle* (London: Routledge & Kegan Paul, 1975).
3   Chad Gordon, 'Development of evaluated role identities', *Annual Review of Sociology* (Calif. Annual Reviews, Inc., 1980), p. 406.

4 Kenneth Roberts, *Contemporary Society and the Growth of Leisure* (London: Longman, 1978), p. 102.

5 Rapoport and Rapoport, op. cit.

6 Douglas Kleiber and J. Kelly, 'Leisure, socialization, and the life cycle', in *Social Psychological Perspectives on Leisure and Recreation*, ed., S. Iso-Ahola (Springfield, Ill.: Charles C. Thomas, 1980), pp. 91–137.

7 George McCall, and J. Simmons, *Identities and Interactions*, rev. edn (New York: The Free Press, 1979).

8 Chad Gordon, C. Gaitz and J. Scott, 'Leisure and lives: personal expressivity across the life span', in *Handbook of Aging and the Social Sciences*, eds, R. Binstock and E. Shanas (New York: Van Nostrand Reinhold, 1976).

9 J. R. Kelly, 'Family leisure in three communities', *Journal of Leisure Research*, vol. 10, 1978, pp. 47–60.

10 George H. Mead, *Mind, Self, and Society* (Chicago: University of Chicago Press, 1934).

11 R. H. Turner, 'Role-taking, role standpoint, and reference group behavior', *American Journal of Sociology* no. 61, 1956, pp. 316–28.

12 Gordon, op. cit.

13 M. J. Ellis, *Why People Play* (Englewood Cliffs, NJ: Prentice-Hall, 1973).

14 Elizabeth Child, and John Child, 'Children and leisure', in *Leisure and Society in Britain*, eds, M. Smith, S. Parker and C. Smith (London: Allen Lane, 1973), pp. 141–2.

15 Janet Lever, 'Sex differences in the games children play', *Social Problems*, vol. 23, 1976, pp. 478–87.

16 J. R. Kelly, *Leisure* (Englewood Cliffs, NJ: Prentice-Hall, 1982), ch. 11.

17 J. R. Kelly, 'The problems of parents', *Swimming World*, March 1976.

18 E. H. Erikson, 'Growth and crises of the healthy personality', *Identity and the Life Cycle – Psychological Issues*, no. 1, 1967, pp. 101–71

19 Rapoport and Rapoport, op. cit., p. 36.

20 Gordon, op. cit., p. 417.

21 ibid., p. 427.

22 Kelly, 1982, op. cit., 12.

23 James Coleman, *The Adolescent Society* (New York: The Free Press, 1961).

24 Seppo Iso-Ahola, *Social Psychological Perspectives on Leisure and Recreation* (Springfield, Ill.: Charles C. Thomas, 1980), p. 27.

25 Kleiber and Kelly, op. cit., p. 102.

26 Rapoport and Rapoport, op. cit., p. 122.

27 J. R. Kelly and S. W. Masar, *Leisure Identities through a Life Course Transition* (Champaign, Ill.: University of Illinois Leisure Research Laboratory, 1981).

28 Rapoport and Rapoport, op. cit., p. 186.

29 Gail Sheehy, *Passages: Predictable Crises of Adult Life* (New York: Bantam, 1977).

30 Sar Levitan, and W. Johnston, *Work Is Here to Stay, Alas* (Salt Lake City, Utah: Olympus, 1973).

31 William R. Torbert, *Being for the Most Part Puppets* (Cambridge, Mass.: Schenkman, 1973).

32 Eli Chinoy, *Automobile Workers and the American Dream* (Garden City, NY: Doubleday, 1955).

33 Robert Dubin, 'Industrial workers' Worlds', *Social Problems*, vol. 3, 1956, pp. 131–42.

34 Rosabeth M. Kanter, *Men and Women of the Corporation* (New York: Harper & Row, 1977).

35 J. M. Pahl, and R. E. Pahl, *Managers and their Wives* (London: Allen Lane, 1971).

36 Roberts, op. cit., p. 136.

37 K. Roberts, F. G. Cook, S. C. Clark and E. Semeonoff, 'The family life cycle, domestic roles, and the meaning of leisure', *Society and Leisure*, vol. 8, 1976, pp. 7–20.
38 Kelly, 1978, op. cit.
39 Lillian Rubin, *Worlds of Pain* (New York: Basic, 1976).
40 Kelly and Masar, op. cit.
41 Kanter, op. cit.
42 Daniel Levinson, *The Seasons of a Man's Life* (New York: Knopf, 1978).
43 Levitan and Johnston, op. cit., pp. 17–18.
44 Elmer Spreitzer and E. Snyder, 'Work orientation, meaning of leisure, and mental health', *Journal of Leisure Research*, vol. 6, 1974, pp. 207–19.
45 Kelly, 1982, op. cit., ch. 8.
46 J. R. Kelly, 'Leisure adaptation to family variety', in *Leisure and Family Diversity*, ed., Z. Strelitz (London: Leisure Studies Association, 1979), pp. 2, 1–2, 25.
47 Robert Stebbins, *Amateurs* (Beverly Hills, Calif.: Sage, 1979).
48 Rapoport and Rapoport, op. cit., p. 243 f.
49 Gordon, op. cit., pp. 322–6.
50 Rapoport and Rapoport, op. cit., p. 270.
51 Robert Atchley, *The Sociology of Retirement* (New York: Schenkman, 1976), p. 23.
52 ibid.
53 Linda K. George, *Role Transitions in Later Life* (Monterey, Calif.: Brooks/Cole, 1980), p. 80.
54 Helena, Z. Lopata, *Women as Widows: Support Systems* (New York: Elsevier, 1979).
55 J. R. Kelly, 'Leisure and later-life satisfaction', paper presented at National Recreation and Park Association, Phoenix, 1980.
56 M. F. Lowenthal, and B. Robinson, 'Social networks and isolation', in R. Binstock and E. Shanas, eds, *Handbook of Aging and the Social Sciences* (New York: Van Nostrand Reinhold, 1976).
57 Jonathan Long, 'Retirement, leisure and the family', in *Strelitz*, op. cit.
58 Frances McGuire, 'An exploratory study of leisure constraints in advanced adulthood', Ph.D. thesis, University of Illinois, 1979.
59 Peter A. Witt and T. Goodale, 'The relationship between barriers to leisure enjoyment and family stages', *Leisure Sciences*, vol. 4, 1981, pp. 29–50.
60 S. R. Parker, 'Leisure and the elderly', *Society and Leisure*, vol. 5, 1973, pp. 49–62.
61 Robert Atchley, *Social Forces in Later Life* (Belmont, Calif.: Wadsworth, 1977).
62 Amelia Harris, and S. Parker, 'Leisure and the elderly', in M. Smith *et al.*, op. cit., p. 173.
63 George, op. cit., pp. 81–3.
64 Gordon *et al.*, op. cit., p. 323.
65 I. H. Simpson, K. Back and J. McKinney, 'Continuity of work and retirement activities', in I. Simpson and J. McKinney, eds, *Social Aspects of Aging* (Durham, NC: Duke University Press, 1966), pp. 106–19.
66 Gordon, *et al.*, op. cit., p. 323.
67 Lopata, op. cit.
68 O. G. Brim, 'Theories of the male mid-life crisis', *The Counseling Psychologist*, no. 6, 1976, pp. 2–9.
69 Levinson, op. cit.
70 Stebbins, op. cit.
71 Kelly, 1982, op. cit., ch. 9.
72 Gordon *et al.*, 1976, op. cit.
73 J. R. Kelly, 'Social position and leisure participation as factors in leisure and life satisfaction', paper presented at National Recreation and Park Association, Las Vegas, 1977.

74 J. R. Kelly, 'Leisure stereotypes: the state of the artefact', paper presented at Canadian Congress of Leisure Research, Edmonton, 1981.
75 Kelly, 1982, op. cit.
76 Kelly, 1981, op. cit.

4

Personal and Social Identities

The simplest distinction would be that a personal identity is the definition of the self to oneself and a social identity is assigned by others. However, in a dialectic approach to social interaction the two are so interrelated that self-definition must be seen as a process rather than a completed product. My personal identity is always being revised by how others respond to my presentations and by my interpretation of my assigned social identities. At the same time, how I enact my roles is in part shaped by my personal identity, how I see myself in the role. Recognizing this dialectical nature of identities we can still employ the distinction of perspective:

> *Personal identity* is one's self-definition in a role context.
> *Social identity* is the definition by others of our taking a role.
> *Presentation* is the mode of enacting a role in order to receive social definitions of an intended personal identity.
> *Role identity* is how a role is enacted, a style of behavior.

In this approach I may be defined as the instructor of a class (social identity), who presents himself in such a way in that role (role identity) as to reinforce a self-concept as a professor who seeks to provoke interaction with students rather than simply impart information (personal identity). However, there is always some discrepancy between that personal identity of 'senior colleague' and the actual definition by others of my self-presentation. As a consequence, various signs of that discrepancy may cause me to alter either my presentation, my personal identity, or both.

Any interaction episode has some boundaries of time and space as well as definitions of meaning. Leisure episodes are no exception. Some are clearly defined with absolute parameters of schedule and location. Others are defined in the process of their occurrence. However, within those parameters something happens that is more than the observable action. In fact, the real meaning of the event may be in the identity presentation and revision process. The role – that of guest or host, for example – may be only a context for a processual working out of personal identities and altering or reinforcement of social identities.

Meanings of Leisure: a Review

The models of leisure from Chapter 3 may be understood a bit differently from this perspective. Styles of leisure are not just combinations of activities, but are the stages on which we present our identities and receive feedback on our role identities. In the balance model there is the premiss that leisure is integrated into the overall patterns of life. Therefore, since we take many different roles not only through the life course, but in any single period, it follows that we would seek a balanced variety in our leisure to complement the diversity of our roles. There would be the informal interaction sequences with those closest to us, singular events to give variety and the possibility of activity contexts in which we can maintain and develop relationships with those whom we enjoy but whose lives do not intersect ours daily. Further, that balance might express the diversity of our personal identities in which we know ourselves to be multidimensional.

The core plus balance model recognizes that the time–space contexts of our lives are not infinite, but are bounded by sets of regularities. Within those boundaries we have relatively ready access to a number of associations, locales and resources. Further, those resources complement a series of role relationships that include expectations for interaction. Leisure, then, for most persons in a life course cohort tends to have a number of leisure engagements in common. This common core of leisure is closely tied to our primary roles of familial and household interaction. Although many such activity contexts have been pejoratively labeled 'passive', as though they were essentially inferior to getting out and doing something, quite the contrary may be true. That core may incorporate just those ongoing sequences of interaction that enable us to sustain our most important relationships and to enact critical roles well. The problem may arise when there is no balance over and above the core, when all we have or do is the daily round without highlights of the special and different. Further, it may be in those core activities and settings that we receive most surely the affirmation of our personal identities that enables us to launch new presentations of self.

The role identity model opens a new possibility for understanding leisure. The fundamental meaning of some leisure may not be so much in what we do or in the outcomes as in *how* we do it. Much of the meaning and satisfaction may be in the enactment of the role, in the identity-building dialectic of the episode. As a consequence, we may make leisure choices not just because of the activity or the environment, but because of the enactment potential of the opportunity. Exactly what we are doing, where we are, or even who else is there, may not be as important as how we take and carry out the role itself. We will explore various aspects of this theme in this chapter.

The concept is not that leisure becomes just another role context in which we meet expectations and receive some validation. Rather, leisure would seem to be a social space in which we develop both expressivity and role enactment. It is important that we have the latitude to enact a leisure role in ways that express our personal identity. An essential characteristic of much leisure would be the openness to 'play' with role identities, to do more than respond to norms, to be and become *ourselves* in the event. Gordon proposes that there are four dimensions of this expression and development of self that may be worked out in leisure: competence, self-determination, unity and moral worth.[1] There would seem to be no single self-concept, a 'real self' seeking to come out in our multiple role contexts. Rather, we are multidimensional in our personal identities. We seek to demonstrate that we can do things well, that we may to an extent shape our own destinies, that there is a self underlying our varied actions and that this self has value. We, then, seek approval, results, acceptance and respect as symbolic rewards validating our selfhood. This process may take place in any part of our lives, including leisure.

The Development of Selfhood

Basic to this approach is the concept of the social self, of the learned self-definitions that change through the life course. George Herbert Mead's approach to the self is that a person may act not only toward others, but also toward him/herself.[2] The self is an object of consideration, not just an acting unit. We act in ways that take into consideration the social and environmental context and also who we are when taking the action. In this process we not only have a *self-concept*, but we are continually reshaping that definition of the self. We are in a process of learning who we are – and more, of becoming somewhat different selves in the process. We are, to an extent that has real consequences, who we believe ourselves to be. Further, what we believe ourselves to be is always being learned and relearned in social situations in which there are interpreted responses of others.

Without delving into some of the details and complexities of this view of social action, we can take the basic starting-point. The primary implication for our understanding of leisure is that this process of becoming the learned social self is going on all the time. Leisure is not set apart from the process even though its relative salience may change, even from day to day.

Ralph Glasser began in 1970 to offer an 'identity theory' of leisure that sees it as central rather than residual. In the years since, there has been a slow growth of research and theory-building to support the point-of-view. Glasser stresses that each person has a kind of ideal identity toward which he/she strives.[3] Whether or not the process is this teleological for most individuals, there is an evident development process taking place. We are becoming – sometimes in line with a goal or model we have chosen, sometimes by being defined so rigidly by others that we seem unable to break loose from those social identities and, perhaps, most often in the dialectic that includes both aims and acceptance.

Childhood Development

Mead was not the only one with a theory of the development of selfhood in a process that included leisure and play. Jean Piaget was also an influential contributor to the approach. For example, Piaget argued that in play the young child manipulates such social objects as dolls to begin to experience the social world as real.[4] In middle childhood that social world expands dramatically as do the child's cognitive and emotional abilities. In late preschool and early school years the child learns in many contexts, including games, to take the perspective of others and become less egocentric. Learning how to comprehend expectations and take roles through the negotiation of contracts and agreements is basic to social interaction. Piaget analyzed how changes in cognitive ability are met with new social competence.[5]

However, it is Erik Erikson who placed clear focus on developing a sense of competence.[6] A child is capable of perseverance in goal-directed action and so experiences success and failure in achieving aims. Peers as well as teachers, parents and other adults provide evaluation in many ways, both direct and indirect. Inclusion or exclusion by peers may be most critical in play settings, where to be left out is interpreted as a lack of competence or a failure of others to perceive actual ability. Play and games offer not only such evaluation and opportunity to develop a self-definition of competence, but also the main context for trying out self-concepts and presentations. The relative openness of play coupled with quick feedback makes play a social space for the experimentation of self-development.

Despite many changes in sex role socialization, relatively recent research still supports findings of differences between boys and girls. The dynamics of etiology in such differences remain less clear than we might desire. Significant others, especially partners, have expectations of sex-appropriate behavior that shape the self-definitions of children in their earliest consciousness. By the time they are in school, the more competitive group games of males contrast with the dyadic and small-group social interaction of females.[7] On the other hand, some care needs to be exercised when research is done in settings such as school recess, when adults have generally decided which groups will have access to space and equipment. Increasingly, research attention is now being given to those least-determined episodes, such as neighborhood groups of general inclusion, in which girls participate fully in active and competitive games and often exercise leadership. In any case, it is evident that leisure/play is a significant arena of development for children, in part due to its relative freedom from adult designs.

Adult Development

In a bureaucratic world in which economic roles tend to be determined by the structures of the corporation and public agency, leisure offers relative freedom. As suggested previously, for some leisure may even offer the fullest possibility of experiencing productivity. In many leisure episodes there is an immediate feedback of an outcome that measures performance in some way. As a result, leisure offers the potential of freedom, productivity and measurement in ways that may be integral to developing self-definitions in adult years.

Some of the limitations in many work relationships lead to a loss of centrality of meaning. While some occupational settings offer relative autonomy, a variety of interactional possibilities, a relationship to outcomes or products and a context for ongoing development, many do not. The requirement of the bureaucratic structure, whether office, factory, or retail outlet, that individuals always be replaceable by others, reduces the opportunity for personal investment or developmental return. Further, realization of such limitations increases through the life course for so many who are employed that a high degree of disillusionment is common. The work situation is valued for what it offers – income, some interaction, a social identification as 'employed' and some schedule framework for the week. However, when the requirements of a job have been mastered for years and there seems little chance for enlargement of scope, then different social spaces may be sought for investment and enhancement of selfhood.

A Case Study

One case study of leisure investment that involves some risk, investment of time and income, and a high level of physical exertion suggests that both socialization and deprivation are elements in participation. The activity is 'motocross' – the offroad competitive use of motorcycles in simulated cross-country races. In the United States participants were found to be disproportionately of working–class backgrounds and occupations. Construction workers, mechanics, factory hands and other 'blue–collar' men are joined occasionally by students, teachers, or clerks who usually come from working–class families.

One explanation is based on socialization opportunities. For such men, motocross with its stress on machinery, speed and competition, is a natural and attractive possibility. They have grown up with other males who have the same interests and who have placed a high value on mechanical skills and on masculine competition. Both driving and working on cars were anticipated in early teen years and made a central element of life when the license was received. The sound of the engine conveyed feelings of independence, control of power and direction, and motion. At the same time that some youth were camping with their families, going to country club dances, or practicing the french horn, these young men were into engines and transmissions.

After all, used cars and cycles are not only valued, but are generally available. They may require payments, but not wealth. Necessary knowledge and skills are generally available. Therefore, the working-class youth who moves from used cars and cycles to motocross *with* his friends is following an easy path. On the other hand, the attorney's son who leaves the country club to compete on the dirt-track has all kinds of social barriers to overcome.

Yet socialization probabilities are not an adequate explanation of why of all the sports and activities available, some take up this particular demanding activity when most do not. Sometimes there is the influence of a friend or family member, most often a father or brother. Some may be attracted by seeing the sport on TV. However, there would seem to be something more at work here. There is something about the activity that provides the 'right' context for the working out of identities. The world of work provides little opportunity for most young men to demonstrate their mastery of such a skill, especially not in competition with others. Motocross is an arena for the development and exhibition of physical control and strength, for acting out the aggressive activism and individualism learned in boyhood,[8] for testing the self in competition that rewards courage, stamina and tactical skill. It is a social space in which a personal identity as a man can be presented and validated.

There are many other examples of how the form of an activity combined with social access make it especially viable for the expression of self-definitions salient to men or women with value orientations learned in their cultural milieu. However, another related phenomenon is social identification through either participation or symbolic attachment. Various kinds of insignia and clothing may identify the motocross rider when he is away from the track. In parallel ways individuals who do not themselves join in a sport may gain some social identity by their symbolic association with those who do. The extreme seriousness with which the win–lose record of football teams that 'represent' one's city may be taken testifies that there is more operating here than interest in the game. Somehow a person who identifies closely with a team may feel him or herself more of a person when the team wins. Whether or not the underlying cause of the significance of such identification is an alienation from other sources of identity and meaning,[9] the rise and fall of the moods of such fans related to outcomes and the collective demonstrations of triumph and anguish suggest that it is more than a diversion, a game to enjoy casually.

Elements in Identity Development

It would be possible to find elements of almost any aspect of human development in the play/leisure of a culture. There have now been innumerable analyses of the ways in which play, games, sports and other leisure carry out the fundamental themes of a culture.[10] Leisure, then, is a social space *of* the particular culture with its social structures and values, its socialization processes and elements of differentiation. While there may be dimensions of leisure that are more or less universal, at least in societies that are measurably above a subsistence level, the contributions of leisure to identity development always reflect the culture. Identities are always learned with both the resources and the values of a culture embedded in the process.

Therefore, the contributions of leisure to identity development are rooted in both the nature of leisure and the ethnic forms it takes in a culture and in the structures and value orientations of the culture itself. The relative salience of the kinds of leisure found especially significant in our culture would be different in another culture and are, in fact, constantly changing in this one. However, before going on to analyze the relationship of leisure to personal and social identities in more detail, a suggestion of such salience places the argument in perspective.

Competence: As suggested for children, self-definitions of competence are central to development that enables a person to take the risks of entering any social context that is new or different. 'Can I do it?' is the perennial question that can be answered only by trying it. However, too many outcomes that imply inability make further risk difficult. Robert White's research on the need to demonstrate competence is augmented by Kurt Lewin's on success in setting goals and achieving them as a necessary exploration of the environment.[11,12] There are evident limitations in most work situations that make it difficult or impossible to demonstrate such competence. The tasks do not permit experimentation or, in many cases, even simple improvement. As a result, some leisure spaces may be the most available outlet for competence testing and building.

Indeterminacy in leisure: One element of much leisure that makes such competence development possible is indeterminacy. Not only does much leisure, especially many games and social interaction episodes, not have predetermined outcomes, but the social expectation fosters and permits exploration, a trying of the untested. There are frequent and immediate measures of skill-learning. However, they are not so final or consequential that trying is inhibited. As in a card game, there is an outcome for the episode as well as intermediate outcomes throughout the event. Yet there are also enough problematic elements in determining the outcomes that the results are not overwhelmingly fateful for participants. There is a kind of measurement process that is relative and cumulative without being immediately or ultimately threatening.

Self-containment of play: The measured outcome is possible because the leisure episode is largely self-contained. Although outcomes may have cumulative impact on our self-definitions, each episode is segmented enough from ongoing social roles that seldom is a central role position threatened by the outcome of a single card game or cocktail party. Some leisure is non-social with only internal measurement of effects. Some is so role-segregated and vague in outcomes that meaning is largely in the immediate experience. Even in leisure with measured and recorded results there is a definition of it being 'non-serious' in relation to central roles. Much leisure is like the out-of-town tryout of a play in which evaluation is sought and alterations anticipated based on negative responses. The tryout is a deliberate experimentation with the 'real thing' still ahead when the play reaches New York or London. For much leisure, competence can be tested in a context that is not fateful even though evaluated.

On the other hand, the most common associations of leisure – family and regular friends – suggest the other side of the matter. Leisure performance may be quite significant for those relationships. Family role identities may be worked out in leisure contexts in ways that pervade all of these central relationships. Competence may be tested and developed in leisure investments that include or may even be primarily directed toward family role identities.

The Presentation of Self

The concept of the presentation of self is based on the metaphor of drama and was developed by Erving Goffman in his early study of the Shetland Islands' crofters.[13] From this perspective, an individual – the actor manages his speech, body, demeanor, attire and other communicative symbols and gestures to present a certain impression to others. This impression management is designed to elicit a preconceived interpretation of the self from the presumed audience. In slightly different terms the actor presents an identity for social validation. The response to this identity presentation – the definition by others of our role identities – shapes how we enact the role on subsequent occasions.

Within this dramaturgical metaphor, social interaction is said to be 'something like' a play in which different actors take the same parts in different ways, the staging is managed to reveal some elements of the performance and conceal others, and there is a reciprocity among actors. Each presentation of a play is somewhat different from all others as the processual interplay of role enactments develops. This approach does not imply that there is no coherence to the presentation of self. Rather, despite variations in role identities from one social setting to another, there tends to be persistence in our self-definitions. Personal identities are situated in the social context of the episode, but also remain *ours* – a presentation of the personal identity that mixes what we believe we are with what we would like others to believe us to be.

Further, it is in this process of social presentation that our personal identities are developed. We learn who we are in the perceived definitions of others, especially in face-to-face interaction in which the responses of significant others are most directly perceived. What must be understood here is that despite the employment of such terms as play, actor, impression management, occasions and drama, this is very serious business in the commerce of life. It is in such interaction that we really live, come to define ourselves and perhaps accept our self-definitions, and attempt to alter and expand those identities. We may enact and perform parts (social roles), but in the process we work out who we are in the world of others who are important to us.

Identity and Presentation

Two aspects of such presentation require special attention: signs of identity and the settings in which we present our selves.

Signs of identity: What is the meaning of the following symbolic presentations? A young mother does her shopping at the supermarket in her tennis togs. A production-line employee drives into the company parking lot in a pickup truck equipped for hunting expeditions. A high-school student wears his letterman's sweater to history class. In a university class with thirty students a careful count finds eighty-four pins, badges, Greek letters and labeled articles of clothing desig-nating the wearer as a particular kind of athlete, member of a fraternal organization, student, or in some way 'special'. On the back of cars there is a variety of stickers identifying the owner as a pilot, sailor, horsewoman, waterskiier, or visitor at a distant national park.

Or consider the preparation for participation in a cocktail party. What is to be worn? With whom should one arrive? When should one arrive? How should the entry be made? With whom should one speak first? Who will be there who is likely to give an initial greeting of welcome and inclusion? What lines of interaction can be developed during the party? The fundamental question is that of self-presen-tation. How do we want others to identify us – at the market, workplace, or in class? What symbols can we use to produce the identification we desire? Or in an occasion that is only partly predict-able, what can we do in advance to increase the probability that our role identity will be perceived by others as we intend it? How can we announce ourselves in ways that are likely to gain responses that inaugurate lines of action that reinforce our personal identities?

Gregory Stone argued that appearance is central to social interaction because it at least inaugurates the identities of the actors.[14] When we dress for a social occasion, we dress 'toward' the presumed audience from whom we seek validating responses. Gender differences in attire not only reflect the sex role expectations, but also how the specific man or woman wants to be defined by same and other-sex interac-tants. In some cases the symbolism of clothing refers to occupation. A trucker may wear a cap with a symbol of his firm or brand of truck. A businessman or woman carries the appropriate briefcase. Or in some cases uniforms are worn when off-duty. However, more common in the neighborhood and community are leisure symbols. Running shoes, bowling shirts, football jackets as well as fishing hats, hiking boots and skijackets all tell others that one has a significant leisure identification. There is a symbolic 'leisure ethnicity' in which actors seek not only symbolic identity, but also to signal others with the same leisure identification.

Leisure settings for presentation: There is no adequate analysis available of the relative salience of leisure, work and other settings for the offering and validation of identities. However, it is clear that leisure settings are significant for many people.

One kind of evidence is derived from the many case studies of leisure settings. For example, the poker game has been studied in several different contexts.[15,16] In the bounded and problematic arena of the poker table men present selves as competent and controlled risktakers who can participate on equal terms with other men. The demeanor and acceptance may be as important as the skill validation of winning or losing. *How* one plays the game, adhering to not only the rules, but the local conventions, calls for definitive role enactment. However, a good performance is rewarded by continued inclusion and reciprocal assurance of doing it well. There is more going on than a contest involving the exchange of money on the fall of the cards. Poker, generally a sex-segregated activity, is an arena in which one receives confirmation as a man who can deal with other men – in the interaction as well as the game.

A leisure event is one that may be especially amenable to being 'framed'. In Goffman's terms an episode of interaction has agreed-on parameters in its meanings to the actors as well as in time and space delimitations.[17] The meaning of the interaction is first of all within that frame. Further, there are signs or communications of the limits in the event. When these are indirect or implicit in certain gestures or verbal signs, they may be termed 'metacommunication' and even taken-for-granted in the interaction.[18] This does not mean that the episode has no consequences for identity validation or development, but rather that the first-level meanings are within the agreed-on interaction frame.

Leisure is especially rich in episodes that can be analyzed with such an approach. In leisure events much of the meaning is developed in the delimited interaction rather than having its primary meaning in the carrying out of specified institutional roles. For example, the primary meaning of an episode may be within the interrelated presentations and responses rather than in the form of the activity itself. The campground, gym, or playing-field may be a setting in which the 'action' involves an interaction drama as much as performing the functions of the designated activity.

The forms of leisure in designated settings are too varied to permit simple generalizations. In some there is the problematic element of a contest, the element of chance and some kind of score-keeping. In others 'nothing happens' except the socializing. Some leisure may be highly ritualized in structures and conventions.[19] Rules and roles may be clearly specified in some games and quite open in some informal episodes. However, in any social interaction there are the elements of role expectations, role enactment, evaluations and interpreted responses, and presentations. In most there is some line of action in which presentations, communication and actions are aligned toward an end. There is both structure and openness.

Examples may need no more than an introduction for those who have been part of the interaction settings:

- There is the presentation of sexual identity in the high-school male who moves down the school hallway with a gait and demeanor intended to announce an identity of masculine physical competence.
- There is the cocktail party episode in which symbols fail to communicate an identity. Until such a communication can be offered and received, two strangers may be quite ill-at-ease in a conversation because they do not yet know what kinds of deference and response are appropriate. At a university, for example, it is important to differentiate faculty from graduate students. At a party it is important to know who is accompanied by a spouse – and sometimes who that spouse may be.
- There is the volleyball game in which one player presents a kind of joking distance from the game itself and its score-measured skills and performance. In body language as well as studied remarks a player may try to announce that he or she is at a skill level superior to this setting and therefore cannot treat the outcomes seriously. Such a presentation may be augmented by a tee shirt enscribed with evidence of participation in a major volleyball tournament or membership on a high-level team.

The point is that there are many modes of participation which have to be announced and interpreted in order to carry on the interaction through validating and appropriate responses. Of course, there is also the possibility of a deliberate refusal to accept the presentation and an insistence that all players take the game with equal seriousness.

Self-definitions and Investments

One level of analysis of leisure interaction concentrates on the framed episode with its direct and indirect communication about meaning. Another begins with the person who acts in such episodes and who generally tries to piece together a coherent selfhood out of sequential episodes. The young man in the school hall presents himself in ways that are congruent with demeanor in other settings at school and even at home. The ill-at-ease person at the cocktail party has some persistent identity that he wants others to affirm in a variety of contexts. And the volleyball player who defines the situation as beneath his skills attempts to establish himself as a physically competent person in work and study settings as well as in games. The effective and appropriate modes differ, but there is some persistence of identity.

It is precisely this persistence that leads to the paradox of meaning in leisure episodes. On the one hand, they are relatively self-contained and non-serious, even when their outcomes are given momentary salience.

The containment of consequences permits much leisure to be used to try out and develop identities that would be too risky in work or even family contexts. On the other hand, role identities that are given trial runs, refined and received validation in leisure settings may become central to the actor's repertoire and brought into role after role. Further, certain leisure identities and investments may be found so satisfying that they take a central place in a person's life.

Self-definition in the Life Course

A return to the life course from the presentation-of-self perspective adds to the previous analysis. The sequence would be as follows: a person essays a new or revised presentation in a leisure episode that is relative segregated from other roles. This presentation, seeking to establish socially an element of selfhood previously unattained, meets with a measure of approval from some significant others. After such confirmation is repeated and confidence in the portrayal is gained, it may then be transferred to settings in which failure would be more costly. At the same time, the portrayal itself may be so satisfying that it becomes more important to the actor.

In the changing roles and relative salience of roles through the life course there is always a mixture of acknowledged obligations and investments. Again the dilemma between individual freedom and expression and security in social roles continues as an ongoing dialectic through the life course even when the roles and relationships change. This dialectic persists in leisure as well as in more institutionalized contexts. Leisure, too, is a mixture of role constraints of greater or lesser importance as well as of opportunity for exploratory and intrinsically satisfying investments of self. In fact, the independence vs integration dialectic may be seen most dramatically in leisure where choices can be measured.

Presentations of self are an action dimension of leisure that is complementary to other roles and of leisure that is more autotelic and expressive. Identity development through a presentation–response–interpretation process takes place in familial role-determined leisure and in the least-constrained situation. It may even take place in the imaginative constructions of solitary daydreaming. In all kinds of leisure episodes and events self-presentation and feedback occur that have impacts on our self-conceptions. They may reinforce established self-definitions, threaten them, question their appropriateness for a new period of the life course, provide a subtle shading of change or refinement, or develop into a highly valued investment.

In retirement a craft activity that had previously been thought to be too time-intensive may come to provide a significant expression previously found in work. The parent of a young musician may find great fulfillment in the performance of a school choir or orchestra that would have previously been thought of too inferior a quality to be worth an evening. A game or a friendship, a trip, or a home-improvement project, may come to have a previously unrecognized significance when involvement yields a new set of satisfactions, intrinsic or relational. Further, we may become somewhat different persons to ourselves as well as to others in the leisure investment. One dramatic kind of shift in self-conceptions results when a man in his fifties or a woman discouraged from such unfeminine activity demonstrates a previously unrealized physical competence through disciplined and directed exercise or sport involvement. The involvement changes the self-concept which in turn yields satisfaction in performing the new role identity well.

Central Life Investments
So often in the past leisure has explicitly or implicitly been defined as peripheral to 'real life' – to the central institutional roles of the society. As a result, it seemed to come as something of a surprise when Robert Dubin and his colleagues found that work was not the 'central life interest' of most workers.[20,21] Unfortunately, this research approach did not go on to develop research strategies that would identify just which interests were central through the life course. We have suggested that in general adults find the relationships and investments of the family and home roles and contexts central. Leisure is understood in its contribution to those roles as well as to the development of identities.

However, there are some individuals for whom leisure is a central life interest. They design their lives around leisure investments rather than shape their leisure to complement family or work roles. They may be in the minority in contemporary societies, but they do represent a possibility that reveals something of the potential of leisure in adult human development.

The most thorough investigation of such persons has been carried out by Robert Stebbins. His book, *Amateurs: On the Margin between Work and Leisure*,[22] examines the extraordinary involvement of some amateurs in theater, baseball and archaeology. However, his interest in 'amateurs' began with his own own deep involvement with chamber and orchestral music as a string player. He noted not only his own investment in this disciplined and demanding activity, but that of others who confessed that they could not imagine their lives apart from such music. When leisure is viewed as relaxing, residual and complementary to what is more important, then how can we account for those who engage in music, theater, or a sport with such devotion that much of the rest of life has to be shaped around this 'leisure'?

Stebbins defines the amateur as one whose standards of performance are essentially the same as the professional, but who does not receive his primary income from the activity. In first-rate amateur theater, for example, cast and crew devote long hours for weeks preparing a play that is intended to be a valid and even definitive presentation. No excuses are accepted for aims of mediocrity. Even though limitations may in the end yield a product well below professional standards, the intent remains. Production of good theater is not just a pastime, a pleasant social interlude, or fun with and for some friends. It is *theater* in every sense of the term.

When leisure is viewed as an element in life that can provide central meaning and absorb major investment of the self as well as resources, then the problem of such amateurism being leisure is quickly resolved. What is not dealt with so easily is why and how such major investment may be made by some in leisure, in activity for which the reward is essentially personal. How can amateur musicians schedule their work, so that both practice and performance retain centrality? How can amateur theater performers let their families fend for themselves for extended periods of evenings and weekends to take a small part in a community production? How can an athlete with no realistic hope of ever making a living at his or her sport give up a job that interfered with skill development and even move a family 500 miles and look for another job?

There are a number of factors: from the perspective of the author's paradigm, the two kinds of satisfaction may be intensely experienced. Doing the activity itself is found to be expressive, exciting, fulfilling engrossing and even self-transcending at times. Also the intimate community that develops around the activity may become our most valued associates, those with whom we experience a regular sharing of the investment and its meanings. Even further, the activity often evolves into a subculture that provides a major source of social identity. A person may come to define him/herself as a painter rather than a bank clerk, a cello player more than a lawyer and even a character actor more than a mother. In more cases a kind of dual citizenship is established in which the lawyer has at least the two central identities, or the mother cannot imagine giving up either her family or the theater.

How does this happen? To begin with, such leisure results in much more than pleasure.[23] The dimensions of amateur acting may include self-expression, the development and enrichment of self-concepts and actually becoming more of a person. Some of the ancient Aristotelian concept of fulfillment is achieved. Such fulfillment is multifaceted and a process rather than a prize gained once and for all.

Further, amateurs continue in their engagement with the activity when such outcomes are central to their identities. Such an investment provides continuity in life that may experience change or disillusion-ment in other roles. Amateurs persevere in their commitment to skill development as well as participation because the investment has come to be central to their self-definition. The activity not only provides regular associations, a time framework and intermediate goals that can be chosen in a world that often seems to be cast in concrete, but it provides that social space in which we are able to define ourselves and demonstrate to others that we are someone special. We may experi-ence an acceptance in the subgroup, recognition in larger circles and, perhaps most crucial of all, a self-concept that we have *done something* and *are someone*. It does not require a premiss of alienation or anomie in the social system to allow for the possibility that some persons may develop their identities most fully in leisure.

In one of the cases from the study of leisure in the transition to early establishment a young woman had shaped her life around her leisure.[24] She entered no long-term commitment of marriage or family that would inhibit her devotion to a variety of outdoor rec-reation pursuits such as backpacking and skiing. Her employment was chosen because it involved a regular association with others having the same interests rather than as a career with long-term goals and ad-vancement. She centered her life around environments, associations and opportunities that required that less importance be attached to either work or family.

There is no evidence that such devotees or 'amateurs' are a major segment of the population in any modern society. Whether or not they are a growing group remains to be measured. What is evident is that there are certain periods in the life course in which persons are most likely to make such leisure investments. The first is adolescence, a period in which the school and family roles are distinctly unsatis-fying for many and in which a leisure role may provide the fullest opportunity for working through tasks of independence and social integration. A second period, especially for those who experience university education, is the time prior to taking on commitment to family and work roles of early establishment. A third period occurs in the middle years, when family roles may have diminished and work roles been re-evaluated. Some of the amateur scientists – archaeolo-gists, geologists, or astronomers – are redeveloping an investment laid aside during the earlier establishment period.

One other dimension of the phenomenon of leisure centrality remains to be noted. It is that such investments often produce *subcul-tures* with distinctive symbols of identification, vocabularies, schedule commitments and interaction rituals. Such a subculture may develop around a lack of other commitments as in Whyte's study of a *Street Corner Society*.[25] In this ethnographic study of a slum group of young men bowling is a context of interaction, the club an instrumental organization and the corner a meeting-place. The real meaning of their 'club' is in the mutual acceptance of their identities and relationships. Even though many members also have other interests, their most stable and identity-confirming relationships are in the group that does more 'hanging around' than scheduled or directed activity.

Other subcultures develop around an activity and the social organization required for its exercise. Among examples would be the parents of elite age-group swimmers, who share not only vocabularies and hours of waiting at swim meets, but also the significance of tenths of a second and 6 a.m. practices. In some cases associations continue long after the children have ceased to swim.

Various kinds of horse-showing also eventuate in special leisure groups that can dominate members' lives and associations. All those who commit themselves and their resources to the showing of a breed of horses or a class of equestrian competition are not wealthy. In the United States many devotees of quarterhorse breeding, racing and showing live very modestly and describe themselves as 'horse poor'. However, on the weekend – at the fair or show – they become special persons who are recognized and accepted as accomplished in their art. Since the refinements of such competition are incomprehensible to the outsider or casual spectator, the subculture of communication and acceptance becomes the critical context of selfhood.

Such subcultures may develop around almost any activity, tennis tournaments, sailing competition, or skydiving. The development of subcultures is facilitated by the necessity to leave home and associate in a designated place with others, by the need for special equipment or apparel, having to learn skills from others and media of communication such as special-interest magazines. In these cultures a participant may describe herself as a 'different person'. Whatever the measure of personality persistence, there is an attitude of being able to present a different identity in that frame and receiving validating feedback from the group.

Leisure and Identity losses

Most of the preceding discussion has outlined the contributions that leisure makes to identity development through the life course. There is always the other side of the coin, the possibility of damage and loss. Either leisure may be one element in a social system that is dehumanizing, or there may be aspects of leisure that have the potential of doing damage during human development.

Mass Society and Identity
One possibility already introduced is that leisure provides opportunity

for the expression and development of identities that are denied to some people in other roles. One approach to this theme is based on analysis of the so-called 'mass society' produced by industrialization, urbanization, mass media and a routinization of services and social organization. Mass media, mass transit, mass retailing, and so on, have replaced the urban neighborhood or the small town in which individuals are known by name and in which there is a personal quality to most interchange. We are identified by numbers and plastic cards rather than the personal recognition of the clerk, physician, or police. We gain our knowledge through impersonal TV and even identify ourselves with corporations or football teams when no officer or player would even recognize our names. In this mass society we need to gain some kind of social identification, some act or relationship that gives us a place in the anonymous scheme of things.

It is such anonymity that turns so many adults to home and family as their primary investments. Here one is known, one's presence is recognized and absence noted. Here what we do makes some impact. Further, the home seems to provide a relative permanence and the family even the possibility of doing something that lives on. However, in a society in which families tend to be less secure and more marriages sequential, such investment may also be found less than fulfilling for the entire life course.

Even when home and family investments remain relatively stable, there are changes in those roles. Parenting becomes less engrossing in the latter third of the life course. As with work, disappointments and re-evaluation are often a part of the process. Besides, the family may not be an adequate link to the large world. Some appear to need more.

In one influential analysis of the consequences of mass society Orrin Klapp proposed a number of ways in which symbolic identification may be sought.[26] The conventional ways of seeking self-definitions of relatedness and significance are through the stable institutions of the society. Along with family and work, there are the myriad voluntary organizations of the community. Ethnicity and religion provide two central and often related means of symbolically identifying with an ongoing segment of the society that is less anonymous. Ethnic identification gives one a sense of having a history. Religion may yield a sense of being related to eternal meaning as well as to a community of those who reinforce belief in such meaning. It is endemic to their social function that ethnic and religious institutions be essentially conservative, representing links to the past and to meaning that has endured.

However, Klapp goes on to suggest that the intensity of such identification may not be enough for many in contemporary society. They feel the need for more vivid and emotionally gripping attachment. They seek symbols and relationships that are immediate in their offer of identification. In religion they attach themselves to sects and cults that offer excitement, identification with a face-to-face community, an assurance of being special and promising a unique grasp of ultimate truth. Such sects have the fervor of being new, the social identity of being set apart from the masses and the charismatic center of a leader. They provide symbols of identification in behavior and immediate communities and often in dress and diet as well.

In less intense forms various kinds of leisure attachments may also provide some sense of social identity in a mass society. The various analyses of the social meaning of football in European and South American countries all presuppose that spectators have symbolically attached themselves to the team and its fortunes. The 'religious' metaphor suggests the capacity of football to integrate and symbolize the values of the society in its rituals.[27] When games are preceded by chants and even the singing of ethnic hymns, then the parallels are obvious.

The 'social control' theory presupposes that workers alienated in their political and economic roles may be distracted by symbolic attachments to the trivial outcomes of public contests. The violence that occasionally accompanies matches is explained as a misdirected form of protest by those who are powerless and exploited. And the emotional fervor of the crowds and various displays of emotion are seen as demonstrations of 'collective behavior' in which individuals lose themselves in the mass and engage in acts that would not be permissible in another context. In all these theories and any combinations there is the underlying premiss that opportunities for meaningful and existential attachments to social meaning are so limited in a mass society that the sport spectacle becomes a surrogate for identification with real community or productivity.

In general, even in the Green Bay Packer country of central Wisconsin, the identification seems somewhat less vivid and violent in the United States. Partly due to the professional nature of the game and the association with cities rather than ethnic regions or nations, there is a perspective of containment in American professional football that leads to less violent or emotional collective acts. Nevertheless, the emotions that are displayed suggest that football is more than a convenient topic of common conversation among men. Personal attitudes do rise and fall in winning or losing seasons and the jackets, badges and car stickers are more than decoration.

As with motocross, one suggested element in such attachment is the 'loss of labor'. The evidence that many workers do not experience a meaningful attachment to the labor process or product leads to the question of whether or not such a meaning must be found elsewhere.

For those who believe that labor in the sense of identified contribution to socially necessary production is a human quality and not just an optional activity, surrogate identifications are assumed necessary. Home and family are one common avenue of investment. Can leisure be another?

It would appear that for some of those 'amateurs' their leisure receives such a major investment and yields such a central identity that it might be a substitute. The problem is that some of those with such leisure investment are also deeply involved in relatively satisfying work. What is needed are much more careful studies to delineate the patterns of identity development in relation to leisure roles. At present, the distributions and patterns are clear only in theory and supported by enough research to indicate their viability for some:

- Some who do not realize a satisfying identity in their work seek it in a leisure investment. That leisure may or may not be closely aligned with the home and family.
- Some who have the fullest and most satisfying leisure are receiving much the same meanings in their work.
- Some are so deeply invested in work that all other attachments and identities are secondary and complementary.
- Some find that there is little deep meaning in either work or leisure.

One research question would be based on alienation and mass society models. Do those types of leisure that provide social identity – affective involvement, symbols of identification, a face-to-face community of acceptance and a myth of overarching meaning – draw a disproportionate number of persons whose other roles contribute little to satisfying self-concepts? Is there a push into leisure investments as well as a pull of attraction? Further, do measures of alienation, anomie, disenchantment and routinization predict such leisure?

A second approach to the same issue would begin with the positive attributes of leisure. If leisure or play is characterized by the potential of intense involvement, the excitement of problematic outcomes, self-containment that permits experimentation with presentations and identities, learning and self-development and the enhancement of primary relationships, then does it become a legitimate social space for human development and expression in a mass society that by its nature has lost some previous opportunities for investment? In an urbanized society does leisure offer needed contexts for intimacy? In a rationalized culture does leisure provide a chance to seek personal meaning and to test self-definitions? In a media-saturated culture can leisure offer firsthand experiences of doing something that has a result?

On the other hand, the 'leisure solution to work' is viewed negatively. It is a false promise, an investment that cannot yield long-term human fulfillment. On the other hand, leisure is seen as an appropriate opportunity for personal investment and human development. Recognition of the inadequacy of other roles for many people does not then mean that leisure is inherently inferior. If leisure is emerging as an increasingly significant social space for the development and enrichment of intimate communities, personal identities and social identification, then non-utopians may prefer that to truncated opportunities for many in today's world.

A Critical Perspective

The issue becomes a philosophical one at this point. The critical argument, based on neo-Marxist premisses and augmented by a variety of other perspectives, is that in a modern consumption-oriented society leisure may become a means of disguising alienation and dehumanizing conditions of life. The version of Herbert Marcuse that adds the human need for sensuality from a neo-Freudian perspective has been one of the most influential in developing the critique.[28]

In general, the argument proceeds as follows: humankind require meaningful engagement with productivity and community in their economic, political and social relationships. In work being human calls for both direction and engagement with the production process and with other workers. The state should consist of governing and serving structures that are responsive to the expressed needs of the citizens. In social institutions, including the family, there must be the actualization of intimacy and sensual expression uninhibited by bourgeois convention and repression.

However, ownership and control of the means of production by economic elites and subsequent control of not only the 'market', but also all secondary institutions of the society including the polity and the church, allows the elites to shape the system according to their interests. If economic participation by non-elites becomes reduced or threatened, then the stability of the system might be placed in jeopardy. Therefore, it is in the interest of capital-controlling elites that relatively powerless majorities believe they have a stake in the system. Since they cannot be permitted any real control over the institutions or even the fundamental contexts of their lives, then another perception of reward must be found.

In a capitalist or capital-dominated society the obvious means of control is through consumption. Obtaining and possessing commodities believed desirable and life-enhancing are defined as the goal of life. This 'commodity fetishism' is carried out in every social space – in the home, church, market and leisure. Owning a home is defined as fundamental attachment to a *place* in the system. Providing a home and other consumer goods for one's family is seen as the central personal goal. Churches are evaluated by their buildings, communities by their constructed monuments of government and service, sexuality by conception and birth of a useful number of children, leisure by possessing toys and work by the means to purchase these 'goods'.

Leisure, then, is not primarily expression and community, freedom and intimacy. Leisure is 'fun', and fun is measured by cost. An expensive trip is more fun than a walk down the lane. Camping in a new caravan is more fun than tenting. Playing ball in new uniforms is more fun than in old jeans. And even public leisure services are defined in terms of provision of shiny 'sports palaces' and destination resorts modeled on Disney World. The premiss is that investment – economic investment – produces satisfaction. Leisure loses its essential freedom by being tied to credit and payments, possessions and parking. It is another commodity, available on the market for a price as a reward for cooperation in a social world over which one has no control.

Whether or not we accept the entire argument, there is at least a significant warning here. Since leisure is ethnic, of the culture, then the value-orientations of that culture permeate not only what is done, but how it is chosen and valued. The danger that the essential freedom of leisure may be diminished or lost when it becomes tied to possessions and payments is quite real. Whether or not this is a social control scheme of a ruling elite, commodity fetishism can come to dominate leisure to the extent that satisfaction is equated with price. The concept that the primary investment in leisure is the self may be lost in the panoply of leisure toys and locales that are on the market. The human development outcomes of leisure resulting from self-investment may be vitiated by engagement with technologies and products. Again the research question implied requires coming to understand with greater depth just what is happening to people in their leisure and how varying modes of participation yield different personal outcomes.

Identity Damage in Leisure
Without entering the complex debates as to the consequences of various play contexts and leisure interactions for participants, we do need to recognize that the potential for benefit assumes the possibility of damage. Here a few examples will introduce the 'other side' of leisure.

We have already introduced the significance of self-concepts of competence that may be developed in leisure as well as in work and school. Such self-definitions may be determinative in decisions as to whether or not to attempt to learn something new. In the same way, learned identities of acceptance and ability in a variety of social situations may encourage or inhibit entrance into new sets of social settings and opportunities.

In childhood such self-definitions are learned in all the games that involve measurement and a ranking of outcomes.[29] They may be intensified by the record-keeping and award systems that characterize so many sports run by adults for children. In so far as the reward system identifies losers as well as winners and the play context is central to the child's world, then the potential is there for learning self-concepts of inability and inferiority.

Further, many play episodes involve some choosing and the possibility of exclusion as well as inclusion. That exclusion may be made on grounds other than competence in the activity. Sometimes the basis may be some kind of social identity of being 'different' – by race, sex, ethnicity, religion, or just being new in the neighborhood. In any case, personal identities are being developed that take such exclusion into account for those on the social margins of a play group.

From a social-psychological perspective, the other side of the development of competence is the personal identity of helplessness. One analysis of little league baseball suggests ways in which the attribution of failure, the aim of the other team or even other players to reduce effectiveness by imputing lack of ability, and accepted measures of individual failure in the sport may lead to a self-concept of helplessness.[30] Further, if such a self-concept learned in a childhood context carries over into adult life, then the damage could be quite serious. The analysis only outlines the possibility and such damage has not been documented by research. Nevertheless, processes by which such learning takes place have been documented and the structures of such team competition for children verified. The possibility of such negative learning and long-term results is there. It is not possible simply to assume that all play, game, or sport participation is beneficial for children. The potential for damage is real, and dangers for identity development should be reduced when possible.

The same process is at work in school recreation. Especially when an activity such as team sports holds high salience in the social system of the school, classification by measured outcomes and competition and the inclusion–exclusion procedures would be expected to have significant results. So much school recreation is competitive that 'losers' inevitably outnumber winners. Especially when second place is defined as losing, the consequences are skewed toward the negative.

In the life course learning process we all tend to generalize from our specific episodes and events. We may come to define ourselves by the outcomes of a sequence of events in which innumerable variables affect the outcomes. Especially when a contest measures rate of physical development more than anything else, temporary lag in resources and ability – to be altered in time may be internalized and retained as definitions of the self. Then future presentations incorporate such internalization in ways that elicit further confirming responses by others.

In a culture in which so much of one's personal identity is defined in comparison with others, and in which leisure reflects competitive value orientations, leisure includes the possibility of learning incompetence as well as competence, exclusion as well as inclusion, low as well as high ranking. In some contexts evaluation of the self is actually *against* others. All the awards for the few winners, the rankings by cumulative statistics and the stress on scores and monetary rewards, lay the groundwork for inhibited performance. Freedom is reduced when we fear failure and do not take the risk. Community is narrowed when we are unsure of our acceptance and fail to enter a new social setting. We learn in leisure – in ways that may develop identities and may also inhibit development.

Leisure and Identities – a Summary

This interactionist approach to leisure has led us in some rather different directions from the traditional sociological study of leisure. Although the fit of leisure with the institutional structures and value orientations of the society remain an important part of the picture, the focus of the meanings of leisure to social actors has added identity development and expression to the work-related functions of leisure. While the power of institutions to shape leisure and the possibility of their domination by ruling elites is recognized, there is also attention given to the interpreting actor who makes sequential decisions and develops lines of action. The analysis is existential as well as social and interpretive as well as structural. From this approach, we come to three conclusions that are also somewhat different from previous theory.

The Centrality of Leisure
At the end of Chapter 3 it was suggested that leisure through the life course might be found in some periods to be central rather than residual. Now we can reinforce that statement. The significance of leisure in human development and especially in the formation of personal and social identities precludes any definition of leisure as

residual. Whatever else it may be, leisure is not leftover time. Not only because most people have little such time, but because leisure in some times and places takes a high priority in decision schemes, it is an element of life that must be dealt with in its own right. There is always the possibility that leisure *can* be central, determinative of other aspects of life and a major element in the process of our self-definitions and development.

This does not mean that leisure is never leftover, of low priority, or essentially recuperative. Some leisure is low intensity, low impact and of only secondary significance. But so is some family interaction and work time. The point is that we have to allow for a wide range of meanings, intensity levels and personal consequences in studying leisure.

There are special cases in which leisure may take an especially central place. For the 'underemployed' who are not able to invest their abilities and interests in their work in ways that yield a return in satisfaction and fulfillment, leisure may provide that social space for critical investment of self. As a result, leisure may be that life space in which identity is most fully expressed and developed

The rising specter of technological unemployment in industrial societies may be a sign of fundamental contradictions or a cost of a transition to a postindustrial society with different economic structures and value orientations that define productivity quite differently. In either case, crisis or transition, the personal costs for those pushed outside expected productive roles in mid-life or earlier may be overwhelming. The extent to which leisure can begin to take a central place in the identities of the able unemployed remains to be seen. It is, in any case, a dramatic test of the viability of the 'leisure solution to work' in which the deficiencies of work roles are compensated for in leisure roles.

The evidence that later years and retirement can find fulfillment in leisure that is expressive, creative and productive is accumulating slowly, but clearly.[31] Retirement, whatever the age or process, is a period in which schedules require revision and time use calls for altered priorities. The evidence that many anticipate retirement and have an abundance of investments that will not only fill time, but continue personal development, suggests that the possibility is there for others.

One valuable way of examining the contributions of leisure through the life course is to focus on transitions rather than more stable periods. In critical role transitions leisure may not only provide continuity in personal and social identities, but open doors to new relationships and investments of high salience for the succeeding period. For example, the overlap between regular leisure associations and support networks for widowed women indicates that leisure and social support cannot be easily separated. Social networks may be multi-faceted with primary attention shifting in relation to the needs of the moment or time of transition. Leisure is one element in overall social integration, at times a central one.

Little studied but quite common in North America is the geo-graphic move, usually related to occupational change. Not only the old neighborhood, but the old metropolis, is frequently left behind, especially by those who serve the great corporate or government bureaucracies. Leisure is often a critical buffer in such moves to a new social locale. Voluntary organizations and churches provide a context of developing new friendships. A leisure activity – arts, sports, or child-related – may offer entry into a community of commonality even more than the neighborhood. For the child or adolescent, proficiency in some leisure skill may be the primary entry into a new set of associations. Leisure, then, is a source of continuity when roles and relationships suffer severe change.

Just as important is the possibility of shifting priorities in adap-ting to life course transitions or traumas. Any major change – a geographical move, an occupational shift, a family addition or reduction, or some combination of such changes – may be accom-panied by role and identity transitions. When we are placed in different social positions and when major sets of expectations and opportunities are gained or lost, we may come to define ourselves differently. The woman whose identity and productivity were engulfed in the mother role may find new avenues of personal development in employment or a return to school. A competitive athlete may turn his high scoring to sales charts. A student on leaving school may shift from leisure of informal socializing to scheduled events. For anyone, a relatively peripheral activity may take on increased salience during a transition period. Leisure is, among other things, opportunity for investment and development as well as for rest and recuperation. As such, it may take a central place in life as well as a secondary one.

The Integration of Leisure

One assumption of leisure studies has too often been that leisure is segmented from the rest of life. Especially from a recreation point of view, attention has been given to 'activities' that fill time remaining after other roles are fulfilled. From a time perspective, this view is inaccurate since so much leisure is 'interstitial' – found in the midst of the ongoing round and routines of life in every setting. Leisure happens, often not planned or chosen at all, in work interactions and in transportation lulls as well as at home and in the woods. Further, such interstitial leisure may be at least as important as planned events and scheduled investments in the overall balance of life.

However, a second line of attack on the view of leisure as separate and segmented has been outlined in this chapter. Not only may leisure make some contributions to the development of identities, but leisure-based identities may be central for many persons. Leisure may have a persistent centrality in the life course as well as shifting salience through role changes.

Underlying this is a set of premisses as to what is involved in being human. Granting that the forms of these premisses are considerably shaped by the culture in which they are expressed there is the possibility that in some sense both freedom and community are essential to the development of human life. These are not separate and unrelated dimensions, but exist in a dialectical relationship with each other. Beyond survival and basic maintenance, there are dimensions of development. At various points in the life course, they take on somewhat different emphases and forms. For example, freedom as a striving for independence and community as a thrust toward non-familial intimacy may characterize the late adolescent. A major dilemma is to carry out both of these tasks without splitting the dialectic and losing one essential element – autonomy in judgement and decision or the security of stable community in family and friends.

Life does not consist of separate realms and a simple opening and closing of doors as we go from one to the other. Rather, our work, family and leisure roles intersect in countless ways. How they influence each other depends on a number of factors including the overlap of associations from one to the other. However, the emphasis in this chapter has been on learning. The self we are continually learning to be may differ from one role context to another. In fact, one cause of tension in some relationships may stem from a failure to make the transition. Nevertheless, what we have learned in any role context in some measure goes with us to others. How we have learned to define ourselves in leisure may have an impact on how we enact work roles. Identity presentations that are validated in one set of relationships may be tried in another. Even more, we come to believe that we are persons of worth, that who we are has some significance. Such a self-concept is not abandoned the moment we leave a room or court. Rather, the significance of our lives – expressed in freedom and confirmed in community – may be learned anywhere.

Fulfillment and Role Identity Performance
Both work and leisure have been analyzed in terms of intrinsic and extrinsic satisfaction. Whether in a two-factor theory[32] applied to

work or a distinction in differentiating leisure from other activity,[33] the meaning of an activity has been divided between the attainment of external goals and the experience itself. But such a dichotomy omits a central element of meaning – the carrying out of the role.

Examples are limitless since any role may be defined as important enough to yield such satisfaction. Parental roles were suggested in Chapter 3 as ones in which performance may be satisfying both at the time and in contributing to persistent identities. In Chapter 5 we will examine the possibility that it is in such a role identity that we are best able to account for the fact that leisure that is most constrained may be most valued.

However, more leisure-directed roles can also provide satisfaction in *how* they are enacted. The hostess strives to meet and even exceed expectations to be evaluated in that role. The skating instructor finds satisfaction in doing a good job in teaching the skill. A potter finds meaning not only in the product and in the experience of creating something, but in *being* a potter whose skills are exercised. Even at a reception or other social event, there is satisfaction is mingling and interacting well.

In some cases the roles are too central to other commitments such as family and occupation to ever be considered essentially intrinsic. However, in many cases neither the choice of participation nor performance is simply a matter of meeting obligations or ful-filling expectations. Rather, with all the constraints, there is still satisfaction in performing well. Much leisure is neither unrelated and self-contained experience – however expressive or creative. Nor is it just performing in a role as expected. Often we enjoy the process of how we enact a role. The primary meaning is neither in the activity itself nor in any gain we might anticipate outside the experience. It is in the enactment, the performance of the role. And such satisfaction is enhanced by direct and indirect evidence that we have done it well.

In this sense much leisure is both personal and social in meaning. We present ourselves in a role, develop and establish an identity, receive confirmation or correction on our performance and enjoy the process. We enjoy the experience of successful role enactment and find our self-concepts enhanced in the process. Some roles are quite central and others peripheral; some pervade many social set-tings and episodes and others are quite discrete and transitory. However, creating our portrayal of a role identity has its own satisfaction at the moment and in our building of selfhood.

References: Chapter 4

1   Chad Gordon, 'Development of evaluated role identities', *Annual Review of Sociology* (Calif.: Annual Reviews, Inc., 1980); pp. 405–33.
2   George, H. Mead, *Mind, Self, and Society* (Chicago: University of Chicago Press, 1934).
3   Ralph Glasser, 'Leisure policy, identity and work, in J. Haworth and M. Smith, eds, *Work and Leisure* (Princeton, NJ: Princeton, 1976), p. 42.
4   Jean Piaget, *Play, Dreams and Limitation in Childhood* (New York: Norton, 1951).
5   Jean Piaget, *The Origins of Intelligence in Children* (New York: International University Press, 1952).
6   Erik Erikson, *Childhood and Society* (New York: Norton, 1963).
7   Janet Lever, 'Sex differences in the complexity of children's play', *American Sociological Review*, 1978, pp. 471–83.
8   Thomas Martin, W. Berry and Kenneth Berry, 'Competitive sport in postindustrial society', paper presented at the Midwest Sociological Society, Milwaukee, Wisconsin, USA, 1973.
9   Paul Hoch, *Rip Off the Big Game* (Garden City, NY: Doubleday/Anchor, 1972).
10 Brian Sutton-Smith and J. M. Roberts, 'Play, games, and sport', in H. Triandis and A. Heron, eds, *Handbook of Developmental Psychology*, Vol. 4 (Boston, Mass.: Allyn & Bacon, 1981), pp. 425–71.
11 Robert W. White, 'Motivation reconsidered: the concept of competence', *Psychological Review*, vol. 66, 1959, pp. 297–333.
12 K. Lewin, T. Dembo, L. Festinger and P. Sears, 'Level of aspiration', in J. McV. Hunt, ed., *Personality and Behavior Disorders* (New York: Ronald Press, 1974), pp. 333–78.
13 Erving Goffman, *The Presentation of Self in Everyday Life* (Garden City, NY: Doubleday/Anchor, 1957).
14 Gregory Stone, 'Appearance and the Self', in A. Rose, ed., *Human Behavior and Social Processes* (New York: Houghton Mifflin, 1962), pp. 86–118.
15 Thomas M. Martinez, and Robert La Franchi, 'Why people play poker, in G. Stone, ed., *Games, Sport, and Power* (New Brunswick, NJ: Transaction, 1972).
16 Louis Zurcher, 'The friendly power game: the study of an ephemeral role', *Social Forces*, vol. 49, 1970, pp. 173–86.
17 Erving Goffman, *Frame Analysis: An Essay on the Organization of Experience* (New York: Harper & Row, 1974).
18 Gregory Bateson, *Steps to an Ecology of Mind* (New York: Ballantine, 1972).
19 Erving Goffman, *Interaction Ritual* (Garden City: NY: Doubleday/Anchor, 1967).
20 Robert Dubin, 'Industrial workers' worlds: a study of the central life interests of industrial workers', in E. Smigel, ed., *Work and Leisure* (New Haven, Conn.: College and University Press, 1963), pp. 52–72.
21 John R. Kelly, *Leisure* (Englewood Cliffs, NJ: Prentice-Hall, 1982), ch. 7.
22 Robert Stebbins, *Amateurs: On the Margin between Work and Leisure* (Beverly Hills, Calif.: Sage, 1979).
23 ibid., p. 98.
24 John R. Kelly, and S. W. Masar, *Leisure Identities Through a Life Course Transition* (Champaign, Ill.: University of Illinois Leisure Research Laboratory, 1981).
25 William F. Whyte, *Street Corner Society*, 2nd edn (Chicago: University of Chicago Press, 1955).
26 Orrin E. Klapp, *Collective Search for Identity* (New York: Holt Rinehart & Winston, 1969).
27 Stephen Edgell and David Jary, 'Football: a sociological eulogy', in M. Smith, S. Parker and C. Smith, eds, *Leisure and Society in Britain*, (London: Allen Lane, 1973)), pp. 214–29.

28 Herbert Marcuse, *One-Dimensional Man* (Boston, Mass.: Beacon, 1964).
29 Douglas Kleiber and J. Kelly, 'Leisure, socialization and the life cycle', in S. Iso-Ahola, ed., *Social-Psychological Perspectives on Leisure and Recreation* (Springfield, Ill.: Charles C. Thomas, 1980), pp. 102–8.
30 Seppo E. Iso-Ahola, 'A social-psychological analysis of little league baseball', in Iso-Ahola, ibid., p. 192.
31 Chad Gordon, 'Leisure and lives: personal expressivity across the life span', in R. Binstock and E. Shanas, eds, *Handbook and Aging and the Social Sciences* (New York: Van Nostrand Reinhold, 1976), pp. 310–41.
32 F. L. Herzberg, B. Mausner and B. B. Snyderman, *The Motivation to Work* (New York: Wiley, 1959).
33 John Neulinger, *To Leisure: An Introduction* (Boston: Allyn & Bacon, 1981).

Part Two

Social Contexts of Leisure

Leisure can take place almost anywhere. Although some social contexts may be so rigidly task-oriented and organized that even moments of interspersed leisure are unlikely, the possibility of activity done primarily for the experience itself can be ruled out of few settings. Episodes of interaction that are primarily self-contained rather than directed toward work or family requirements may occur in the midst of tasks as well as in manifestly leisure events. Nevertheless, there are social contexts for leisure that encompass a high proportion of leisure action and interaction.

For youth, social frames of face-to-face informality are central to leisure. Many scheduled events are a context for the real leisure action – not the event, but all that goes on around and through the focal activity. This may be true at a concert or an athletic contest as well as at a party or school convocation. For adults living in nuclear families, various combinations of family companions and activities are central to leisure. Not only doing leisure activities with the family, but interaction *as* the activity become the common substance of leisure.

In the next three chapters we will examine three social contexts of leisure. The first is the family. The dilemma of the family and leisure is that the same set of relationships that are seen as a primary leisure resource are also defined as a source of constraints and limitations. The second context will introduce the variety of face-to-face situations which have their meaning in the episode itself rather than in some exterior task or role. Thirdly, we will attempt to draw out some of the implications of the approach developed in the previous chapters for the planning of leisure provisions – public and commercial.

In the final chapter of the book we turn the relationship of sociological theory and leisure research from a one-way flow to a dialogue. Directly and indirectly, there is now enough known about leisure identities and interactions to begin to contribute to explanatory theory about how social situations emerge and social groups form, continue and dissolve.

5

Leisure and the Family

The relationship of leisure and the family begins with a paradox. If leisure is defined as having an essential element of freedom, how can the most pervasive set of obligations in our social worlds not be in conflict with leisure? There are some social roles that are relatively discrete and segmented, carried out in social spaces cut off from other roles. Some work roles are quite segmented in time, place and associations. Some leisure roles are quite specific to an activity setting. But familial roles tend to pervade our allocations of resources – time, space, financial and personal; our modes of interaction; and our definitions of responsibility. How long can we ignore the expectations of the immediate others in our nuclear families? How often can we expend time or money without some consideration of the needs and obligations of home and family? The family is the *budgeting* unit of Western societies in relation to all resources.

It is no wonder that Joffre Dumazedier proposed that most family activity is at best *semi-leisure* and too laden with obligations to be leisure for its own sake.[1] Family activity is just not free enough to be authentic leisure according to this view. The other pole of the paradox is represented by the accumulated evidence that a high proportion of non-work activity is done with other family members as companions or is essentially familial in its substance. Further, such activity is generally valued most among all the range of leisure choices and investments.[2] How can family-related leisure be both constrained and preferred, least free and most valued?

We will explore this paradox more fully in this chapter. However, the basis of an explanation has already been offered. Leisure is not separated from the central identities and investments of life. Rather, from childhood on, leisure is related to primary role identities – in the self-development of play, the acquiring of social skills and self-concepts of competence, and in the beginning and building of primary relationships. Leisure is community as well as freedom, intimacy as well as expression. And there are times and places in which the two dimensions are in tension.

As described in Chapter 4, there is a life course transition for most young adults from a family of orientation to a new nuclear family of productivity. However, some do not begin a second nuclear family, some leave and some are members of several nuclear families in sequence. In discussing leisure 'family' is used here to refer to a primary group of intimates who share residential provisions. 'Quasi-nuclearity' characterizes the social arrangements of many people for whom day-to-day interaction is based on such primary-group stability. In the following discussion the residential family is denoted and extended kin designated when intended. The focus is on the regular interaction and related role expectations and definitions.

The Social Spaces of Leisure

Terminology can become overly precise and precious. Nevertheless, there must be at least general understanding of how terms are used to minimize confusion. *Social space* is used here almost interchangeably with terms such as social context or social world. However, the reference to space suggests that there is a time and space set of parameters that give some structure to the interaction. Further, the nature of the time and space have some influence on the interaction. *Social world*, used to refer to the same occurrence, connotes the agreed-on set of cultural values and symbols that also give some structure to the interaction. *Social context* is perhaps the most neutral term and includes all those elements of setting in which an interaction episode takes place. In each case there is the denotation of parameters or boundaries. Events, leisure or other, occur in social contexts with time parameters of beginnings and endings, space boundaries and role expectations that are relatively precise or open. Our argument is that leisure can occur in almost any such context, but that the nature of the setting has consequences for the leisure.

Any individual has many roles. Some of these are closely related to other roles and some are relatively discrete. The assumption that leisure happens only in discrete role contexts is both inaccurate and mislead-ing. Rather, activity that is essentially done for its own sake, whether structured or not, may be in social contexts in which many kind of roles are being enacted. For most adults, the primary and most pervasive social roles are related to work and family. Other roles of importance may be related to institutions of education, the community, religion, or leisure. In general, despite vast differences in their relative salience for different persons or for the same person at different times in the life course, work and family roles tend to be dominant in their absorption of resources, especially time. Three diagrammatic models suggest possibilities of the relationship among roles (Figure 5.1).

The problem with diagrams that approach any representation of reality is that they are seldom neat and clearcut. The first two models do

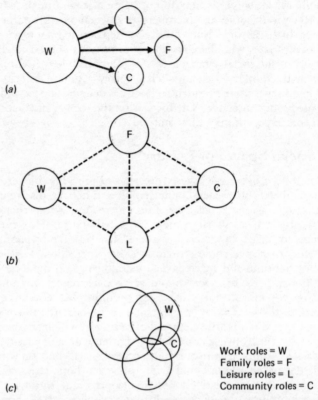

Figure 5.1   Three models of role relationships: (*a*) model presupposing some form of economic determination; (*b*) model requiring independence among roles; (*c*) model displaying overlap among roles that remain both distinguishable and partly independent. The relative size of the circles tends to change through the life course.

not represent current research findings. Leisure is not a separate social space determined directly and indirectly by work. Nor are the four social spaces essentially separate and connected only by occasional or tenuous influences. Rather, there is considerable overlap in time, resources, companions and meanings. Influences may be reciprocal as well as unidirectional.

Further, the relative salience of the four social spaces varies. Suggested in the third figure is that family may be the most significant in relative importance and community the least. That would not be true for the unmarried young professional, the student and for at least some persons at any point in the life course. Nevertheless, more often than not, for adults the family and related investments take priority in life. A study of industrial workers found that they believe their family roles to be of first importance followed by work and leisure.[3] The greatest spillover was between family and leisure rather than work and leisure, especially for men who are employed. It is this relationship that we will explore in this chapter.

Research on Leisure and the Family

Only in the decade of the 1970s has the leisure–family issue emerged in research and theory. Prior to 1970, the work–leisure issue dominated the literature and seems to have obscured the more obvious relationship. However, that oversight is now being remedied.

In the United Kingdom Kenneth Roberts devoted a chapter to the family-leisure question in his little 1970 book. He summarizes the work–leisure issue as quite complex and certainly not simply a matter of determination. Then, he begins the next chapter: 'Family life is exceptionally closely woven with leisure.'[4] The evidence that follows draws on a series of community studies that have been a major thrust in British sociology. In general, he suggests that gender, period in the family life cycle and type of community are factors in adult leisure. More recently, he analyzed trends in time use to find that just being with one's family is a major element of leisure.[5] Further, the dominance of TV in the use of time cannot be understood apart from its connections with familial interaction. TV-watching is not as solitary and passive as some suggest, but may provide a context and a set of extramural topics for family conversation.

Studies of the leisure of industrial workers in the United States have followed a trend that may reflect social change as well as the altered focus of the research community. That blue-collar workers engaged in sex-segregated leisure and for the most part left their unemployed wives behind was a truism in the literature until the 1970s. The mutual quoting that supports and extends such sociological truisms was much in evidence. Mirra Komarovsky's study from the 1950s reports that husbands prefer wives as companions in only 25 percent of their most enjoyed activities and 32 percent of moderately enjoyable ones.[6] She further found a common split in families not only in mutual activity, but in communication and support.

The possibility of change has been reported in more recent research. For example, Gavin MacKenzie reports that the majority of skilled workers enjoy most leisure as couples with only three of the 194 studied omitting their wives from their discussion of leisure.[7] Outings with other males are not completely abandoned, but are occasions in the common round of more familial interaction. Even in 'hard living' families with conflict-ridden patterns of interaction, husbands and wives engage in considerable informal exchange.[8] The familial basis of weekend leisure in extended ethnic families may involve men and women separating part of the time, but still in an overall family event.[9] When a group of California steelworkers were given extended vacations, their home-based activity increased and they believed that their family life has been enhanced by the greater opportunity for interaction.[10] Even in a study of wives that paints a rather bleak picture of opportunities and personal development, there is an expectation that husbands will share their offwork hours with their wives and families.[11] Whatever the accuracy of earlier studies, the weight of evidence from even those studies that begin with traditional perspectives now seems to be that working-class families engage in a considerable amount of leisure interaction. One problem with earlier studies was the definition of leisure as 'activities' that gave undue attention to identifiable events rather than the ongoing round of life. Now, even for the 'worst-case' industrial workers, we may presume some integration of family and leisure.

The Case for Integration

From research that begins with a leisure focus, we are taken somewhat further in analysis of the ties between leisure and the family. One line of research has been based on investigations of outdoor recreation. It begins with the simple evidence that activity at beaches, lakes and rivers takes place with other family members or family and friends in over 80 percent of cases for informal activities, 75 percent for boating and 65 percent for fishing.[12] Lower percentages are registered only for more youth-oriented activities. Then, in a greater variety of leisure settings, similar findings were analyzed to support the thesis that regular interaction groups or communities form around leisure activities and locales. Of these, the most common and most mobile is the family.

Taking the family as the focus of the research strategy, Dennis Orthner studied the nature and meaning of marital leisure experiences.[13] He distinguishes between activities in which a couple participates jointly and parallel activities during which both are present with little interaction. He finds that joint activities which are chosen for their potential of mutual involvement tend to reinforce patterns of communication and other kinds of sharing in the marriage. His findings support a theoretical perspective in which the sharing of spontaneous and planned activity is an element in building the total relationship in a marriage. However, his analysis reveals both cohort and life cycle differences. During the parental phase of the family life cycle, children are more the common focus of communication and planning. Younger couples, however, seem to have higher expectations for leisure-sharing and interaction that those whose children have been launched. He suggests that those entering their marriage careers more recently expect levels of leisure-sharing beyond those considered necessary by their parents. However, in either case, both joint and parallel activities are a central part of their leisure.

A recent study of a transitional area of Greater London supported the significance of marital and family interaction in leisure.[14] Most of the adults indicated they would like greater sharing of leisure with their spouse. Activities at home, occasional short trips and informal interaction are a major part of their leisure. Those who command greater resources of time, money, mobility, education and friendship groups participate in more of a variety of activities. The highest value was placed on interpersonal relationships, especially around the home.

In general, the case for the close relationship of leisure and family seems unassailable. The issues of the extent of obligation in family leisure, of convenience rather than choice and of satisfaction in family-based leisure remain. However, the integration of family and leisure is a 'social fact', whatever the implications and consequences.

Opportunity and Obligation

In a line of research carried out in the United States the author discovered a surprising anomaly. Even though freedom has been stressed as the central element of the meaning of leisure, complementary leisure with higher perceived constraint was found to rank higher in importance to adults than relatively unconstrained unconditional leisure.[15] In the university town study, using a value scale, only 38 percent of the high-value activities were unconditional as opposed to 56 percent of the lower-value activities. In the mill town 68 percent of those activities ranked first by respondents were role complementary, 56 percent of those ranked second, 51 percent third, 46 percent fourth and 39 percent of those ranked fifth.

One possible explanation is that people really prefer constraint and place a lower value on relative freedom. They may find decision threatening and structure comfortable. However, there is a simpler and more plausible explanation. It is that the complementary kinds of leisure that are related to primary roles are valued more highly because of satisfactions attached to those relationships. Family leisure may be more constrained by expectations, but also be more satisfying. When we recognize that 64 percent of such adult activities are usually engaged in with other family members, the picture becomes more clear. It is not that we disvalue freedom, but that family interaction –

even with somewhat less freedom – is valued more highly. For most adults, then, the most important leisure is relational, social leisure chosen because of the positive satisfactions anticipated.

In this line of research respondents ranked reasons for choosing the kinds of activity they would least want to give up. Some of the reasons referred to satisfactions intrinsic to the experience, some to recuperation and compensation for other role constraints, some to positive satisfactions in the relationships and some to role expectations and obligations. The social-meaning statements range from the relational 'I enjoy the companions' through 'it strengthens relationships' to 'it's a duty'. The full set of social reasons in order of increasing role determination is:

'I enjoy the companions.'
'I feel I belong.'
'I like being of help to others.'
'It strengthens relationships.'
'Expected to by family.'
'Expected to by friends or others.'
'It's a duty.'

Except for the generic and essentially contentless 'because I like it', the two reasons ranked the highest overall were 'I enjoy the companions' and 'it strengthens relationships'. The role-determined reasons of social expectation ranked well below such intrinsic statements as 'it's my self-expression', 'I grow as a person' and 'it's exciting'. Expression and self-development along with the experience itself are more significant satisfactions for adult leisure than any except those related to immediate communities of family and friends. In leisure, interaction with intimates comes first followed by identity development and the experience itself.

Family Interaction as Leisure

In the comparison of two new towns – one British and the other in the United States – there were some differences in the kinds of activity selected as most important to the samples of adults.[16] Reading for pleasure, arts and crafts, and family conversation were ranked higher in Reston, the American planned community, while visiting family and friends, short car trips, play with children and going to pubs and clubs were more important in the British town of Telford. However, in both, various kinds of family interaction were the single dominant category of leisure activity for adults comprising either five or six of the highest-ranked types in each (Table 5.1). Allowing for discrepan-

Table 5.1 *Family Leisure in US and UK Towns*

Activity Type	US New Town Rank	UK New Town
Marital affection and intimacy	2	1·5
Activity as a couple	4	9
Play with children	7	4
Family outings	8	9
Family conversation	3	14
Visiting family and friends	11	1·5

cies due to the small samples the agreement remains persuasive. Family interaction itself is a major leisure activity. It may take varying forms through the life cycle. Some marital dyadic interaction may give way to playing with children for parents. Kin-visiting can be altered by moving away. The difference in value placed on family conversation may be cultural, while the greater stress on kin-visiting and short car trips in England probably reflects geography. Most extended families are in the West Midlands in the British sample, while those in a Washington, DC, suburb are usually far from kin. Further, eating out, entertaining and going to church tend to be done with family members as well as friends and acquaintances. Outdoor sports such as swimming and tennis are often done with others in the family. Finally, vacation trips are almost always events for familial interaction.

The point is simple: family interaction itself is the dominant form of leisure for adults living in nuclear families. Research that begins with lists of specific activities, most of which require a scheduled trip, and then contrast them with TV-watching at home misses the primary context of leisure. Whatever the quality of the interaction, leisure most often occurs when two or more family members are together.

This does not mean that such interaction necessarily consumes the most time. John Robinson's time diary research in North America reports that media use, primarily TV, generally takes about 40 percent of the time not devoted to sleep, employment, and family and personal care.[17] About 30 percent goes to social interaction, usually with other family members. However, there are several factors that make this categorization misleading. First, considerable TV-watching is done with other family members, sometimes 'parallel' rather than joint, but often involving some communication and interaction. Secondly, time labeled 'family care' also mixes elements of communication and satisfying interaction. And, thirdly, use of time does not represent importance or intensity.[18] Social interaction may involve a high level of intensity and be valued highly, while some media use may be residual and of low intensity. Even so, family members are the most common companions for leisure.

Orthner's research found that the higher the proportion of time spent together by couples in joint activities, the higher their marital satisfaction.[19] Partners establish mutually reinforcing leisure and marital interaction patterns that change through the family life cycle, especially during the parental periods.[20] The expansion and contraction of the household through the life cycle radically alters the communication and interaction patterns related to maintenance tasks as well as leisure.

However, neither time diary research nor that focusing on joint vs parallel activities distinguishes the orientations of the interaction. If nuclear family interaction is central to most adult leisure, does this reflect more than convenience or availability? If there is something more, is it a response to the expectations of intimates, a positive satisfaction found in the relationship, or some combination of the two?

The author's research is far from final or definitive. However, there are several consistent indications from the multicommunity studies.[21] First, in both the US and UK studies, positive 'relational' satisfactions ranked with relaxation as two of the highest three substantive reasons for selecting important leisure. Enjoyment of companions and strengthening relationships are primary orientations of adult leisure, each at least six times more often mentioned than family expectations.

Secondly, the primary content of considerable adult leisure is family interaction itself. Further, many activities serve primarily as a context for interaction, as social settings. Thirdly, situational factors are important in specific decisions about what to do at a given time. Therefore, the convenience of family companions is one element in such interaction. They tend to be most available, in the same residence and on parallel schedules.

Fourthly, building intimate relationships of sharing and communication is considered a central life concern and goal. Some leisure, then, is in part instrumental – a context for inaugurating, developing, enhancing, enriching and strengthening primary relationships. Fifthly, another element in such familial leisure may be 'role comfort'. All the attention given to role-testing, problematic outcomes and identity presentation should not obscure that on some occasions we prefer not to experiment, compete, or even refine identities. The relative acceptance within intimate communities may be a positive factor in choosing to spend time with others for whom identities are well established and interaction patterns relatively routine. Just as TV-watching may be relaxing and recuperative due to its low investment requirements, so some familial leisure may be valued just because it can be familiar and easy and responses accurately predicted.

Life Course Changes in Companionship

However, we should not assume that family leisure is static through the life cycle. Rather, both forms and orientations change as the structure and roles of the nuclear family are altered. In the same three-community study sequence the family life cycle was found to be a major variable in leisure.[22] Almost 2,400 activities were studied in 374 interviews in a university town, a mill town and a suburban new town in three regions of the United States. The findings on family and leisure were quite consistent among the three communities.

First, over half the activities were usually done with their family members. Even outdoor sports such as tennis, swimming and bicycling are evenly divided between family and non-familial companions. Secondly, four of the seven activities ranked highest actually consist of family interaction – sexual, communication and play – rather than of some activity done *with* family members.

Thirdly, over 70 percent of recreational activities and 80 percent of social activities are usually done with other family members. Exceptions to the family association patterns with overall rank are reading for pleasure (2), arts or crafts (15), hobbies (20), companionship on the job (21) and voluntary organizations other than church (22).

Fourthly, respondents were asked if there might be any consequences were the activity stopped. Just one-third of the activities were perceived as having family consequences of disappointment or damage to relationships. There is little question that meeting expectations is one element in a considerable amount of adult leisure, especially social interaction. However, for two-thirds of the activities, the only perceived consequence was personal loss – 'I would miss it'.

Fifthly, parenthood has a marked impact on leisure. In both the mill and university towns over 30 percent of the activities chosen primarily for their own sake took on significant role expectation components during parenting years. The expectations and obligations as well as the aims and hopes of parenting take a share of both time and financial resources. However, even more they become central to life's meanings, the central investments of this establishment period of life. As a result, leisure becomes more role-related and less unconditional.

Table 5.2 *New Town Leisure Associations during the Family Life Cycle* *

Family Life Cycle	Alone	With Spouse	Association With Family	Family and Others	With Others
Never married	36% (41)	0% (0)	3% (3)	4% (5)	57% (65)
Preparental	21% (40)	55% (106)	2% (3)	14% (26)	9% (17)
Parental	23% (147)	22% (142)	32% (203)	16% (102)	7% (17)
Launching	24% (29)	23% (28)	26% (32)	19% (23)	9% (6)
Postparental	26% (31)	51% (61)	7% (8)	12% (14)	5% (6)
Broken home	45% (17)	0% (0)	0% (0)	13% (5)	42% (16)
	25% (305)	28% (337)	21% (249) N=1198	15% (175)	11% (132)

* Chi square=495; $p<0.001$; lambda=0.166 with association dependent.

Sixthly, this shift is also demonstrated by the associational pattern. Table 5.2 displays the transition from activities done alone or just with marriage partner to family while children are living at home with a shift back after all children have been launched.

All this does not mean that leisure is lost in the parenting period of life. Nor does it imply that what is called 'leisure' becomes merely another activity setting in which the roles of spouse and parent are enacted. Rather, the satisfactions found in the companionship, in enacting the parental role well and developing that role identity, and in fulfilling life goals through self-investment, are turned significantly to the family of productivity.

Leisure companionship is a major, if often overlooked, element in family life and marriage. It is far more complex than just responding to the expectations of others or meeting conventional role requirements. Fulfillment is found in the midst of life's ongoing relationships, not just in moments of esctasy or transcendence. Who we are may be explored in a variety of settings, but is grounded in our intimate communities. Therefore, leisure companionship is a multidimensional phenomenon.

Family members are generally the most available companions for both informal and unscheduled leisure as well as for events that require planning. The family is thus seen as a primary resource for leisure. Enough adult establishment period leisure is organized by and for couples that being without this resource calls for a different set of opportunities for social leisure. The expectation of 'double occupancy' for vacation trips, the games that require pairs for participation and the customs of entertaining are only part of the expectation. Those who lack this resource, both for social events and for ongoing interaction, live in quite a different social world for leisure. The attention given to leisure as a resource for familial development should not be allowed to obscure the reverse, the significance of the family for leisure.

An issue that is only beginning to emerge is that of the expectations associated with the 'leisure role' in the family. Not only is a spouse, parent, sibling, or even child often expected to provide companionship for others in the family, but there are expectations as to the quality of the interaction. Members of the nuclear family are expected to listen, to give attention to the relating of events and attitudes so important to interaction. They are expected to give some priority to the priorities of others, to be ready to enter into conversation, adjust a schedule preference or even commitment, and share the interests of the other. In fact, the quality of leisure companionship may become more and more of an issue in marital stability or dissolution. The increase of divorces during and following launching of children suggests that for a husband to be an adequate breadwinner or a woman an acceptable mother and homemaker may not be enough to hold a marriage together. There is the further desire for companionship, for a sharing of interests and activities not only at home, but outside. The study by Lillian Rubin[23] documents the failure of some blue-collar husbands to meet the companionship expectations of their wives. One factor in meager communication may well be the lack of leisure interaction and sharing.

One of the women interviewed intensively in the study of the place of leisure in the transition from student to early establishment was a person with her life clearly organized around a set of priorities.[24] Not only did her leisure change with the seasons and with the rise and fall of her teaching schedule, but she managed the life of the household to include the desired variety of leisure. Some leisure was intended to enhance the quality of marriage in communication and excitement. Some extended their sharing to friends, who provide a number of contexts for both activity and interaction. And some was more personal and developmental in intent. In such an ordered existence leisure has multiple meanings and contexts. However, the dialectic between building of the marriage and leisure is basic. Leisure and the marriage are reciprocally resources for each other.

The particular forms and settings of such leisure companionship change as roles change. Early marriage as an intensification of the courting period brings about a processual shift of leisure to what is shared with the partner. The birth of children not only adds responsibilities, but breaks the simplicity of the dyad. Now a drastic new set of relationships, responsibilities and roles turn the couple into the more complex family of productivity and also may seriously erode the quality and quantity of dyadic leisure. However, more and more leisure for parents is found in the various support functions that attend childrearing. The transition that accompanies the loss of those support functions during launching does not mean that there is a simple return to preparental dyadic sharing. Rather, the leisure roles must be rebuilt during this latter transition if they are to take a more central place in the investments and allocations of the couple.

Transitions that break the family and marriage, such as death, separation and divorce, and serious physical or mental illness, have a sharp impact on leisure companionship. All the taken-for-granted associations that accompany the 'normal' family life cycle to widowhood are upset. The previous associations developed around interfamilial relationships are disrupted. Previous patterns of intrafamilial interaction are broken. Then the meaning of the family as leisure resource is revealed by its loss. While a new sense of freedom may also be experienced as roles are abandoned or lost, the removal of availability, 'role comfort' and so much of the social support for leisure requires for most a serious process of adaptation.[25]

Satisfactions and Investments

Families provide many things to their members. There are the basic nutritional, shelter and protection functions; the sexual regulation and access functions; the reproduction and nurturing functions; appropriate economic production and consumption; education functions; property transmission functions; and social status and placement functions. It is no wonder that the family has been described cross-culturally as more of an economic than companionship institution. Nevertheless, in our societies the family also provides nurture for development, affective as well as economic support, and relationships of intimacy, trust and communication. The family is the first and basic intimate community, a set of face-to-face relationships with continuity. It is as a family member that most children face the world and are given identity.

The companionship and leisure functions of the family have just begun to find their way into the more structurally oriented literature. Popular journalists have been quicker than scholars to write of men and women who expect marriage partners to be friends, consistent and enjoyable companions in the round of life. The considerable emotional as well as economic investments in the nuclear family are made with the expectation of being given much in return. Among the aspects of return is leisure. What, then, are the leisure functions of the nuclear family?

First, leisure is a mutual interest for the family, a focus of interaction and communication. Generally, adult and youth members of the family join in deciding and planning a vacation trip. While relative influence may not be equal, the planning, anticipation and recollection of a vacation trip may be a common topic of conversation and medium of sharing.[26] In the same way, other common leisure events and investments – entertaining, visiting, a toy such as a boat or game, or any shared event – are concrete symbols around which communication and interaction are built.

Secondly, leisure is a social space for parenting. Not only one-on-one play with a child, but the various forms and locales of playful interaction are the context of considerable development of relationships. Family life that is all task and schedule, without leisure or spontaneity, would be lacking much of the joy and openness that break routine and add affective richness.

Thirdly, leisure is an opportunity for trying and developing new facets of family relationships. While there are values in routine sharing, even doing the dishes, leisure is the context of the unexpected and the novel. It is in leisure that we are most likely to break routine and discover something new in relationships.

Fourthly, leisure may also be an opportunity for autonomy and independence.[27] On the freedom side of the paradox, leisure legitimates independence from the family. Leisure, whether it is a ball game or an evening class, is an acceptable purpose for a spouse or child to go out on his/her own. It is space for the development of non-familial identities that complement the family role identities. One important element of such autonomy, especially for adolescents, is sexual exploration and expression.

Fifthly, leisure is removed enough from the economic and maintenance functions of the family that it may serve as the context for role-enactment that alters and defuses the authority patterns of maintenance. The rigidity of breadwinner, banker, provider, schedule-keeper and teacher roles may be broken and emotional tension reduced through play that allows dominant family members to take less authoritative roles.

Sixthly, the expectation of mutual support in the family depends on some voluntary decisions as well as meeting social expectations and legal requirements. The companionship and trust developed and continued in leisure interaction contributes to the overall relationship that includes various kinds of support through the life course.

The other side of the investment–return issue is based on the significance of the family in the value schemes of adults in contemporary Western societies. Evidence that the family–home investments are most often of greatest salience has been presented. In the context of a fuller analysis of the family this central investment of self and resources may be re-examined. One approach is instrumental. Leisure is understood primarily in terms of what it provides to the stability and richness of family relationships. Leisure may be seen as at least some of the brightness and uniqueness in the overall fabric of family. Leisure is defined as good for the family, a necessary addition of variety and developmental opportunities. Leisure is approached as it makes significant contributions to that central investment of life, the family.

The second approach takes the family as a resource for leisure. Leisure is not defined just in terms of instrumental values, but also in terms of necessary expressivity. One element of the importance of the family is that it provides a social context for much leisure. Leisure, from this perspective, is a necessary space for freedom, expressivity and self-development. Enacting leisure roles has intrinsic as well as instrumental value. After all, in a family there are multiple roles and relationships. Among these is the role of leisure companion, enacted in many activity and environmental settings. Leisure roles are seen as an important part of the set of roles that make up the family institution. Further, family leisure roles enable portrayals that are needed to balance more structured role reciprocity and to facilitate possibilities of change through the life course.

In a society that requires so much from the nuclear family it should be no surprise that it is given such centrality in overall schemes of value. Nor should the close relationship between the family and leisure be considered surprising in a social system that has increasingly separated the workplace and residence, delegated a high proportion of time and other resources to the family, and been no more than ambivalent about the importance of social solidarity. As a consequence, those who remain outside the nuclear families for extended periods of their life course generally have to find some substitute.

Forms of Family Leisure

Most of the forms of familial leisure have been mentioned. However, their variety can be seen more clearly by distinguishing three types.

Informal Leisure

In terms of the amount of time invested, the main kind of family leisure consists of ongoing interaction that takes place chiefly around the home. Evidence that this kind of leisure is most highly valued has been introduced. Such interaction consists of interstitial conversations, play with children, informal episodes in which dyadic interaction is the focus and various interaction sequences that are more processual than planned. They take place in and around the home, in transit to both tasks and events, and often in connection with meals.

While Orthner's distinction between joint and parallel activities for a couple make an important point, the two may be more on a continuum of interaction intensity than clearly divisible. For example, a walk may involve considerable interchange or be relatively silent. Watching TV may spark exchange of comments and even affective responses during a sport contest in which there is identification with a team or involve nothing except proximity before a single screen. Some activities require interaction, some permit it and some block it. Nevertheless, Orthner lists over thirty kinds of activity that are most often parallel and fifty that seem generally to foster interaction.[28]

The meaning of much of the informal interaction is actually found in the communication that takes place. The lack of such communication may be defined as an acute and significant deprivation. Whether such communication takes place at the dinner table, before the TV, in the garden, or even in the garage and around the car is incidental. Such leisure is essentially one element of intimate interaction, perhaps the light side of the ongoing relationship.

Of course, the home is also the locale for a number of events such as entertaining, different kinds of celebration related to life course milestones and general holidays, and definitions that designate an occasion as important. Further, external schedules often enforce a timetable in informal and interstitial social leisure that give it a feeling of having to take place at a particular time or not at all.

Scheduled Events

From one perspective, scheduled family leisure becomes the punctuation in the run-on sentence. Events are the designated high points of family interaction that lend meaning and excitement to the rest. They are the events that require some planning and anticipation as well as a specific allocation of at least one resource, time.

Some such events are regular. They include participation in church worship and organizations, other voluntary organizations, activities that require collecting certain people at the same time and place such as a sport contest or choral concert, and all the special events selected as worth this attention and resource allocation. Some events are related to the social roles taken by family members such as a mother's participation in community theater, a brother's track meet, or a school-related convocation. Such events may be clustered in weekend periods or be routinely scheduled on the 'fourth Friday evening'. Others are seasonal or related to the school or church calendar.

The decision processes related to such events are often complex. In some families the mother becomes the keeper of the social schedule and arbiter of conflicts.[29] In other families the responsibility is shared or delegated according to convenience or salience. There seems to be a close connection between transportation needs and resources and such schedule arbitration in the modern metropolitan family. Juggling all the priorities, schedules, changes, losses and contingencies can be a demanding and complex task in a family with children over 10–12 years old.

Another issue is the extent to which leisure events separate or integrate the family. Some community agencies which claim to serve the entire family actually segregate their activities quite rigidly by age. Activities and events that allow for or require immediate interaction of family members may be relatively rare in many churches, clubs and community recreation programs. It is the self-organized events that are most likely to provide a frame for intimate community-building.

Vacations

Although vacations do not all involve trips, some special use of the time is common. Even in Brent, almost three-quarters of the sample had been away from home on holiday in the previous twelve months and a third more than once.[30] Most of the other 25 percent had been on vacation during the previous three years. Further, such trips are found to have an important place in leisure and life satisfaction.

Such trips have many dimensions.[31] Not only is there the anticipation and recollection as well as the experience itself, but family vacation travel is more than getting someplace. Some parents report finding that just being together in the car with no distracting tasks or interference provides a singular opportunity for communication, especially with older children. Trips themselves are frequently more than transportation. A case study of a California family found that a single summer trip combined interaction on the way, camping in transit, visiting relatives and friends, sightseeing and even routines of eating at restaurants previously found attractive.[32]

Similar analysis of outdoor camping suggested that a variety of activities are contexts for many different role portrayals at a single campsite.[33] Activities such as chopping wood, erecting a tent, and preparing and gathering food, as well as hiking, boating and swimming, are opportunities for the symbolic presentation of various aspects of the identities of different family members. While this may be true for any event of sustained and varied interaction, the possibility of playing out sequences of role identities in company with others of the nuclear family seem especially evident in the vacation trip.

Trends and Transitions

We may continue to distinguish between structural elements of social institutions and those of style. Just as the stylistic 'how' of leisure may be more differentiated than the more structural 'what', so changes in the family are also both those of form and of style.

Structural Trends
The analysis that follows is based on an analysis of structural trends in household composition and women's employment in the United States. The trends are common to other Western countries, but the rates and baselines differ. In general, the following trends seem well established:[34]

- The major increase will be in households composed of single persons and single heads rather than those headed by married couples.
- Fewer households will have children living at home.
- The trends toward lower birth rates and a slight increase in those who do not marry as well as higher divorce rates are actually consistent with the trends of the 1920s and 1930s. The 1940s and 1950s can now be seen as war-inaugurated deviation from long-term changes.
- More women will be employed and more of the employed married.
- As a consequence, there will be more two-worker families, decreased fertility and more continuous full-time employment for women.
- Single-women-headed households, with and without children, will continue to increase dramatically.

These are changes in structure. They may be summarized negatively: the traditional two-parent, single-worker with children family is expected to make up less than 15 percent of households in the USA by 1990. This means that at any given time, 29 percent will be female-headed, 16 percent male-headed and over half will have no children at home. Further, dual-worker couples are expected to be twice the number of single-worker couples. Later marriages and more divorces will increase the number of adults taking roles in work and community without a marriage partner. More persons, at any one time, will be in some stage of transition – in or out of a marriage, employment, or parenting. Further, those transitions can no longer be identified as associated with a particular age segment of the lifespan. At any age people can be single, courting, or separating; beginning or leaving parent responsibilities; and so on.

What does this imply for leisure? First, of course, the 'normal' family life cycle cannot be taken for granted. The Rapoports recognize this change as well as different ways of enacting roles in their analysis of the leisure of traditional and non-traditional families.[35] However, the structural changes alone are highly significant:

- The decrease in the proportion of the adult population engaged in childrearing lessens the resource constraints, but also provides longer periods in which that focus of leisure is absent. The possibility of more discretionary income and time means that adult leisure will incorporate most satisfactions other than those of fulfilling parental roles.
- The life course will involve more change. Transitions in and out of marriage, parental obligations and residential contexts mean that leisure will be called on to contribute to adaptation to such changes. Evidence that the transition periods, such as separation, are especially critical and difficult suggest that leisure can play a major part in providing continuity of associations as well as exploring possibilities for new intimate communities and strengthened identities.
- The common context of adult leisure – the nuclear family – will be an available resource for less of the population. More leisure provisions and occasions will have to be adapted to participation by those who do not come in couples or whose aims are different from those with a nuclear family waiting at home. Along with the missing resource, there comes some freedom. The orientation of complementary leisure with the need to integrate schedules and equitably allocate resources is sharply reduced, especially for those who do not continue as single parents. On the other hand, when all parenting is concentrated into a single unsupported role, then both freedom and resources may be severely limited.
- Two-worker families would presumably have greater schedule constraints combined with increased economic resources. The impacts of rising housing costs and consumption expectations on the allocation of those resources remains to be measured. However, we do know that employed wives and mothers engage in both efficiency and lowered expectations for homemaking and parenting. Further, employed married women, while spending 40 percent less time on homemaking than those not employed, also continue to carry the major responsibilities for housekeeping, meal preparation and the care of young children. They may have greater autonomy due to having an independent income, but there are tradeoffs in time. On aim in leisure may become an increased efficiency in time use for leisure as well as in child care and household management.
- Parental responsibilities are a crucial variable. Ninety percent of single employed parents are women who suffer under the typically

lower incomes received by women. Their time is constricted by parenting tasks and the lack of a partner with whom to share them as well as by the job timetable. Their leisure resources are often acutely scarce in time and money.

- On the other hand, changes in women's roles can be expected to have impacts on leisure orientations and contexts. Women will have less time, and the time available will be more competitive with men. Weekday programs will miss most adult women. However, fewer women will have their leisure dominated by their secondary support roles and by the expectations of their husbands. There will be both new opportunities and constraints.

Transitions and Leisure
There will be an increase of two kinds of family-related transitions that may be summarized as 'in' and 'out'. More and more adults will be in process of making a change in their household/familial contexts and commitments. There will be more formerly marrieds, more adults seeking to become remarried, more children not being nurtured by both their biological parents and, in general, more individuals spending more of their lifespans outside the nuclear family.

An analysis of a national survey in the United States yields some suggestions about those who are in a transition rather than having completed adaptation to new roles, opportunities and identities.[36] They are those who identify themselves as 'separated' – neither married nor divorced. They are still adjusting to a situation in which one change is the loss of a central leisure companion. As a consequence, they are less likely than any other group to venture into bars, engage in social sports such as swimming, or to dine out. They seldom entertain at home and spend fewer evenings with friends who are not kin or neighbors. They are far more likely than any other group to feel bored, are lonely more often than any but widows and are measurably least satisfied with their lives. These bare statistical comparisons suggest that there is a process of adaptation to singleness that has profound effects on what people do, whom they are with, and where and why they engage in leisure. The family context may gradually be replaced with new relationships of companionship, communication and even intimacy; but it takes time and the learning of new behaviors and role identities.

On the other hand, the 'in' transition may be presumed to be similar in some ways regardless of age or previous family history. Leisure becomes a context of building a new relationship, sharing and learning interests and experiences, and of developing intimacy in communication and trust through a variety of events and occurrences. Leisure is also one social context for establishing new and renewed relationships of the emerging dyad with other dyads, institutions and groups.

Other Changes Ahead

Are there other changes and trends that are likely to have an effect on family leisure? The close ties between leisure and the social context of the family and the spatial context of the home combine to suggest further change.[37]

First, the increased costs of housing and construction will allow for less interior and exterior private space for most households. While this will be partially offset by smaller family units, some of the former luxuries of space, especially in North America, will in the future be bought only at very high costs in income obligations.

Secondly, reductions in family size and an increased proportion of single adults will reorient the intimate communities of leisure in two ways. Leisure companionship will become acknowledged as a more central element in relationships, especially in later years. Also leisure will more and more be a social space in which those temporarily or permanently single seek and develop close relationships. Human sexuality will also be recognized as an accepted dimension in leisure relationships.

Thirdly, most adults will continue to find their primary context for leisure in home and immediate community. However, that primary community will less and less be the childrearing nuclear family. Further, failing to meet expectations for leisure sharing in marriage will become more frequently a basis for divorce even when breadwinner, homemaker, sexual and parental roles are being fulfilled adequately.

Fourthly, women will be less bound to the home in their leisure as well as in work roles. They will have more control over financial resources, more regular relationships with men as well as other women away from home, and less time free from non-familial obligations. While there may be less pressure on the marriage to provide so much companionship, the change will call for a new balance of freedom and dependence for many marriages and for cultural definitions of marriage.

Fifthly, the central implication for leisure of such structural and stylistic changes may well be in the relative importance of leisure to many adults. As traditional family roles take less time and offer less pervasive role expectations, then leisure roles and identities may take on greater importance. Leisure as opportunity for personal meaning and for fulfilling community will be more and more crucial to how life is understood and evaluated. Family changes will alter both the contexts and orientations of considerable adult leisure; but leisure changes and expectations will have impacts on resource allocation and salience in the family life cycle.

Leisure and Intimacy

One important step in the study of leisure has been to recognize that it is understood better in the context of family roles and contexts than as the second half of a 'work and' formula. In the light of structural and stylistic changes in the family, a next step may be to begin to address 'leisure and intimacy' rather than 'leisure and the family'. Family, especially the adult family of productivity, may be only one context of the development of intimate communities – for both children and adults.

To begin with, the pervasiveness of sexuality and sexual identities is being brought into a more central place in leisure studies.[38] Intimacy itself, the sharing process of communication and trust, can be leisure with meanings that are deeply experiential as well as freely chosen and related to the expression of selfhood. The narrower range of meanings and interactions of sexual activity can also be leisure. Sexual intercourse is not just a role obligation or a functional task; it can be enjoyable, exciting, engrossing to the point of time-and-space transcendence and eagerly anticipated. Intercourse, in its many forms, may be engaged in primarily or entirely for the experience itself. We are not only sexual beings in all our leisure, but sex as activity is a major kind of leisure. Further, the meanings of salience of sexual activity vary through the life course. The meaning of intimacy is not exhausted by sexuality, but sexuality and sexual identities are a significant element in leisure and intimacy.

However, it may be more inclusive to refer to the less connotative term of 'community'. Intimacy denotes 'deep community' or intensive relationships. Intimate relationships are firsthand, profound and shared over some period of time. Some sexual intercourse is not intimacy by this definition, while most intimate relationships involve no sexual intercourse at all. Intimates are significant others with whom we have an ongoing and usually multifaceted relationship in which we go beyond self-presentation to sharing. Such intimacy may be found in the family and also in work and leisure. Further, intimacy is a basis for the more inclusive integration of a society. The concentric circles of our social lives move outward from intimacy to momentary, anonymous and instrumental interchange. But at the center are those relationships in which we are most deeply confirmed in our identities.

From this perspective, leisure is an interaction environment more than a set of activities. Some of the activity in this environment is explicitly instrumental – directed toward the development of intimate communities. Leisure is a social space in which the relative freedom allows us to concentrate on relationships as well as experiences, on intimacy as well as role identities. Leisure is not *the* environment for anything. Rather, leisure has characteristics that permit and even facilitate personal and social development that is most central to who we understand ourselves to be in relation to our social environments.

Cheek and Burch are correct, then, in proposing a significant social function for leisure.[39] In our social environments we build from the center outward, from intimate communities to the complex social system. This means that intimate communities are the primary building-blocks of the social structure, the first element in social cohesion. In a mass society we are connected first of all by our immediate communities. We escape alientation because of intimacy more than because we know ourselves to be contributing to some grand purpose or overall design. The family is the first primary-group connection for most of us. However, other immediate communities may be developed through the life course, based on commonalities of family, religion, ethnicity, work, or even leisure.

And, since leisure is a major element in family interaction, in the development of intimacy through the life course, then it has a significant place in the overall scheme of social cohesion. It is not only opportunity and freedom, but the locus of considerable personal investment. When leisure is given a high priority in the allocation of resources and in self-definitions the investment is not entirely misplaced. In so far as leisure provides a context for intimacy as well as the expression of personal identities, it is critical rather than trivial.

References: Chapter 5

1 Joffre Dumazedier, *Toward a Society of Leisure* (New York: The Free Press, 1967), p. 19.
2 J. R. Kelly, 'A revised paradigm of leisure choices', *Leisure Sciences*, vol. 1, 1978, pp. 345–63.
3 Graham L. Staines and Pamela O'Conner, *The Relationship between Work and Leisure*, University of Michigan Survey Research Center, 1979.
4 Kenneth Roberts, *Contemporary Society and the Growth of Leisure* (London: Longman, 1978), p. 41.
5 ibid., pp. 59–61.
6 Mirra Komarovsky, *Blue-Collar Marriage* (New York: Random House. 1964), p. 326.
7 Gavin MacKenzie, *The Aristocracy of Labour: Skilled Craftsmen in the American Class Structure* (Cambridge: Cambridge University Press, 1973), pp. 86–7.

8 Joseph T. Howell, *Hard Living on Clay Street* (Garden City, NY: Doubleday/ Anchor. 1973).

9 Herbert Gans, *The Urban Villagers* (New York: The Free Press. 1962).

10 William J. Klausner, 'Extended leisure and the family', unpublished paper, University of Redlands, 1970.

11 Lillian Rubin, *Worlds of Pain: Life in the Working-Class Family* (New York: Basic, 1976).

12 Donald R. Field, 'The social organization of recreation places', in N. Cheek, D. Field and R. Burdge, eds, *Leisure and Recreation Places* (Ann Arbor, Mich: Science, 1976), p. 26.

13 Dennis Orthner, 'Patterns of leisure and marital interaction', *Journal of Leisure Research*, vol. 8, 1976, 98–111.

14 Rhona Rapoport and Michael Dower, *Leisure Provision and Human Need* (London: Institute of Family and Environmental Research, 1978).

15 Kelly, 1978, op. cit.

16 J. R. Kelly, 'New town leisure: a British–US comparison', *Leisure Studies*, vol. 1, 1981, pp. 211–24.

17 John P. Robinson, *Changes in Americans' Use of Time: 1965–1975* (Cleveland, Ohio: Cleveland State University Communication Research Center, 1977).

18 J. R. Kelly, 'Three measures of leisure activity', *Journal of Leisure Research*, vol. 5, 1973, pp. 56–65.

19 Dennis Orthner, 'Leisure activity patterns and marital satisfaction over the marital career', *Journal of Marriage and the Family*, vol. 37, 1975, pp. 91–102.

20 Orthner, 1976, op. cit., p. 109.

21 J. R. Kelly, 'Situational and social factors in leisure decisions', *Pacific Sociological Review*, vol. 21, 1978, pp. 313–30.

22 J. R. Kelly, 'Family leisure in three communities', *Journal of Leisure Research*, vol. 10, 1978, pp. 47–60.

23 Rubin, op. cit., p. 311.

24 J. R. Kelly, and S. W. Masar, *Leisure Identities through a Life-Course Transition* (Champaign: Leisure Research Laboratory, 1981).

25 J. R. Kelly, 'Leisure adaptation to family variety', in Z. Strelitz, ed., *Leisure and Family Diversity* (London: Leisure Studies Association, 1979), pp. 2, 11.

26 Orthner, 1976, op. cit.

27 Chad Gordon, C. Gaitz and J. Scott, 'Leisure and lives: personal expressivity across the life span', in *Handbook of Aging and the Social Sciences*, eds. J. Binstock and E. Shanas (New York: Van Nostrand Reinhold, 1976), pp. 405–533.

28 Orthner, 1976, op. cit., p. 104.

29 J. R. Kelly, 'Parents have problems too', *Swimming World*, March 1975, pp. 11–12.

30 Rapoport and Dower, op. cit., p. 11.

31 J. R. Kelly, *Leisure* (Englewood Cliffs, NJ: Prentice-Hall, 1982), ch. 16.

32 ibid.

33 William Burch, 'The play world of camping: research into the social meaning of outdoor recreation', *American Journal of Sociology*, vol. 69, 1965, pp. 604–12.

34 George Masnick and Mary Jo Bane, *The Nation's Families, 1960–1990.* (Cambridge, Mass.: Harvard MIT Joint Center for Urban Studies, 1980).

35 Rhona Rapoport and Robert N. Rapoport, *Leisure and the Family Life Cycle* (London: Routledge & Kegan Paul, 1975).

36 Kelly, 1979, op. cit., pp. 2, 11.

37 Kelly, 1982, op. cit., ch. 15.

38 Kelly, 1982, op. cit., ch. 12.

39 Neil Cheek and William Burch, *The Social Organization of Leisure in Human Society* (New York: Harper & Row, 1976).

6

Face-to-Face Interaction

Not all leisure is social. Some, such as reading, is usually and prefer-ably done alone. One occasional aim for entry into natural areas such as forests is solitude, to get away from association with others includ-ing family and friends. Further, there are moments of daydreaming or contemplation that are not social even when other people are present. Nevertheless, most leisure events are social, involving some elements of interaction with other persons. Whether the event is going some-place or informal activity around the home, more often than not there is an interactional dimension.

The varieties of leisure have already been introduced. Leisure may occur in moments lodged in the time and space of institutional roles as well as in set-apart environments. Leisure may be in a complex event that requires the organization of resources and people to come together in a time of interaction such as a party or the annual picnic of some organization. Leisure may be self-contained in its meanings or provide the social space for the development of intimacy in primary relationships. It may be spontaneous or routinized with predeter-mined or problematic outcomes. In such variety the social roles as well as the activity and the environment make a difference in mean-ings and outcomes.

One dimension on which leisure varies is that of intensity. Both in relation to the activity itself and to the other people, the intensity of involvement may be quite casual or profound. In some events the social elements are intense and the activity only a setting. In others the activity is the focus and the interaction routine and instrumental. The two dimensions of intensity are displayed in Figure 6.1.

The 'doubly casual' (1) kinds of leisure, low in both activity and social intensity, would include much watching of TV at the end of the day when both attention to the program and interaction are intermit-tent. Such leisure is valued for its relaxing and recuperative qualities as well as the low-cost entertainment.

'Socially intense' (2) leisure, in which the activity intensity is low and the interactional high, illustrates that the diagram suggests con-tinuous dimensions rather than categories. For example, some times of deep communication would be more intense than the interaction at

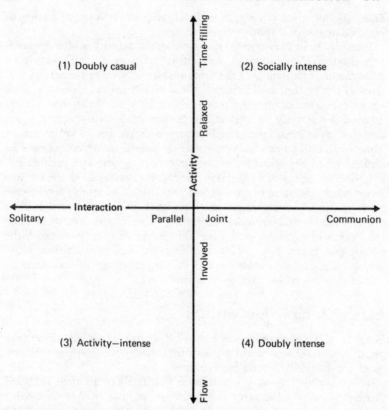

Figure 6.1 Intensity of leisure experience.

a party which might in turn be higher in intensity than much 'fooling around'. In all the intensity level might change during the occurrence, even though the activity and setting would remain constant.

'Activity-intense' (3) leisure is that in which there is a high level of intensity in the activity but not the social interaction. Some kinds of artistic production as in a musical group would have this pattern. In a somewhat different way, even a team sport might fall into this classification at times when the interaction is more or less routinized. Of course, solitary activity such as reading or painting would clearly have its intensity in the activity.

'Doubly intense' (4) leisure is found in activity in which a high level of communication as well as action is required. Such communication may be largely non-verbal as in sexual intercourse or involve many modes of interchange as in developing and rehearsing a dance or planned attack in a sport.

Intensity may vary due to the nature of the activity which demands a high degree of attention and effort or cannot incorporate such investment. The nature of the relationships as well as the setting and aims of the episode will influence the social intensity. During a given episode the level of intensity may rise and fall in relation to the ebb and flow of the activity as well as the conversation. Some activities are designed to alternate peaks of intensity with periods of relaxation or 'time out'. Csikszentmihalyi argues that intense involvement may be highest when the structure of the activity is regular and permits full attention to be given to the skill.[1] However, certainly there are also times when uncertain outcomes and problematic identity presentation raise emotional involvement to a high level. In any case, it should be evident that leisure episodes, including those incorporating face-to-face interaction, are not all alike. The same activity with the same people may reach different levels of intensity at different times. Now we may begin to explore some of the elements of variation in face-to-face social interaction as leisure.

Leisure Interaction settings

What are the environments of leisure? If we agree that leisure *can* take place almost anywhere, do we also find that some environments are most conducive to leisure interaction?

There are, of course, environments that facilitate leisure. They are those that protect the actor from obligation, that enhance freedom. For some, such protection is first of all against role expectations. By eliminating or reducing communication links with others who can exercise a claim of role obligations – work, family, or other, we may choose activity or inactivity that is expected to benefit the self. Such environments may be outdoors and away from telephones or indoors and separated from interruption.

There are also environments that facilitate leisure because of what they offer for activity or interaction as well as their separation from contact with role obligations. For some, leisure is enhanced by quiet or by music, by broad vistas of flowing water, by the pounding surf or the wind in the treetops. For others, it is the special space of the playing-field or court, the racetrack or the club, that provides a place that makes involvement in valued leisure activity possible.

However, in many cases it is the activity itself that is the leisure environment. Leisure does not require a special space as much as a shared definition. This will be found especially true in face-to-face interaction. When two or more persons share a definition of the moment that it is play, non-serious in intent and done for its own sake, then leisure occurs wherever the interaction takes place. Such a definition may be communicated in the workplace as well as the cocktail party, in the kitchen as well as the garden.

Further, whenever the primary intent of the episode is playful interaction, then the activity may become secondary. Such face-to-face leisure is most likely to occur when there is some latitude in expectations and openness in timing. Events that rigidly structure every moment are not likely to permit free and spontaneous interaction. However, even the tennis lesson, the choir rehearsal, or the planning conference may become a context for play.

What are the elements of social contexts that increase the likelihood of leisure interaction? In explicitly leisure settings the shared definitions would seem to be least problematic. It can be assumed that when people have gathered in a manifestly non-work situation that the aims of activity and interaction are intrinsic rather than extrinsic. For example, work colleagues who meet in a pub or rooftop bar after employment hours on Friday are there to relax, have fun and, perhaps, to make arrangements for some event during the weekend. At a cocktail party the aim of the event is to facilitate conversational interaction. In many cases a person who attempts to transact business will be told to save it for another time and place. In contrast to the work context, the expectation for self-contained interchange is prior. Therefore, playful comments, joking, story-telling, fantasizing and other conversational modes intended to develop enjoyable interchange rather than accomplish some informational exchange or decision can be inaugurated most easily.

In contexts in which the activity rather than the interaction is the focus there are dual approaches to leisure in the setting. For example, during a softball game or bowling match, there is the activity and the contest, presumably enjoyed as a demonstration of skill, exercise and excitement with a measured outcome that has no long-term consequences. However, during the course of the game, there will also be considerable interchange – often related to the game – that has no serious meaning. Part of the 'fun' of the event is the bantering and joking that are expected in the social atmosphere of the game. As at a cocktail party, such interchanges are anticipated and require no special sign that 'now we are not being serious'.

On the other hand, in the non-leisure environment, such signs must be given and preferably acknowledged before a playful interchange can be transacted. If, in a business office, one person stops before a colleague's desk with the announcement about the value of the pound, it will be understood as information related to the business. However, if a signal has been given that what is to follow is in fun, then the 'pound' reference may be interpreted metaphorically as an attempt at joking.

One kind of interchange that calls for careful signaling and testing of meanings is in heterosexual exchanges, whether at a party or the office. 'Flirting' that is understood as non-serious is a common form of leisure interchange. It is a playing of 'let's pretend' with the possibility of 'serious' outcome eliminated. Gestures of affection, questions and responses are kept within the self-contained definition of the situation. However, there is always the possibility of a shift in meaning. One person may use the definition of play to explore whether some further sexual relationship might actually be possible. With this potential for changing definitions, the game takes on a heightened excitement and interest just because the outcome is not entirely preordained. Such flirting becomes a game with rules that may change. The communication devices, verbal and other, must then be employed and interpreted with subtely and a recognition of the processual building of their meaning within the episode. 'What if' questions may receive reponses that call for a second level of 'could you mean?' queries that do not overrespond in commitment or interpretation. And the process *is* the leisure interaction!

The setting, then, predisposes social actors toward particular definitions of the situation, but does not fully determine them. While play is more common on the racket court than in the law court, it is possible in either place when signals are exchanged that at least for the moment what follows is not serious.

Occurences: Moments of Leisure

Johan Huizinga was primarily concerned about the relationship of play and culture when he composed his philosophical essay *Homo Ludens*.[2] He recognizes that games as such may be engaged in with the greatest seriousness while playful elements of the comic, jest and laughter can be found in a variety of social contexts. Play, for Huizinga, is characterized by freedom, enjoyment, non-seriousness, disinterestedness, parameters setting it apart in time and space, order, the formation of community and representation. Play is both separated by social definition from the 'real world' and yet represents some element or elements of that world. All play is not 'a play' but contains some dimension of drama – of a self-contained outcome that is something like outcomes in social institutions. It is this combination of outcomes and representation that makes play especially amenable to trying out and developing identities. The roles of play/leisure are much like those of the institutions of productivity, but do not have the same fateful consequences from their outcomes. Further, they are attractive because they are enjoyable.[3] They call for self-investment rather than demand it.

Some such play is a matter of *occurrences* rather than events. Leisure can be momentary and fleeting as well as planned and scheduled. Moments of social play, by Huizinga's definition, can occur almost any time. What is required is choice and a definition that sets the non-serious episode off from the consequential.

From an experiential perspective, such moments may be peaks of self-transcendence. Csikszentmihalyi's 'flow' experience is more than a non-serious episode. Occurring in work or leisure, flow incorporates concentrated attention, enriched perception, total involvement and intensity, loss of time–space perceptions and anxiety, and high enjoyment. The fleeting nature of such experience is paralleled in low-intensity moments as well. A social interchange that is playful may interrupt 'serious' negotiation for only seconds. A flash of imagination may remove attention from a task for moments. In either case the moment of play provides a break from attention to the serious.

Some occurrences of play are mental, taking place in the imagination. The most common is some form of daydreaming. Freed of the physical constraints of ordinary activity, the mind may leap instantly to distant environments and times, bring together persons actually far apart and construct interactions that have never occurred. Yet, paradoxically, with all the freedom of the imagination, there are still constraints. There remains continuity with the identities and environments of actual experience. We tend to act and define ourselves as persons with the actual histories we have known. We interact with recognizable others, who may respond in novel ways but retain their identification. Water remains wet, heights anxiety-producing and hunger unpleasant. In our daydreams we both dramatize some of the constraints of our real world and construct imaginary worlds with many of the same limitations. We may imagine persons never actually encountered and yet find them consistent with our preconceptions. We may fulfil dreams and yet have to experience the fulfillment within the limitations of our self-definitions and self-images. At least, when we become quite different in our daydreams, we are aware of the transformation.

Nevertheless, daydreaming is a central form of leisure occurrence, precisely because of its availability and freedom. Without the actual limitations of resources and abilities, we may act with unaccustomed spontaneity and respond without our usual doubts and hesitations. We may, in that moment, kick the winning goal, rescue the lovely maiden, or tell off the overbearing boss. We may be with the distant lover, transcend the pain of illness, or complete the dreamed-of poem. And, in the moment, some of the meaning and satisfaction is real, present in our minds and received with joy.

There are also interactional occurrences that may be experienced in the midst of events with well-defined goals and procedures. The routinized 'coffee break' has become an institutionalized recognition of the need to intersperse tasks with respite. A bank official who was uncertain just why 'spare time' was worth investigation was asked how much of the day she and her nearby colleague spent in non-business interchange. The quick answer 'about half' was probably nearer the truth than her amendment following the recognition that it sounded as though she were not really *working*.

Donald Ball analyzed the everyday meanings of the telephone in North American culture as a special kind of conversational exchange.[4] The lack of visual reference gives both a freedom and an impoverishment to the conversation. In such a dyadic interchange the lack of visual reinforcement of face-to-face exchange such as nodding and smiles must be replaced by periodic aural responses including non-verbal sounds as well as an occasional 'yes' or 'right'. For some, the telephone has become a ready means of inserting social interaction into periods otherwise spent alone. It is no wonder that housebound, unemployed mothers or those who lack mobility use the telephone as a major instrument for leisure occurrences.

In face-to-face behavior some interchange never passes beyond greeting. An acknowledgement of the other may convey termination as well as greeting. However, a pause offering continuance can lead to a leisure occurrence on the sidewalk, in the office, or in the factory. Such occurrences are most common at the customary intersections of life. For example, before or especially after a regular event such as a church service is a regular intersection for some and provides a context for exchange that goes beyond greeting. Such interchange may be formal and serious, a transmittal of information or arrangement for some task-oriented event. However, the exchange may also be quite spontaneous and playful. A sermon with a serious theme can be the springboard for a parody that is offered and completed in a few seconds. The aim is enjoyment as well as providing a sign of a relationship that calls for more than greeting.

Some such occurrences are routine. The expectation is built up over time that something non-serious will be offered and that a playful response is expected. In other intersections the orientation of the exchange is signaled by the mode of greeting, by a non-verbal sign, or by some discontinuity in the conversation. Further, a playful comment – one related to but distinct from the 'real world' – may receive a disclaiming response that turns the exchange quickly back to 'business'. Much more needs to be known about the construction and function of such moments of play in the midst of routined and task-oriented environments. One possibility is that they are often critical to getting through the day. It may well be that such play is necessary in order to work or to maintain emotional poise amid highly structured role expectations.

Events: Structured Leisure Times

When reference is made to leisure, more structured events are usually denoted rather than face-to-face occurrences at the social intersections of life. Such events are similar in their possibility of developing playful interchange in the midst of the activity. However, the entering definition of the situation tends to be different. Leisure events are constructed for enjoyment rather than extrinsic production.

Poker: Uncertainty and Structure
Take, for example, the card game. A regular game of poker among players who may have some other social connection but are essentially a group formed for the single purpose is deceptively structured. The surface informality obscures a structure that is revealed only in repeated systematic observations. Several analyses of such games have been published and others produced for analysis in classes on the sociology of leisure. The profile that follows combines a number of these reports. Card-playing most often takes place at home or in the home of friends. Crespi found that relatively few cite it as their favorite activity, but that none the less card-players tend to do it with regularity.[5] The participant observation analysis of Louis Zurcher is perhaps the most acute in revealing the levels of rules and conventions.[6] The general rules of poker prevail, but augmented by 'house rules' concerning the amounts of money that can be bet, the range of games permitted, and responsibilities for banking the chips, providing refreshment and inviting guests.

However, second-level rules also provided basic structure to the event. Betting stakes are to be high enough to be consequential, but not so high as to be serious. Players should care whether they win or lose, but not be risking family maintenance support, carfare, or tuition. In some groups women are not permitted in the room during play and in others they are allowed to observe quietly and serve refreshments. In none of those studied do women play poker with the men. Further, conventions regulate keeping the table clear for the game, quitting times and announcements, withdrawing a dime from each pot for beer and the range of conversation permitted. Some of the second-level rules are best revealed in the process of recruiting and selecting new members. Usually a guest is invited and 'tried out'. The house rules are explained. However, the alertness of the potential initiate in picking up on the second-level conventions and in responding to cues when violations occur largely determines whether or not an invitation to participate regularly will be issued. Sanctions following violations of rules and conventions generally follow the order of subtle cues, informational suggestions, joking, ridicule and, ultimately, exclusion. Core players are willing to instruct a new member for a time, but expect a willingness to learn and abide by the consensual structure. Only when that structure is largely taken-for-granted can concentration on the game yield maximum satisfaction.

Zurcher identifies a number of such satisfactions, some clearly related to the presentation and confirmation of masculine identities. The 'scripted competition' allows for self-testing without long-term consequences. Opportunities to exhibit skill are coupled with demonstrations of emotional control and mastery. What Erving Goffman terms the 'action' of the measured contest provides an excitement and experience of participation in a social event in which something is happening.[7] Within the event there are outcomes that are recognized and signaled, both for each hand and for the evening. Further, the subtleties of learning to interpret the playing style of others – their likelihood of taking risks, bluffing and attempting to deceive other players – calls for a depth of personal understanding more profound than simply knowing how to play the game. The evening also includes some retrospective analysis and consideration of missed opportunities. It is a common experience for shared communication.

Poker has problematic outcomes. No two nights are the same and every evening provides a chance to start anew, equal in the beginning of the evening no matter what the cumulative results of the past. On the other hand, the rules, conventions and social rituals provide a clearly communicated and agreed-on structure for the event. The excitement is not that of a children's game in which rules, boundaries and teams are negotiated and renegotiated throughout the event. Rather, the first- and second-level regulations are there to permit a concentration on the game itself. As Huizinga suggests, the play is set apart not only in its results, but also in the parameters of the drama. The setting and the rule-bound activity are a context for involvement that incorporates presentation and testing of identities with interpretable results.

Structure and the Problematic

Erving Goffman has analyzed in a variety of settings and situations the dialectic between structure and freedom. On the one hand, there is the dramaturgical intent of enacting a role in such a way as to elicit a particular definition of identity from the audience observers, from the 'alters' in the situation.[8] This presentation is partly designed for the occasion and partly made up of habitual and confirmed elements that have produced the intended responses in the past. An 'action' framework is one that involves enough of a problematic outcome to test the presentation.[9]

On the other hand, such occasions and events are not limitless as to the roles or even the styles of role enactment permissible. Not only are there manifest rules and regulations, but also a series of covert and taken-for-granted elements in the structure of the social context. Failure to recognize and properly interpret these elements will usually result in a failure in the presentation. There are many kinds of leisure events that illustrate the dialectic between the contingent and the structured.

One is partly based on the setting itself, the bar. North American bars are different from the British pub in several ways, one being the increasingly specialized clienteles. Nevertheless, the bar is generally defined as a place where conversation with strangers is permissible. While some kinds of cocktail lounges are designed for relative privacy, bar entry signifies being open to the contacts of others. In fact, some specialized bars have fostered a social definition as places where particular kinds of people may meet. Bars are now known in urban areas as businessmen's bars, gay bars, student bars and bars where middle-class individuals may meet for sexual encounters. Sherri Cavan has analyzed the physical signals employed by those who would like to engage others in conversation or who would not.[10] Where they sit, posture, demeanor, responses to 'looks' and 'remarks' as well as declarations not directed to a specific person are means of communicating readiness to inaugurate interchange. Topics of conversation include the bar or pub itself, the quality of various drinks and public events related to money and jobs. In male-oriented bars local sports may absorb a large percentage of the conversation. The point is that the bar is a place for 'meeting' – friends and neighbors in the old neighborhood bar and strangers with similar interests in urban establishments. Of course, people also drink.

Bar encounters are not only facilitated by the social definition of the setting, but also provide means of closure, so that they need not lead to greater involvement than either party desires. In an increasingly anonymous metropolitan area, there are always many persons who are not integrated into social networks that provide adequate stability in relationships, companions and communication. One response for younger people has been the emergence of the 'wine bar' where decor and physical arrangements facilitate mingling. Most arrive in same-sex pairs or groups. Seating arrangements and crowding allow for the exchange of 'looking' signals that may be followed up by the offer of wine either at the table or when coming to the bar or sandwich display simultaneously. Those who come alone may gather at the bar where they are merged into a collectivity that minimizes recognition of their aloneness. The aims are social. Such establishments announce the kind of clientele they intend to serve by their location, decor, name, and food and beverage offerings. The locale then becomes a place for the inauguration of social exchange as well as a meeting-place for those already acquainted. One such establishment in California, advertised as the place 'where a lady may buy a gentleman a drink', actually retained the traditional male-first conventions. Further, a measure of safety was maintained by the norm that almost all conversations were begun through a third party known to both the man and woman. The main clientele was from the new set of offices near San Francisco's wharves.

For the most part, bar interaction – however simple or sophisticated the social environment – demonstrates the structure vs openness dialectic. There are conventions that reflect both the social status of the actors and the designed intentions of the establishment. However, there is also the possibility of conversation with unanticipated outcomes and of relationships with unpredictable developments.

Hans Zetterberg began the analysis of one crucial element in such environments in his paper on the 'secret ranking'.[11] The ancient 'rating-dating complex' of William Waller served as the springboard for the analysis of erotic ranking in a corporation. Such a ranking, always secret, is the likelihood that one can gain sexual compliance on some level from a person of the other sex. It is a social stratification based on a special form of power, related to but distinct from other forms of power. Zetterberg suggests that sexual intercourse is only one form of sexual compliance or surrender in a heterosexual environment such as an office. Social regulations and conventions may be general to the social strata and culture. However, the particularities of the environment shape the forms of cooperation, conversation, body language, touching and secondary compliance. The obvious elements in the secret hierarchy such as physical attractiveness, age, status in the organization and marriage condition – being single, somewhat married, or very married – are only the beginning. As sexual identities are negotiated, there comes to be a generally acknowledged sexual hierarchy not only for each sex in general, but for segments of the collectivity defined as appropriate for various levels of exchange. The modes of presentation, self-offering, recognition, rejection, affirmation and encouragement vary according to the elements of the hierarchy. The same signal, as touching a shoulder with the hand, may have quite different meanings depending on the hierarchical position of the pair. Again, there is both structure – manifest and covert – and an existential element of the problematic. Social interaction, of which sexual exchange is only one element, is negotiated as well as determined with a myriad of interrelated items that must be grasped and interpreted to continue interaction.

Everyone doesn't 'do it right'. When a person who does not comprehend the nature of the hierarchy makes an inappropriate gesture or overture, there is the possibility of a rupture in the social scheme of the office. Therefore, it is necessary to signal a negative response in a way that does not embarrass the person who failed to understand the hierarchy. This is often done by deliberately not understanding the communication, by joking, or by a non-verbal sign declining without giving full recognition to the overture. Illustrating the reality of the structure by repairing a possible break in its tacit set of social definitions, a whole realm of meaning can be communicated by the kind of smile with which one turns to the typewriter or telephone.

Camping as Theater
One of the problems with considerable recreation research has been the assumption that a set of behaviors can be subsumed under an activity label such as swimming, playing cards, or camping. Agencies who manage resources for recreation often differentiate the type of resources to classify swimming as 'lake' or 'pool' and camping as 'developed' and 'dispersed'. However, there remains the failure to deal with the diverse modes of activity and interaction in the activity setting.

'Swimming at a pool', for example, encompasses sunbathing, flirting, ball games in the water, reading, playing cards on the deck, conversations while watching small children, a variety of parties, strenuous practice for competition, health-related swimming laps, and a multitude of ways of playing in and around the water. The pool is a gathering-place more than an activity-specific resource for most of the activity.

Styles of camping also vary widely. A few carry minimal gear into primitive areas, in small groups or sometimes alone and practice self-sufficiency hoping to encounter very few others. Many more come to the campground with considerable equipment, often a mobile dwelling, and expect to meet others in a setting that offers far less privacy than the residence they have left. In the western United States there is a style of 'sports-car camping' engaged in by younger couples who have space for very little equipment, buy food, make short stops on their itinerary and carry one set of dressy clothes for an occasional night out on the town with friends when they visit a city.

William Burch introduced the approach of theater to the analysis of camping.[12] In his study that involved observation as well as interviews, he identified some of the roles that campers play in that environment. One factor is the persistence of roles with such sex role differentiation as women being expected to manage food preparation and men to set up the camp and provide firewood. The role of *provider*, traditionally male, includes the industrious chopping of wood and leaving females behind when males forage for food by fishing or hunting. The role of *caretaker*, traditionally female, is found in the unspoken assumption that women will have food prepared and watch younger children. In some cases the roles are enacted with an elaborate display of sex-specific presentation as the 'mighty hunter' returns with his three small fish to lay before the admiring nurturers. In this setting there is the possibility that the blurred characterizations of the urban community can be demonstrated with clarity. The worker whose family has never seen him on the job can enact the masculine roles in a clear and direct way. He can then receive an affirmation from his primary community that is much more vivid and reinforcing than any response to bringing home a paycheck or handing over cash at the supermarket checkout. Further, there is the satisfaction of enacting this simple role identity with concrete and identifiable results. The load of wood or pan of fish are right there to be seen and counted.

The relative exposure of life in camping, while obtained at the cost of the stress-reduction of privacy, is a context for such role enactment yielding immediate feedback. So much life is enmeshed in all kinds of protective screening that there is no evident product or firsthand audience. In camping with others there is more opportunity to act out a full sequence of a role in the view of significant others. The world of camping, then, is more than a response to the natural environment. It is also a constructed social world with particular features that facilitate identity development. It is 'theater in the round' with a simplicity of staging and an openness to observation.

Leisure as Constructed Events
Without underrating aimless 'being together' as leisure, there are also many kinds of leisure that are constructed events. They have forms that are developed and agreed on by the actors in order to enable them to perform an event. The interaction is given a structure and frequently an outcome. Such a constructed event may reflect some cultural values and thus be celebrational.[13] The event itself is a context for holding up and reaffirming some elements of the cultural value system, often through celebration of an historical event or personage. Constructs such as parades, concerts, games, dances and services of worship have such a basis in the culture.

On the other hand, other constructed leisure seems to be more self-contained with the primary aim to provide for the interaction. In modern game theory logical and even mathematical analysis is brought to bear on the outcome of conflict.[14] The game is constructed to provide a relatively even beginning with resources evenly divided. Further, the rules of playing the game are designed to ensure that the outcome will be reached according to differentiating variables within the contest. Excitement may be engendered when the internal variables include chance as well as skill. The best player or team does not always win. In any case, the game construct is a social context for attempting to manipulate outcomes. By exercising skill, playing the odds, or in some way inducing opponents to err, we try to achieve our desired outcome. The game, with a bounded beginning and end, incorporates various means of assessing success or failure.

This means that although the game is self-contained in its outcome, it may be an arena for attempting to try and accomplish all sorts of things important to us. In the game we may develop strategies for establishing our identities, opening or closing relationships, attempting to demonstrate power or dependence, and a number of other social intentions that lead beyond the game itself. It is also important to note that these games are face-to-face encounters. The opponents and colleagues are not faceless and unidentified beings, but become others with whom various levels of communication take place within the game context. Whether or not we ever see those others apart from the game, we are engaged in this bounded exchange with two levels of outcomes. There is not only the outcome of the contest itself, but also what happens to us – to our personal identities and self-images in the process. In recollection what we recall from the game is often not the final score, but how in an episode we demonstrated recognized competence or failed with resulting embarrassment. It is precisely the order of the constructed event, the game, that permits such evaluation, episodic as well as overall.

Erving Goffman has suggested several elements of such constructed leisure in his book *Interaction Ritual*,[15] The approach revolves around the concept of 'action' which he defines as activities that are 'consequential, problematic, and undertaken for what is felt to be their own sake'. In other words, they are leisure games. Action consists of a sequential process of engagement of 'squaring off', determination, disclosure and settlement within a timeframe brief enough to hold attention. While Goffman refers to types of gambling, by his definition *action* can be a social encounter, sport, game, or interstitial exchange. The governance of rules is balanced by the problematic outcome. The concern with maintaining one's identity or *face* is supported by the reciprocity in which actors generally seek to avoid embarrassing other players.

The setting of the occasion may be adequate to define the nature of the interaction. However, on some occasions it is necessary to signal that an episode of action is about to begin through some metacom-munication, verbal or non-verbal. There must be some agreement on the rules and intent in order for the action to commence. In playful action there is a kind of consensus that within the frame of the occasion the outcome has meaning even though it is non-serious in relation to other roles. Goffman locates such action in commercial recreation provisions of sport, games, entertainment and the inter-action enabling that setting he calls 'fancy milling'. Action may be primarily activity or interactional with the form and result measured by a numerical score or by some interactional compliance or response.

One problem with this approach to leisure as constructed action is that it omits what is perhaps most playful, the episode in which the outcome is unmeasured or totally inconsequential. What about the exchange in which literally *nothing happens* except for the communica-tional construct, in which the enjoyment of the encounter is really self-contained? Granting that there are some sort of identity agendas operative in most social occasions and that action is taken seriously as a symbol of efficacy, competence, or favor, are there not some oc-casions in which the action really is entirely for its own sake? Can the episode become so engrossing that its meaning is fully autotelic, intrinsic to the moment? In other words, is there ever complete spontaneity in a leisure occasion? Goffman generally comes out on the side of agendas and manipulation, of playing *to* an audience and of real concern with the outcomes. We need to know more about the extent to which we may, at least at times, become so engrossed in the enactment that we forget any kind of measurement.

There remains in constructed occasions the dialectic between struc-ture and the problematic. However, in such games, the action takes place in a context that is constructed to provide for the process of engagement, determination and settlement within a relatively brief span of time. Whatever the persistent meanings of identity develop-ment and maintenance, there is meaning in the outcome made possible by the nature of the game.

The Occurrence of Leisure

The other side of the issue refers to interstitial leisure, play in the midst of work or any other roles. This is leisure in which the meaning is built up in the episode rather than, as with the game, prestructured. Some such interaction is essentially conversational, an exchange of opinions, information, stories and arguments with appropriate responses. Some such exchange is routinized, expected when two or more associates meet in a regular time and place. Some is tied to family or work roles and includes information functional to those roles such as the scheduling of the family car or the names of workers out sick.

However, there is also the possibility of a unique construction of the episode. Often built with materials from previous exchanges and shared experiences, the interaction may take the forms of kidding, joking, embellishment of the commonplace, humor in deliberately inappropriate responses and other verbal play. The study of British shipbuilders suggests that play in the yard is more than just verbal. It is one essential aspect of 'being one of the lads', of maintaining reciprocal identities in the social world of work.[16] It requires not only a responsiveness to the overtures of others, but knowledge of the vocabularies and lore of the workgroup, a sensitivity to the identity presentations of others and familiarity with the history of banter. The lack of such knowledge is a central factor in the common teasing of anyone new in the situation who has not yet gained the resources for full participation. The seeming spontaneity of workplace banter may deceive the casual observer who does not recognize the rituals operative, the symbols that call up shared experiences and the codewords that signal all regulars that a particular game is about to be run on a newcomer. In the Old West, for example, a traditional game was to offer a new hand an unprepossessing horse who under certain circumstances was likely to launch into especially unsettling bucking.

Such leisure is social and interstitial. It not only occurs in the midst of work or family roles, but often incorporates their forms and history. An incident in which a person has been embarrassed or in some non-harmful way has violated a role expectation may be recalled and a repetition arranged. In an ongoing social group all sorts of previous interaction becomes a fund of material for the construction of play. While such interstitial play is most often verbal, it may take the form of an arranged environmental discontinuity such as hiding a tool or removing a 'wet paint' sign from a wall.

Building on the meta-communication concept of Gregory Bateson, Rob Lynch developed an approach to explaining how ordinary conversation turns to such play.[17] Metacommunication is indirect signaling about the nature of the communication. For example, there are many ways in which one actor or party in a conversation may indicate that 'what I am about to say is to be treated as fantasy'. Lynch gives the illustration of the exchange of social scientists that develops an entire methodology and rationale for the study of the phenomenon of 'garage sales'. On another occasion two sociologists 'proved' to a cooperative dupe that the state of Wycoming did not exist. The key is the sign 'this is play' and some reciprocal signal that 'I am playing, too'. In the episode there is also need for eventual agreement that the play is over or taking a different orientation.

Most such interaction is neither wholly spontaneous nor structured by strict role norms. Rather, interchange tends to be *extempore* in the speech sense of having some context and orientation, but with considerable allowance for innovation within the context. In fact, much of the play meaning in social interchange comes from the unexpected, the insertion of the incongruous into the flow of conversation. Humor is more a reciprocal disjointedness of communication than a freestanding story or joke. Deliberate or not, it is the unexpected that generally sparks the beginning of play in the midst of the serious. In time play roles may come to be assigned in a social world of an office or school. Particular persons are expected to be the instigators or catalysts for breaks from the tasks.

At present we have not developed any comprehensive methods for investigating such interstitial leisure. One approach is to ask people to review the last hour or two in which they were in contact with others. A question such as 'did anything happen that wasn't serious?' can elicit accounts of leisure in the midst of non-leisure roles. Other methods include participant observation with some device for recording incidents, diaries with the agreed-on focus of the non-serious, or some means of sampling segments of time through the day. However, any method that breaks into the sequences of interaction is likely to interrupt the construction process. The shifts of conversation from a request for information, to an incongruous response, to an acknowledgement of the incongruity, to a transitional remark and, finally, a closing answer to the original question is a fragile construction. It may be terminated simply by an outsider walking within hearing as well as by a countersignal of serious intent by either party. Further, such episodes begin and end so quickly that they are hardly noted or remembered.

Play in Work
Such play occurs in work situations. In the classroom a student asks for information about an upcoming examination. The instructor responds that the material to be covered encompasses 'the history of Western civilization since Pythagoras with special attention given to material in English, Latin, French and Aramaic'. The students smile, if wanly. From there, the sequence can continue the banter as another student inquires whether Scandinavian primary sources should be reviewed as well or return to the 'serious' as the instructor specifies the chapters on social stratification and race relations as material to be reviewed.

Some playful constructions may be quite elaborate. A single remark can become the foundation of a complex construction of fantasy with the subtle weaving in of a wide variety of themes, shared experiences and references. 'It's a hot day' may lead to a response of 'but not as hot as. . .' and in moments two or more actors collaborate in spinning a tale woven of history and fantasy that crosses all sorts of time and space boundaries.

That such constructions are common at the cocktail party or even in the pub would be expected. That we cannot be expected to be *serious* all the time is also taken-for-granted. A study of a secondary school in England went beyond the usual concentration on roles, authority and structures to examine the informal interactions and communication.[18] A surprising proportion of ongoing interchange was more spontaneous than structured, more playful than businesslike. In fact, there were indications that much of the social fabric of the institution consisted of play rather than 'work' with a variety of metacommunication signals that the conversational mode offered is that of play, intrinsic in intent.

What is the significance of such interstitial leisure? We might believe that its frequency alone is evidence of its functional significance. Can regular social interaction continue unrelieved by play? Can tasks be completed with total attention to the product and without at least moments of leisure? It has been common to say that some leisure provides compensation for the prices exacted by other roles,[19] but the reference has usually been to events and investments that clearly contrast with work conditions and constraints. Even more significant may be leisure in the midst of work; the relief of humor, the break of daydreaming, the redirection of playful conversation and the enjoyment of autotelic activity. Is leisure, indeed, what 'gets us through the day'?

Play in Non-work

Perhaps leisure in non-work settings should be taken for granted. However, it is not necessary. All sorts of serious and product-oriented activity can take place in non-work times and spaces. Leisure as intrinsicly motivated and self-contained activity can be shoved aside by all sorts of tasks and obligations at any time. Winning may be all-consuming in a game or sport. Impressing a significant other may be the sole meaning of a party exchange. Gaining some physical condition improvement may obliterate all other meanings of some form of exercise. Leisure is found in the *how* and *why* of activity, rather than the separation from work or maintenance.

Nevertheless, play may be expected in some settings. We may be expected to be entertaining rather than informative at the department party. Kidding and banter may be the customary conversational mode during a ball game. Affection and support may be the persistent meaning of an evening conversation.

Even in the leisure environment the episode requires the sequence of announcement, recognition, development and termination. Further, ambiguities in communication can open possibilities for different responses that then determine the orientation of the interactional episode. For example, an opening gambit at an urban bar can be designed to permit a variety of responses:

(1) Opening of male buying a drink directed to female who appears to be drinking alone:

'Can you relax with just one drink on Friday?'

(2) Range of possible responses:

Positive: 'I'm about ready for a second.'
Ambiguous: 'It's been a long day' or 'on some Fridays'.
Negative: 'I'll have another with the friend I'm meeting' or 'Sometimes' while turning away.

Generally, the aim is to offer the possibility for further exploratory conversation while allowing for a negative response that is non-personal and informative. The ambiguous responses permit a number of lines of communication that neither commit either party to continuation nor close the possibility. The point is that whatever happens is a communicative construction in which both verbal and non-verbal symbols are employed to carry on or terminate the exchange. The general norms of heterosexual approach are complemented by those specific to that kind of social context. Further, the processual episode – however brief or long and complex – occurs within the structure of interactional expectations yet retains a problematic course. In fact, some of the enjoyment may come from working through a series of ambiguous responses and offerings to an agreed-on resolution. Further challenge can be added to the interchange by mixing signals – verbal and non-verbal – so that an appropriate response to such ambivalence requires further ambiguity. Indeed, the episode becomes a kind of game with both rules and an uncertain outcome.

Perhaps there has been too much stress here on verbal exchanges as leisure. The central place of communication in social leisure and the adaptation of vocabulary and syntax to play is an area with many possibilities for further research. However, play is also activity – engaging in physical as well as mental and singular as well as social action through some process of choice. It is relative freedom and anticipated enjoyment of the process of reaching an undetermined conclusion. And in that process is the self – seeking and selecting activities, environments and interactions that are opportunities for such action.

Leisure Redefined

If there has been any likelihood of conceptualizing leisure as a *thing* an entity that has certain specified properties, it should now be laid aside.[20] Leisure is processual with freedom as well as structure. Leisure occurs, happens and develops. Leisure is process rather than form.

Further, leisure is experience rather than a defined time and place. There is no 'leisure time' designated by clock or calendar; there is only time in which leisure occurs – potentially almost any time. What makes an experience leisure is its quality. However, it is not a matter of listing qualities that experiences must possess in some absolute manner. Rather, leisure experiences are characterized to a relatively high degree by all or most of the following dimensions:

- Leisure experience is relatively free, accompanied by a minimum of constraint. However, the chosen environment, social frame, or form of the activity may be highly structured. In such a case the freedom is in the choice.
- The satisfactions of leisure are primarily instrinsic. Leisure is, to some degree, enjoyable as an experience.
- Leisure is playful in the sense of being relatively self-contained, having meaning within the occurrence. Its outcomes are, as such, non-serious even when they have significant consequences for personal development.

In a sense it is easier to say what leisure experiences are not than what they are. Leisure may be spontaneous or formal, but it is *not* activity as such. Leisure may be interstitial or an event, but it is *not* designated time. Leisure may be solitary or social, but it is *not* segregated from other social roles and identities. Leisure may be developmental or just for fun, but it is *not* unrelated to the self, presentations, or definitions. Leisure may be experienced in special environments or in the midst of routine and required activity, but it is *not* limited to designated places or resources. In short, the defining dimensions of leisure are not so much in *what*, *where*, as in *how* and *with whom*.

In order to analyze the critical dimensions of leisure, the role identity model provides one approach to distinguishing the primary meaning of the engagement to the self and the significance of the presence or absence of other actors. Who we are in choosing a particular leisure occurrence and the nature of our relationship to fellow-actors are crucial to following the processual nature of a leisure occurrence. The activity form and environment influence meaning and time and at least provide parameters for the action. But a social-psychology of leisure with adequate weight given to both social role and identity elements is required to investigate the meanings of leisure as experience. Further, the analysis of face-to-face leisure interaction reveals that such a social-psychology of leisure must be equipped to follow the developing process of the experience rather than freeze it into a monothematic event. A leisure experience occurs, but it also develops; and the meaning may be in the process.

References: Chapter 6

1   M. Csikszentmihalyi, *Beyond Boredom and Anxiety* (San Francisco: Jossey-Bass, 1975).
2   Johan Huizinga, *Homo Ludens* (Boston, Mass.: Beacon Press, 1955).
3   M. Csikszentmihalyi, 'Leisure and socialization', *Social Forces*, vol. 60, 1981.
4   Donald W. Ball, 'Toward a sociology of telephones and telephoners', in M. Truzzi, ed., *Sociology and Everyday Life* (Englewood Cliffs, NJ: Prentice-Hall, 1968) pp. 59–75.
5   Leo P. Crespi, 'The social significance of card playing as a leisure time activity', in ibid., pp. 101–10.
6   L. Zurcher, 'The friendly poker game: a study of an ephemeral role,' *Social Forces*, vol. 49, pp. 173–86.
7   Erving Goffman, *Interaction Ritual* (New York: Anchor, 1967), p. 262.
8   G. McCall, and J. Simmons, *Identities and Interactions*, 2nd edn (New York: The Free Press, 1978).
9   Goffman, op. cit.
10 Sherri Cavan, *Liquor License* (Chicago:Aldine, 1967).
11 Hans Zetterberg, 'The secret ranking', *Journal of Marriage and the Family*, vol. 28, 1966, pp. 134–42.
12 William Burch, 'The play world, of camping: research into the social meaning of outdoor recreation, *American Journal of Sociology*, vol. 69, 1965, pp. 604–12.
13 Harvey Cox, *The Feast of Fools* (New York: Harper & Row, 1970).
14 Thomas Kando, *Leisure and Popular Culture in Transition*, 2nd edn (St Louis, Mi: Mosby, 1980), p. 33.
15 Goffman, op. cit.
16 R. Brown, P. Brannen, J. Cousins, and M. Samphier, 'Leisure in work: the occupational culture of shipbuilding workers, in M. Smith, S. Parker and C. Smith, eds, *Leisure and Society in Britain*, (London: Allen Lane, 1973), pp. 97–110.
17 Robert Lynch, 'Social play: an interactional analysis of play in face-to-face social interaction', unpublished Ph.D. thesis, University of Illinois, Champaign, Illinois, USA, 1979.
18 Peter Woods, *The Divided School* (London: Routledge & Kegan Paul, 1979).
19 J. R. Kelly, 'Leisure as compensation for work constraint', *Leisure and Society*, vol. 8, 1976, pp. 73–82.
20 John Neulinger, vol. 8, *To Leisure; An Introduction* (Boston, Mass.: Allyn & Bacon, 1981).

7

Leisure Planning and Provision

Freedom is more than a feeling or attitude. Although we may define a decision as embodying real freedom even though there are acknowledged constraints, freedom to decide requires opportunity. One significant factor in leisure choice is opportunity. While some leisure is relatively resource-free, other kinds of activity and interaction require resources of environment, equipment and social context. In modern urban societies some resources are provided by the market, some by the household or the self, and some by public agencies.

In general, public recreation providers operate in a condition of relative scarcity. There are seldom enough indoor or outdoor space, competent personnel and budget to provide all the opportunities that might be suggested or desired. Some set of criteria is necessary in order that decisions may be made to use resources more efficiently and equitably. The approach introduced thus far can offer one mode of basing such planning decisions on the development and expression of the individuals involved. The developmental and life course perspectives offer a framework for identifying some of the most significant resource needs.

Usual Bases for Planning

Considerable attention has been given to public planning for leisure in recent years. Such planning has taken place on national, regional and local levels – usually not in concert. However, the bases of such planning have not always been consistent with the aims.

Tradition
In any agency responsive to publics of users and financial supporters, there is always the weight of tradition. However some provision may have been inaugurated, there will generally be a negative reaction if it is withdrawn, Further, in conditions of scarcity almost anything receives some use and support. As a consequence, without some clear and persuasive overall set of priorities, it becomes quite difficult to

drop any program or close any facility. When financial resources are not increasing measurably, this tradition factor allows for little in the way of new offerings and initiatives. Most of the budget is already locked in.

'Demand' Statistics

Demand is usually measured by use. Therefore, any provision that is used is assumed to be in demand. There are three problems with this assumption for planning. The first is that in a condition of resource scarcity an opportunity may be used because nothing more satisfying is available. For example, in eastern US cities, children may play stickball in the street because no grassy area is available for softball. The second problem is that of *identification*, the shaping of use by opportunity. We cannot assume that use implies preference. Rather, campers may use a crowded campground because it is what they can get to even though greater privacy would be preferred. Nevertheless, when we base future provisions on present use, we lock the process into 'more of the same' without regard for other alternatives. And thirdly, there are some segments of the population whose resources, personal and social, are so limited that they require special consideration if they are to engage in recreation at all. In an opportunity spectrum that ignores their needs, they do not participate and fail to indicate 'demand' by present use.

Long-term Resource Limitations

Some kinds of leisure resources are subject to damage and degradation due to high levels of use. The water in a lake may become polluted if too much camping takes place in areas that drain into it. Fragile groundcover may not be able to support intense use for hiking or games. In contexts where there is little likelihood of renewal or substitution, some consideration must be given to resource fragility if future users are to share in the resources.

Access to Resources Varies

Just providing a sports complex somewhere in a community or a park in a county does not mean that all potential users have equal access. Distance and the various costs to travel are not uniform. Those close to the resource need invest less time and money in getting there. Those with private transportation, a car, are both more mobile and more flexible in their use potential for more distant resources. There is quite a difference between jumping in your own car for a ten-minute drive and waiting fifteen minutes for a bus trip that will require two transfers. And small children are just not able to cross many barriers that adults take in stride.

The Fullness of Leisure

Further, leisure is not just events and activities. In order to plan most efficiently and equitably for a community, those doing the planning need to comprehend just how the provisions they may offer fit into the whole range of leisure. They need to understand how their kinds of resources and activities provide satisfactions significant to the development and expression of the various groups of potential users. Further, they need to know which resources out of the panoply of private, commercial and public provisions are truly scarce. Planning calls for bringing together the needs of the population current and possible resources so that some priorities can be assessed and turned into action. For most people, public provisions are a supplement to the more common home and commercial opportunities.

The Leisure Resource Spectrum

The varieties of activity and interaction outlined in previous chapters suggest that resources are more than playgrounds and craft houses. There are resources of time and space, skill and equipment, privacy and companionship. And these resources vary according to personal history, family condition, social status, geographical location, and place in the life course:

Personal resources: There are the personal resources of developed skills and interests, competence and experience.

Social resources: There are the social resources of companionship and access, institutional affiliation and social identities.

Economic resources: There are the economic resources of discretionary income, in a market-oriented society so crucial to gaining access to facilities, learning opportunities, distant resources, equipment, popular culture in the home and community, and even the clothing needed to present oneself acceptably in many leisure contexts.

All of these resources may be relatively and differentially scarce. In a stratified society such resources are possessed in abundance by a few, in considerable supply by many more and largely denied to some. Further, the role constraints accompanying some conditions or periods in the life course place individuals in conditions of temporary deprivation. That is, they are *vulnerable* – in a condition of scarcity in regard to one or more resources necessary for some kinds of satisfying leisure. The vulnerabilities may be due to conditions that will change in time such as age, temporary infirmity, or being the mother of an infant. Other vulnerabilities are persistent such as being the victim of racial discrimination, having a permanent physical disability, or being assigned a limiting social position. Some vary through the life course. To alter others will require major change in social circumstances. Further, some limitations are cumulative, so that a child reared in the poverty of an urban slum may reach adult years having lacked even the perception that some kinds of leisure might be possible and personally enriching.

Historically, the dual basis of public provisions in recreation are resource scarcity and equity. Some kinds of resources, such as forestland or urban outdoor space, are simply too scarce and expensive for households to provide for themselves. Other resources must be protected for current and future use due to their singular attractiveness and relative accessibility. Further, the personal, social and economic resources of some people are so limited that public provisions are made to compensate partially for their lack of opportunity. Equity has been a consideration since the rise of the industrial city and its lack of leisure resources for workers and their families.

Further, there is considerable variation in the resource requirements of leisure opportunities. Some leisure, such as informal interaction, is relatively *resource-free*. Other leisure, such as TV-watching and popular culture, is available through *commercial* provisions. A third set of leisure opportunities require *public* provisions for all except the very wealthy. Lakeside campgrounds and access to the lakes and shores themselves, sportsgrounds in urban areas, swimming-pools and opportunities to initiate the learning of arts skills are outside the realm of resources that most persons or households can provide for themselves.

Therefore, those planning from either a commercial or public perspective need to take into account not only the number of possible participants with access to provisions, but how that participation falls into a full spectrum of leisure opportunities. The argument to be developed here is that such an analysis requires incorporating the meanings of leisure and their changes through the life course.

A Model for Need-based Planning

Basing recreation on the needs of persons rather than on opportunity-based participation rates or on the lobbying of interest groups would be a move in the direction of programming for human fulfillment. It would not completely replace reference to participation since past behavior is still the best predictor of future behavior. However, beginning with people does provide a perspective on planning that could correct some current inequities as well as

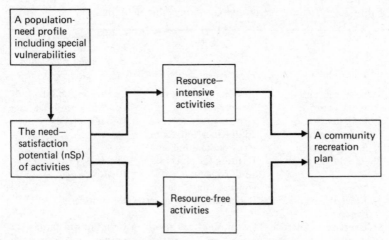

Figure 7.1   A community recreation planning sequence.

enhance human satisfaction with greatest efficiency. The order of planning would be as indicated in Figure 7.1.

Planning would begin with a simple analysis of census data for the community. Particular needs of population groups taking account of life careers and temporary and lifelong limitations do not vary greatly from community to community. Therefore, no new indepth study will be required once the basic need-satisfaction analysis is developed. Rather, the critical needs will be correlated with the population characteristics to produce a need profile for the community. In the community profile recreation needs will be listed by the size of the population groups having those needs.

Secondly, the kinds of activities that tend to meet those needs will be listed under each segment of the population–need profile. Activities with the need-satisfaction potential (NSP) to meet such needs and which are either resource-free or for which there is abundant opportunity may substitute for some that are resource-intensive.

Finally, the program and budget planning for the institution or agency can concentrate on providing opportunities for which public resources are required and that are important in the leisure need-satisfaction of groups identified in the population profile. Further, vulnerable groups will have been noted and their needs given specific attention. The community recreation plan will then concentrate its resources on activities with the need-satisfaction potential to meet the critical needs of those who lack substitute opportunities and resources.

Table 7.1 *Leisure Needs and Corresponding Activities*

	Activities	
Leisure need	*Predominant satisfaction for*	*A major satisfaction element for*
(1) Rest, relaxation, work contrast	Reading for pleasure, TV-watching	Swimming, hobbies, concerts, family outings
(2) Skill development and mastery	Arts, crafts, hobbies, adult education, tennis	Other sports
(3) Self-expression	Arts, crafts, hobbies	
(4) Personal growth	Reading for pleasure, adult education, concerts, museums, etc.	Hobbies, meeting friends
(5) Excitement and a contest	Racket and other sports	Reading, arts, crafts
(6) Exercise and health	Swimming, pair sports	Other sports, family outings
(7) Companionship and belonging	Family outings, meeting friends	Going to concerts, museums, tennis, other sports

Activity NSP

Relatively little research has been completed that sheds light on the NSP of various kinds of leisure activities. The new town study has analyzed the reasons for choosing the activities most important to adults. From that analysis a number of general relationships of activity to perceived or anticipated satisfactions can be derived.[1]

There is no single satisfaction for each category of activities. However, some are perceived to yield greater proportions of particular satisfactions. For example, cultural activities such as reading, watching TV and going to movies are most likely to satisfy needs for relaxation and escape from constraints. On the other hand, sports like tennis and cultural activities such as developing art and craft skills satisfy needs for self-expression and the development of mastery and competence. Travel combines satisfactions, but is oriented towards recuperation. Family activity also is mixed, but tends to complement role relationships in positive relational satisfactions and in meeting the expectations of others. Conversely, further analysis of the reasons given for choosing particular activities provides a preliminary list of activities with the NSP for certain needs.

Even though the sample in the new town study was too small to provide an adequate number of choices for analysis of most of the ninety kinds of activities suggested to respondents that might be

Table 7.2 *Types of Satisfactions by Type of Community Recreation Program*

Program Format	Achievement	Autonomy	Physical fitness	Social enjoyment
Leader-led		—	+ +	—
Leagues/tournaments		— —		
Instruction		—		
Open facilities			+	
Special events	+	+	+ +	+
Program Type				
Physical fitness	+		+ +	
Organized sports		—	+	
Mental/linguistic			—	—
Arts		—		
Social	+ +		+	+ +

+ = measured outcome; + + = strong indication; — = outcome lacking;
— — = strong negative measure.

leisure for them. Table 7.1 suggests how a more complete NSP study might be developed. The crucial step is to find the needs that are especially salient for various groups in the population to be served. Both intrinsic and social reasons for selecting activities are important to adults and may be combined for the same activity. Ideally, activities with multiple NSPs might meet different needs for a variety of participants with a single set of resources.

Public Community Programs
More recently Robert Rossman completed an analysis of the satisfactions of 725 persons participating in sixty-seven different public recreation programs in an Illinois community.[2] Factor analysis of a wide range of items produced four predominant types of satisfaction related to such programs: (1) achievement and skill mastery, (2) autonomy/control, (3) physical fitness and (4) social enjoyment. Of lesser importance were items related to escape from family, risk and attractive environments. These satisfaction elements were then correlated to the types of programs to discover which kinds of community recreation programs were most likely to produce the varied outcomes. The results, which did not vary significantly by age or sex, were as in Table 7.2.

While the results are not surprising, they do suggest two important conclusions: first, the type of program and how it is organized makes a difference in the perceived satisfactions. Programs designed for physical, social, or instructional purposes tend to have outcomes related to the design. However, there is also overlap with social and physical benefits perceived from a variety of programs. Secondly, community public recreation programs are only one type of leisure and cannot be expected to provide a full range of meaning and satisfactions. Their organization and locales and grouping by age, sex and formats include only one band of the entire spectrum of leisure. As such, they provide opportunities to gain certain important kinds of satisfaction, especially those of learning, achievement, physical development and social interaction. Other kinds of satisfaction are more likely to be experienced in less organized and directed activities and in social environments with intimates.

Life Careers and Leisure Needs

The aim of the book by Rhona and Robert Rapoport[3] is to begin to delineate patterns of leisure in relation to employment, education and family careers. They propose that at any stage in the life cycle, persons have 'preoccupations' derived from the basic biological, social and developmental tasks. These preoccupations, in turn, lead to 'interests' in the kinds of activities and relationships that will predominate in that period. Through the life course these interests change as preoccupations and social roles change. Finally, the opportunity structures present activities that provide arenas to carry out these interests. The 'preoccupations–interests–activities' scheme is only one possible way in which to examine the secondary and flexible character of the specific activities that are intended to provide satisfactions related to the changing needs of a person moving through the life career. However, its employment is commended by the inaugural work done in England.

The main point is that leisure interests are not some separate segment of life that may be altered at will. What a person 'wants' in leisure complements identity and social role development through the life course. Leisure is not determined by work, education, family and community roles; but neither is leisure separate from them. Activities would ideally be chosen to satisfy needs integral to biological, personal and social development just as employment, marriage and community relationships may be chosen to enhance leisure roles that are valued. Chapter 3 introduced the three major periods of the life course and the significance of leisure in each. The developmental tasks and dilemmas of each period lead to investments on leisure with identity-building outcomes.

Greater detail in combining developmental theory with studies of persons in each life career period will permit this quite general approach

Table 7.3 *Preliminary Outline of Need-based Planning for Adolescents and Young Mothers*

Need profile	Activities with Related NSP Resource requirements: P = public, C = commercial, F = Resource-free	Probable Community Planning Priorities
	Adolescents	
Social identity: Competence Exploration role-testing	sports (P), arts (PC), crafts (PC) contexts for meeting friends (PCF), team sports (P), service projects (PF), travel (PC)	Space: informal meeting-rooms, halls for events, sports space Program: learning arts, crafts, sports skills, open opportunities for informal participation
Heterosexual role development	limited-commitment events (PC), games (P), gatherings (PCF)	
Self-development and enhancement: Independence Expression Excitement Withdrawal and relaxation	fantasy (F), outdoor activity (P), camping (PC), travel (PC) arts (P), music (PC), creating, (PCF) sports (P), concerts (PC) reading (PCF), TV (F), fantasy (F)	Space: for arts/crafts equipment, camping locales and transportation Program: arts/crafts, music – both learning and participation
	Young Mothers	
Social: Peer community Preparental continuity Parental disengagement Marital interaction	meeting friends (PCF), crafts (P), adult education (P), trips (PC), gathering– lunch, etc. (PF) clubs (P), child care (P) child care (P), travel (PC) outings (PCF), concerts (PC), travel (PC)	Space: lounge, lunch, arts/ crafts equipment space, child care Program: lunch and other occasional gatherings, trip events arts/crafts and other learning
Self-enhancement: Expression Physical enhancement Mastery and development Continuing preparental avocations	arts (PC), crafts (P), projects (P), hobbies (PCF) swimming (P), tennis (PC), other sports (PC) arts (PC), crafts (P), adult education (P), hobbies (PCF) variety of activities including all above	Space: pools, courts, equipment for arts/ crafts/hobbies, informal classrooms Program: child care, learning skills in physical activity, arts, crafts, etc., adult classes, group outings, babysitting coops

to gain necessary specificity. However, more detailed analysis of the satisfactions perceived for activities selected as important to older adolescents and adults in the new town does provide a basis for further illustrating the need-based planning approach. The need profile for adolescents is drawn from the Rapoport and Rapoport study and from the three-community sequence by the author. Certain kinds of activities were perceived by participants as providing satisfactions that at least in part meet their needs. Then leisure planners can select those activities requiring public resources of space and/or program and develop priorities for community recreation. A final step, not given in Table 7.3, would be to develop an overall plan for space, program and budget.

The profile for young mothers, found to be a vulnerable group in a number of studies, demonstrates the interweaving of provisions.[4] Child care is required for the mothers of preschool children to participate in many of the activities that may meet social and selfhood needs. Even activities that are creative and expressive with mostly personal and intrinsic satisfactions usually call for the absence of children in the skill-acquisition phase. By beginning with the needs of an identified group, priorities and requirements can be integrated and resources allocated most efficiently.   .

It should also be noted that for both adolescents and young mothers leisure needs are to a large extent social. The role-testing of adolescents and the community/communication needs of young mothers may be quite different in space requirements, degree of organization and in mode of attraction. Youth may prefer a large gathering and loud music, while the young mother may need small and rather informal gatherings allowing for considerable interchange. But the social needs are integral to the leisure profile for both.

Facility Planning Implications
Without going into detail, some suggestions of how this approach to planning might alter the development of a neighborhood park may illustrate the procedures for facility development. Planning for a neighborhood park would begin with a profile of the population to be served. Then, with a need profile for the groups, activities requiring outdoor park resources would be identified. A crucial step would be the designation of those 'vulnerable' groups with the fewest alternative resources. For a neighborhood park, special attention would probably be given to children who are too old to go to a recreation site with a parent, but too young to go more than a few blocks on their own. Transportation possibilities and limits would also be identified.

Once the groups needing priority are identified and their park-related activities outlined, then the use potential of the site itself would be mapped. Space, terrain, soil and access limitations of most sites do not allow for an infinite range of activity provisions. Activities that conflict in space, personnel, or other environmental resources would be weighed and those with the lowest NSP and the greatest conflict potential eliminated.

Finally, provisions of space, access, separation, amenities and schedule would be combined into a plan for the park. For example, the need for 10–12-year-old boys to gather for participatory games and sports in places open enough for possible participants to 'scout the scene' and yet separated enough not to drive younger children away from nearby activity sites would determine the landscaping design part of the park. Flexibility might be sought, so that different groups could adapt space for their needs at different times. The design process would then begin with the life course need profiles of the neighborhood population and end with horticultural amenities rather than vice versa.

Summary of the Approach

In this exploratory attempt to develop an alternate or supplementary approach to recreation resource and program planning a number of limitations are evident. The first limitation is that not enough is known about the satisfaction potential of specific activities and programs for the user groups at various points in their life careers. Nor have the personal and social vulnerabilities associated with life course transitions been fully identified. Further research and program evaluation are required to fill out the need profiles of the many life course phases. Now only the most evident special needs such as space for autonomous gathering for adolescents and escape activities for young mothers can be clearly identified.

The complex interplay of resource contexts, developing identities and changing role expectations is not amenable to quick survey research. Nor has the leisure component been given adequate attention in most developmental studies. Therefore, research with this focus and with cumulative design will be required for the specificity and inclusiveness that planners can employ as a basis for design.

However, enough is known that at least the component of need satisfaction through the life course may take a place in the planning process. If we are serious about our humanistic aims of providing programs for people that facilitate the full development of their lives, then the basis of planning should be the best we know – however incomplete – about leisure meanings and satisfactions. We cannot allow leisure to be trivialized by separating it from the other meanings, relationships and careers of life.

The second limitation is that direct application to any particular park or program or agency requires specific planning. No readymade blueprints for either programs or facilities are possible. Planning should be based on all that is known about the potential user population in relation to the specific environment – indoors or outdoors –and its design possibilities. This model adds to the planning process a set of human dimensions and some clues about leisure meanings and satisfactions. Some 'best estimates', approximations and educated guesses will always be part of the decision process. Nevertheless, bringing what we know about people and their leisure into the process would seem to give a better chance of meeting real needs than requiring that they make the greatest adaptation of their needs to the preconceived preferences and designs of planners. At least, dimensions of human need through identity and role careers and the need-satisfaction potential of specific activities may be brought together with the resource opportunities and limitations to try to redress inequities and make recreation as human as possible.

References: Chapter 7

1   J. R. Kelly, 'A revised paradigm of leisure choices', *Leisure Sciences*, no. 1, 1978, pp. 345–63.
2   J. R. Rossman, 'Development of a leisure program evaluation instrument', unpublished Ph.D. thesis, University of Illinois, Champaign, Illinois, USA, 1981.
3   R. Rapoport, and R. N. Rapoport, *Leisure and the Family Life Cycle* (London: Routledge & Kegan Paul, 1975).
4   M. Young and P. W. Willmott, *The Symmetrical Family* (London: Routledge & Kegan Paul, 1973).

8

Leisure Interaction and the Social Dialectic

There have been attempts to analyze the shaping impacts of theoretical assumptions on leisure sociology[1] and to base leisure study on disciplinary theory in sociology and anthropology.[2] Theory-building in the field has been limited to attempts to develop systematic and research-based explanations of leisure behavior,[3] rather than to submit the implications of leisure sociology as contributions to the discipline.

The aim of this chapter is to begin to transform the one-way flow into a dialogue. The assumption is that the state of the art in leisure sociology has now developed to the point of offering suggestions to sociological understandings of social structure and interaction as well as receiving theoretical maxims and orientation. Further, most study of leisure has been at least implicitly from a systemic or structure-functional perspective and potentially significant conflict, and interpretive issues have received little attention from those designing research.[4] In contrast, the focus here will be on the relationship between Weberian interpretative approaches and leisure interaction.

Three Theoretical Perspectives

In Western sociology there has been general agreement that the theoretical approach usually labeled 'structure functional', system theory,[5] the social facts paradigm[6] or 'normal sociology'[7] has been dominant. This perspective includes the functional approach of Kingsley Davis and Robert Merton, the social system emphasis of Talcott Parsons and the social facts stress of the acknowledged forefather, Emile Durkheim. Here the dimension of an interrelated functional system is taken as fundamental and the paradigm labeled 'systemic sociology'.

Anthony Giddons[8] and others have identified different premisses in approaches to conceptualizing social structure and interaction. From an historical perspective, the three source theorists are Durkheim, Karl Marx and Max Weber. Both Durkheim and Marx begin with the premiss that social forces determine individual action and are the starting-point of explanatory analysis. They differ in their models of society, however. Durkheim and systemic theorists believe that social solidarity is achieved through a consistent pattern of complementary institutions and value orientations. Marx and conflict sociologists find prerevolutionary societies to be based on fundamental inconsistencies that result in profound division and conflict. Weber, on the other hand, while recognizing such social forces, begins explanation with the actor whose perceptions and interpretations are the basis of social action.

Clear distinctions are misleading. For example, Marxist sociologists are concerned with consciousness and ideologies that reflect accurately or falsely the true nature of the society and its power allocations. Such interpretations and world views, however induced, are one element in the development of conflict based on fundamental differences in power and the ability to exploit others. Explanation is basically in terms of the struggle for decisive power and the basis of that power in the economic order.[9] However, even such a social cleavage may be obscured and the realization of the conflict postponed.

Despite such blurring of distinctions, it would seem that the various schools, models, theory groups and orientations of sociological work can be generally subsumed under one of the three theory types: systemic, conflict and interpretive. Further, each of these theory approaches has led to somewhat different questions and research strategies. Before beginning the attempt to suggest possible contributions of leisure sociology to one of the three, it should be useful to outline briefly how each theoretical model has shaped leisure research. The analysis is based on a more complete presentation by the author published under the auspices of the International Sociological Association.[10]

Systemic Sociology and Leisure Research

The systemic model of a society is one in which functions necessary to maintain the system are carried out by its institutions – especially the central institutions of the economy, polity, family, school and church. The equilibrium of the system is maintained by the adaptation and adjustment of those institutions with their specialized functions. Stability and change are defined from within the system. Order is based on a common culture, socialization into the value orientations of that culture and the functional adequacy of the system. Change tends to be gradual, evolutionary rather than revolutionary, adaptive to alterations in external forces or internal technologies and amenable to reformist action.

Research orientations are, therefore, a response to agreed-on problems of adaptation to the system and its functioning. The focus may be on the normative culture, organization structures, or some relationship of the two. The main institutions command most of the research attention with the traditional assumption that most problems are some maladaptation to industrialization and accompanying urbanization.

Not entirely consistently, however, the most common data-gathering method has been the questionnaire and the interview survey that taps the attitudes of individuals and deals with a kind of 'aggregate psychology'.[11] The assumptions seems to be that aggregates of individuals may be formed in terms of their position in the social system. Responses to survey instruments are assumed to represent a reality about the cultural orientations and institutional behavior of the aggregate due to certain persistent properties they have in common. Behavior is predicted statistically in probabilities for the aggregate. Most recently sociology in the United States has had a resurgence of demographic analysis enhanced by the development of a series of sophisticated statistical treatments. The approach is 'structural' in the sense that quantitative measures of behavior are manipulated to discover the complex relationships of behaviors and conditions for increasingly differentiated aggregates.

Leisure research guided by this model of doing sociology has focused on the issues of functionality and relationship to central institutions. The contribution of leisure to the system has been cast in terms of industrialization, the work-determined schedule and the place of recreation in maintaining an adequate workforce. Leisure has generally been defined as residual time leftover from work and required maintenance. Its aim has been assumed to be to return the worker fit for maximum productivity. As a result, leisure has been viewed as recuperative, beneficial for physical and mental health, and an element in the growth and development of children who will one day be workers.

Secondary to this problem of functionality have been the concerns of recreation resource managers, who needed information about participants in order to plan, and the eternal systemic problem of 'deviance'. Deviants, especially youth who engage in antisocial behavior or are not preparing themselves properly to become workers, receive some attention from those who would design recreation to return them to functional institutional socialization.

Leisure and Social Institutions: The strangely non-cumulative history of leisure research in North America up to 1970 included considerable attention given to the subject in various studies of 'Middletown', 'Elmtown' and other communities. Leisure was generally found to reflect the stratification of the community and its cultural orientations.

The more 'in-depth' Kansas City research of Robert Havighurst[12] and others combined attention to social placement with complex analysis of the meaning of leisure to adult participants.

However, not surprisingly, the greatest attention was given to the issue of leisure and work. As outlined in Chapter 2, the determination of leisure by work and the contributions of leisure to productivity were approached in a variety of ways despite a series of hints that the two might not be as closely related as assumed. Here the premises of the systemic model seem to have delayed consideration of other possibilities.

The most persistent theme of leisure sociology has been the attempt to predict leisure behavior by social placement. The basic assumption is that social position as assigned by age, sex, occupation, income and other indices of social status determines secondary behavior such as leisure. The failure of this research strategy on its own terms, useful prediction, has been reinforced by the failure to build explanatory theory on the findings of the countless participation surveys.

The quantitative bent of this mode of research has also supported the definition of leisure as time. Research in Eastern and Western Europe as well as North America has consistently employed the amount of time given to designated activities as the main dependent variable in the design and the time diary as a primary instrument. Limitations of analysis to comparing means of time use have been compounded by recognition that the activity label may include a wide variety of experiences, purposes and meanings.

More recently various means have been developed to investigate the contexts and meanings of non-work activity. As already outlined, the varied kinds of satisfaction, the significance of social contexts, and the dimension of environments, physical and social, have been incorporated in new kinds of research. However, for the most part, such research is still based on systemic premises that leisure is secondary to other institutions. Leisure is defined as resulting from and contributing to the really central social institutions of the economy and the family. Recognition of leisure as more part of the family–community social space and learned in family socialization contexts rather than determined by work does not contradict systemic presuppositions. The new orientation of establishment social science can be expected to explore how leisure enriches childhood learning and adult satisfaction with life. Both, of course, are functional in a social system that requires comprehensive socialization and willing adult compliance for continued equilibrium and productivity.

Conflict Sociology and Leisure
The reverse premiss of Marxist sociology is that the system in pre-

revolutionary societies cannot sustain equilibrium indefinitely. Leisure, often defined as a false consciousness of freedom,[13] is understood in terms of its employment by ruling elites to deceive the proletariat into believing they have a stake in the system. The model is one of a social system with two or more groups, each with different power, different interests and different economic positions. The ruling group, a minority, owns and controls the means of production.[14] In a capitalist society that controlling class determines a system in which investment capital is rewarded and labor exploited. Only the ruling elite has the power to shape their own lives rather than be molded by the requirements of the production system.

The capitalist system from this perspective is the final contradictory society which exploits the majority. Following its collapse or overthrow, it will be replaced by a socialist system in which the alienation of the worker from self-determination will end. With material conditions fundamentally altered, in time a new kind of person will be produced who will work for the common good and be socialized into a new kind of non-exploitive social solidarity.

In contemporary capitalism hegemony over workers is no longer simply a matter of force and state monopoly over armaments. Rather, repression and control now take the form of seduction and the development of a false consciousness of a stake in the system rather than owner–worker conflict.[15] Leisure may be one tool of repression in providing an escape from the reality of alienation in its deceptive space of relative autonomy. However, in fact leisure is one more commodity that is defined as a reward for alienated labor and employed by the power elite to maintain the system.

Research from this perspective is oriented toward revealing the conditions of life in the system and toward change. Ideally, research produces knowledge that can be put into practice. *Praxis* requires change-activity in a capitalist system that is measured by further research with the theory corrected by the empirical results.

Most recent leisure research in Eastern Europe has been similar to that in the West. With the premiss that the socialist revolution has taken place, the main aim of leisure research has been the quantitative analysis of how leisure is now contributing to the postrevolutionary system. Time diary studies are used to indicate changes in behavior in the new system.

In a capitalist society the conflict model would lead to research on leisure as an instrument of control and repression. There has, however, been little attention given to the relationship of leisure to political orientations, class consciousness and personal autonomy. A few research efforts have turned to work constraints and leisure as compensation as previously introduced. The relationships have not been found to be a prime determinant of leisure choices or orientations. However, the designs have, for the most part, dealt with self-recognized values, orientations and behaviors rather than the unrecognized twisting of false consciousness.

Moving beyond previous approaches to a conflict base for research could provide a number of critical issues for investigation. Leisure as freedom and the alienated consumption of programs and products, equity of provisions, equality of access to leisure experiences and actual differences under different modes of production control are only a few such researchable questions. Some of the questions require more than analysis of behavior. For example, the identification of leisure satisfaction with consumption and cost-intensive experiences calls for some tapping of attitudes as well as behavior.

Interpretive Theory and Leisure
Interpretive sociology takes a starting-point different from both the systemic and conflict perspectives. The examination of social interaction starts with the social actor who is interpreting his social situation and taking action within it. Research, then, begins from the perspective of that actor and cannot exclude such interpretation, consciousness, or intentions.

The model of society does not focus on institutional structures, but on the regularities of social interaction that are built up out of intentioned decisions and actions. As a consequence, the attention to decision has prompted some to label this approach as 'existential'. However, regularities are developed in the need to take into account the expectations and definitions of others in the situation. Further, situations come to be defined in relatively consistent ways and to provide regular contexts for action. The learned-role definitions, common culture, common expectations and sanctioning power of others combine to give the problematic process the appearance of stability. Society is both existential, built by decision and action,[16] and structural in the sense of having coercive power over behavior.

The interpretive paradigm has as its prime exemplar Max Weber,[17] whose definition of sociology included a focus on intentioned action and on the social actor who 'means something' by his action. This 'action theory' may be distinguished from the symbolic-interaction model of George Herbert Mead in which selfhood is learned in an interaction process, where actions are invested with symbolic meaning.[18] Phenomenologists follow Alfred Schutz[19] in defining social reality as the related subjectivities of actors. These approaches along with the dramaturgical model of Goffman will be subsumed under the aegis of interpretive or existential sociology in the analysis of leisure and sociological theory that follows.

Leisure Interaction as Fundamental

Focus on face-to-face interaction in leisure does not preclude either functional premises or analysis. The prime example of such a combination of systemic aims with interpretive means is found in the institutional approach of Cheek and Burch[20] in which leisure is analyzed as having a central function in the social system. That function is to provide a context for the development of intimate relationships. Leisure, then, is found less at the margins of the social system in 'leftover time' than at the center of the working out of primary social relationships. In a social ecology characterized by considerable fragmentation and dispersion, leisure becomes a necessary social space for the location, development and enrichment of primary relationships. One implication of this analysis is that any sociology of leisure must deal with face-to-face interaction as well as institutional affiliations. Much leisure is 'relational' in that its central meaning is found in a positive valuation of the relationship that accepts, implicitly or explicitly, the constraints imposed by the multifaceted role of definitions and expectations. Leisure, then, is not 'either/or' in regard to freedom and constraint or intrinsic and social meanings. Absolute purity of self-determination or intrinsic motivation is a definitional 'ideal type' rather than ordinary realization.

Leisure in Everyday Life: While leisure may be defined by the quality and orientation of the experience rather than its form or location in time and space, there is no end to the activities or contexts of modern leisure. Although a relative few may run miles each week in an exhausting and disciplined form of leisure, many more exercise their imaginations on daydreaming that may be the freest of all leisure, engage in rather aimless 'fooling around' with peers, or are semi-engaged before the residential convenience center of TV. City parks may be little-used, while family and friendship groups crowd the shopping center on Saturday. Time at home may be relatively constrained for some parents who experience considerable opportunity for leisurely interchange at the workplace. In fact, there is increasing evidence that much leisure of great importance for maintaining psychological equilibrium may be 'interstitial' and found in minutes and moments interspersed through any day.[21]

Just how much leisure can be identified remains more of a research question than conclusion. Csikszentmihalyi's use of 'beepers' to secure analysis of ongoing activity randomized by time has revealed the futility of dividing the day into blocks labeled work, maintenance, or leisure. The element of play as autotelic and largely self-contained episodes of behavior may be interspersed into even the most task-oriented situation, if only for a few seconds. When 'play' is defined by its intrinsic meaning and lack of constraint, it seems indistinguishable from leisure. However, a subelement of play definition has been its self-containment.[22] The meaning of play is found within the event in a timespan during which the consequential world is bracketed and the play world taken as temporarily real. Play, then, is seen not just as something children do,[23] but as episodes of non-serious interaction with self-contained meaning and consequences.

Kenneth Burke proposed that humor might be used to test social structures and performances within the role-expectation context.[24] Cheek and Burch[25] build on this insight in their suggestion that play is not entirely self-contained, but may be a way of trying out presentations without risking the loss of social position. Especially as persons move through the life course, interstitial play may be an important way of testing role transitions and age appropriateness.[26]

This possibility takes us one step further in the sociological analysis of leisure. If leisure is neither clearly segmented from primary social roles nor from the development of ways in which roles are taken, then a concept is needed to link self-conscious action with its social context. 'Role identity' is an approach to self-definition and the social identity related to social categories.[27] Self-definition within the context of social identity is provided by the 'role identity' in which a person reflexively 'thinks of himself' taking the role and acting in relation to it.

Since social identities change through the life course, role-identity self-definitions require continual adjustment and occasional revision. If leisure and play provide opportunity for developing role relationships and presentations, then some development of role identities might be expected to take place in leisure contexts. Already several studies have provided evidence for precisely this salience of leisure in role identities. Chad Gordon[28] has reviewed the place of leisure in life-course identity formation. Rhona and Robert Rapoport[29] employed case studies to analyze the contribution of leisure to family and other roles through the life course. Kelly and Masar[30] found leisure salient to definitional shifts in the transition from student to early establishment periods. Robert Stebbins[31] has discovered the centrality of leisure investments to concepts of selfhood among adults who have concentrated on a single leisure skill. Such evidence supports McCall and Simmons's understanding of life events as parts of reflexive sequences rather than isolated occurrences.[32] Leisure sociology is beginning to follow a new avenue into the heart of sociology, that of sequential role definition and development.

Existential Theory

Although the differences between structure-functional theory with its assumptions of systemic unity and bias toward harmony[33] and Marxist conflict theory with its distinction between pre- and postrevolutionary societies are profound, in one sense they are alike. Both are deterministic in their models of explanation. Both begin with the assumption that social structures, whether benign or malignant, shape human behavior.[34] Explanation is largely unidirectional from the properties of the system to behavior. While Marxists may see fundamental conflict in the economic relations of a capitalist society that Parsons thought in essential equilibrium due to a consensus of value orientations, both assume that social forces within a system are based on the institutional structures. Explanation is from institutional independent variables to behavioral dependent variables.

Somewhat on the fringes of sociology is existential theory. Although there are many varieties of the approach, all include a fundamentally dialectical mode of explanation. That is, whether the focus is on Weberian interpretive modes of explanation, symbolic-interaction models, or dramaturgical metaphors, there is the assumption that explanation requires accounting for the interpretive decisions of social actors. However marginal to the discipline, there has been a persistent recurrence of varieties of existential theory that insist on a significant element of self-determination in human interaction.

Without denying the pervading power of institutional forces or their basis in economic control structures, existential theories advocate that at least some levels of interaction require the introduction of interpreting actors into the model of explanation. Some variations may focus on the 'small worlds' in which persons develop lines of action.[35] Goffman[36, 37] and others stress the problematic presentation of self in social situations with implicit orientations. In the dramaturgical metaphor interaction is seen as something like the role-taking, interpretation and staging control of the theater.[38] Such analysis of face-to-face interaction episodes is intriguing and almost self-authenticating when well presented.

However, existentialist theory goes a crucial step further. Luckman, Berger, and others, argue that the social structure taken as 'real' in structural models is actually constructed out of such 'small world' interaction.[39] The regularities taken as the concrete forces of the social system are in reality the relatively fragile constructs of problematic negotiation. Therefore, decision is real in its consequences. Persistence is jeopardized as well as reinforced in ongoing interaction.[40] The mediated character of knowledge is accepted 'as if' perception were direct and reliable.[41]

The Social Dialectic: C. Wright Mills[42] found the dialectical nature of society to be central to the sociological enterprise. Understanding the biographies of persons requires comprehension of the historical structures of their social context. Further, much of life involves the playing of roles within specific institutions with existing role definitions.[43] However, within that context is the person whose self-images have been developed in institutional contexts, whose 'vocabulary of motives' consists of learned interpretations, and yet who constructs lines of conduct within the social milieu.

There are indeed social forces, known and unknown, that shape not only behavior, but also its interpretation. Socialization processes include the internalization of cultural world views of 'how things really are'. Nevertheless, within the interplay of forces, not entirely unidirectional, the social actor interprets and decides in ways that have consequences for both the self and for the social milieu.

The Social Self: The simplest statement is that the social self is acting as well as being acted upon. Turner's dictum is that a person may 'enact' a role but not occupy it.[44] Rather, when a person takes a role, it is an act involving evaluation as well as acceptance.[45] Within role contexts a person forms self-concepts which in turn influence which roles are chosen and how their portrayal is essayed. There is a dialectical relationship between the regularities of role expectations and the ongoing process of self-evaluation of the actor. In fact, many roles are relinquished as well as redefined when self-definitions change through the life course.[46] The 'me' is not only a cognitive frame of reference for decision[47] but is always in process of development and redefinition.

From this perspective, attention is focused on the interaction process in its social situation as explored by Simmel[48] and others. Life is 'negotiation' as well as response, and social identities are constructed as well as assigned. In this negotiation the *role identity* from the actor's side of the social dialectic is how the person defines the self in the role.

From this perspective, decisions are real in their consequences. Further, they rest in the situated process of self-definition and the development of role identities. Within the social dialectic, explanation of interaction requires taking account of this interpreting actor, and the persistence of 'social structure' rests on the agreed-on definitions of such actors.

Through the literature developing this existential mode of sociological explanation, there have been occasional references to leisure settings and interactions. The relative freedom and episodic character of some leisure provides illustrative material for interpretive sociology. What follows is anything but complete or final, but from the perspective of the cumulative work in relevant leisure strategy.

Leisure Sociology and Existential Theory

Support for an existential approach to the study of leisure is found in the accumulating evidence that traditional structural variables do not predict differential participation even in outdoor recreation,[49] and that more immediate situational factors such as available companions, schedule synchronization and accessibility are more highly correlated to choices than social position.[50] The decision element in leisure definitions is supported by analysis of adult choices as well as by the variations in activity patterns within aggregates defined by age, sex, education, occupation and even life course period.

Further, all persons who participate in a given activity do not do so in the same way. Variations in style or mode of engagement are related to such economic factors as cost and costly distance,[51] but also to the intensity and orientations of engagement.[52] Groups and individuals may travel, engage in sport or an art, or attend a party in quite different ways. There are differences between the devotee of tennis with a strong skill-development orientation and the occasional weekend convivial swinger. There are differences between drinking at a country-music bar and at an urbane cocktail party sponsored by the symphony guild. Such differences reflect the social context, but the choices and modes of interaction also reflect the role identities being essayed by the actors.

The essential variety of leisure offers an especially apt environment for trying out identities not fully established and the non-serious consequences of play afford opportunity for risk in self-presentations. However, the significance of leisure for the development of social identities and intimate role relationships requires that analysis be sociological rather than, in a narrow sense, biographical or psychological. Leisure is situated in the confluence of social forces and decision, of institutional structures and the negotiation of identities. The preliminary analysis that follows begins with a critical intersection of structural and existential theory, that of the social role, and moves through elements of role identity to face-to-face interaction and the relationship of spontaneity to identity-testing. Throughout, the social dialectic is found to persist even in the most singular events.

Role Theory and Leisure

If the role is the 'primary point of articulation between the personality of the individual and the structure of the social system' as Parsons[53] has declared, then it is crucial to social theory. However, the analysis by J. A. Jackson defines two common approaches, one through Mead and others who emphasize 'taking the role' and the other stressing the functional requirements of the social system.[54] Here the social role is understood as encompassing an 'improvization' of behavior[55] necessary to respond to the perceived expectations associated with taking a particular position in the social system. Role is a line of identity-expressing action as well as a response. While some interaction situations may be quite structured, others are not. Simmel,[56] Goffman[57] and others have approached the management of identity in relatively unstructured situations that lend themselves to dramatic presentation. Although one useful research approach would be to test theory by focusing on role expectations in relatively open settings such as leisure and on varieties of role-taking in bureaucracies, there would also seem to be a place in theory-building for beginning to learn more about identity construction in leisure situations.

Popitz traces the issue to the fundamental ones of sociology, the accounting for both social normation or cohesion and for social differentiation.[58] On a basic level of pragmatic social interpretation, we may have certain normative expectations of a role that place parameters around the performance limits, but also expect that each actor will play the role in a unique way. In fact, in some cases we find the role redefined by the performance. There is a dialectical relationship between role norms and how roles are taken. If, then, roles are the crux of sociological explanation, it is crucial to understand how role definitions come to differ and performance vary as well as how they are predictable.

The analysis may return to that too-familiar phrase 'how each actor will play the role'. Without making too much of the vocabulary, the concept of *playing* roles may lead us back to leisure. Leisure situations are not without their own role expectations as well as incorporating those persistent role identities that each actor brings to the episode. Even in familiar groups there may be some ongoing negotation about the presentation of identities not fully established in the definition of the presenting actor. Nevertheless, the leisure event often has a significant analytical advantage over more regular events. In so far as it is 'play', the leisure episode is to a degree self-contained. It may be analyzed as an event with at least a major component of its social meaning worked out within that time–space frame. Simmel proposes that in social play objective interests are laid aside and the interaction itself is its own meaning.[59]

For example, although external social identities from economic and other institutions are one factor in the negotiations of leisure groups such as a community theater cast or a league softball game, their heterogeneity mitigates the transfer of rigid hierarchies or status expectations in the leisure event. As the role identities are worked out, elements of related skills, interaction modalities and critical invest-ments *in the event* generally take on greater salience. The rehearsal or performance, the practice or game, has its own self-contained mean-ing. Each 'actor' or 'player' is able not only to try a variety of roles in the inaugural episodes of the line of action of play preparation or a softball season, but may reshape the role identities of others in the process.

Further, at least some of the meaning is found within the event or sequence of events. Not only in intrinsic or autotelic meaning for the individual, but also in the significance of that event-bounded role identity, there is meaning for the actor. In the immediate dialectic of the processual taking and developing of a characterization of a role the reciprocal actions of others in the interaction provide feedback that not only continues the role development but yields satisfaction as the role identity is established and verified. There is, then, satisfaction not only in the theater or sport event, but in the role identity development.

While there is not as much research supporting this approach as might be wished, two kinds are relevant. The first is the case study analysis of sequences of leisure episodes such as poker groups in which the structure of the games provides a context for the presentation and establishment of salient identities.[60] Another is from research on the psychological outcomes of wilderness use in which scaled outcomes cluster in ways that suggest that there are types of wilderness users who combine culture and age-appropriate values with modes of activ-ity within the resource and with other users that build up self-defini-tions that differ on social/solitary and risktaking dimensions.[61] However, knowing that choices and desired outcomes vary does not tell us how self-definitions differ either entering or during the event.

Interaction as Emergence
One feature of many leisure events is that they have open-ended outcomes. In some, indeterminancy is a major feature of the activity. This is true not only in sports, but also in social situations such as bars where people come to seek new relationships. In much leisure the problematic as well as the structured is integral to the experience.

In recent years interpretive sociologists have developed several approaches to piecing together the process of interaction episodes. Norman Denzin[62] has been developing a method of analysis of be-havior specimens that employ 'naturalistic indicators' to incorporate the verbal and non-verbal elements in the emergent process of an episode. These rely on interpretive observation as well as careful recording of conversation and cues. Goffman[63,64] calls attention to non-verbal signals in his analysis of how persons announce their identities and carry out lines of action in the social drama. However, he also stresses the taken-for-granted elements in a social situation that give a kind of structure to the staging and presentation management. From a dramaturgical perspective, this taken-for-granted is the structural side of the roles being enacted. There are not only limits beyond which a role portrayal would be unrecognizable, but also expectations related to how a person with a specific social identification customarily enacts a role. For example, age appropriateness is an assumption that provokes the 'act your age' when violated.

The leisure event is especially amenable to the analysis of emergence due to its problematic outcomes. There is a certain openness in the inaugural 'why don't we take a drive?' that begins a leisure interaction episode. In games the outcome is at least partly in doubt. In the arts the quality of the product will vary. In a conversation or a walk the route and the destination of both talk and walk are open to processual development. Unlike a task-oriented production episode, the end is not prespecified. In so far as what occurs in the process is important, then the leisure event would seem to be well suited for analysis of just how a particular signal or sign can turn the direction of the interaction to something unexpected. Analysis of how conversations enter the special and non-serious world of play suggests that a metalanguage cue that 'this is play' must be given and received.[65] However, that metalanguage communication differs in more presentational 'storytelling' episodes from those in which the play is a shared construction. When the problematic and emergent is dominant, then the risk of self-investment is also greatest and may be hedged by a number of 'try-out' conventions that minimize the role identity cost of failure.

Life Course Socialization and Leisure Engagement

There has been a tendency to treat role socialization as rather serious business, especially by those who beleive that the social system is held together by the glue of role-learning. As a consequence, the problematic and play elements in episodes involving role learning have been bypassed in favor of attention to the invariant generalized other.[66] However, the emergent and non-serious character of leisure permits and even encourages experimentation.

Attention here is on the actor who makes decisions that lead to role-learning rather than as a passive recipient of preordained expectations. The active side of the dialectic may be raised to greatest salience in leisure sociology. Mead himself[67] pointed to various games of children and youth as vehicles for learning role expectations. Leisure settings such as interscholastic sports, dances and organized summer camps have been suggested as socialization media.[68,69,70,71] Even with the stress on anticipatory socialization into adult roles rather than in current roles through the life course, leisure interactions have been considered important to children and youth.

What is less accepted is the significance of leisure in later life.[72] A study of men and women making the transition from university student to 'early establishment' roles in the economy, family and community institutions revealed multiple ways in which leisure is adjusted to serve the ends of making a place in the postschool world. More surprising, however, was the salience of leisure identities to the working out priorities. The process of reconciling family and leisure aims for young parents was found to be one of both conflict and integration.[73]

Case studies in England demonstrated ways in which leisure settings and investments change in relation to the role identities assumed appropriate and desirable through the life course.[74] For example, following a failed marriage, leisure often becomes the primary social space in which somewhat damaged identities are altered and tried out in new associational contexts. As work and family roles rise and fall in both salience and satisfaction, leisure is a source not only of new challenges and associations, but also of additional or recovered social identities. The man of 45 returning to sport engagement is doing more than engaging in a healthful regimen or making a last stab at fleeting youth. He may well be seeking to re-establish a social identity as a physically competent person who is ready to subject his skills to the measurement of competition or other scoring. In much the same way leisure socialization is more than taking up new and renewed activities through the life course.[75] It is a development of self-definitions of investment and competence in activities that extend and test the self. The choice of social settings, activity contexts, environments and, perhaps most of all, new companions at any period in the life course is an element in role transitions that are anticipated, worked through and accomplished with varying consequences. At any time, leisure would seem to be a social space for innovation and experimentation with new role identities as well as for the recovery and redefining of old ones with minimal risk to economic or familial roles.

Leisure Role Investments

As long as leisure is viewed as peripheral and residual, then there seems no accounting for a significant kind of human behavior. Athletic coaches and arts instructors often assert that participation in their activity requires too much discipline and investment to be considered 'leisure'. They see only the relaxation and recuperative dimensions of leisure. But what about those persons who are willing to concentrate their affective and mental energy as well as physical effort in a non-work role more than in their employment? Those who make such a commitment to the development of skill in a non-work activity are called 'amateurs' by Robert Stebbins,[76] who finds such persons on the margins between work and leisure. However, another approach to their commitment is simply to accept their investment in the non-work role identity. After all, is it so surprising that work roles may lose or never provide the opportunity for self-development that is found in chosen and disciplined leisure? The ball player or gambler as well as the cellist or archaeologist may find that the risk, measurement, feedback, associations, and creative and expressive potential of leisure are greater than other roles. Further, a leisure investment may provide a line of action that has a beginning and a series of recognizable outcomes in its course of engagement. Non-serious in the sense of not threatening work and family roles, leisure is an opportunity for consequential action.

Some leisure episodes have their appeal in their temporary situational nature. They do not involve long-term or costly commitments. Some leisure relationships are defined as 'easy in-and-out' and some events as quite separate from other roles. In fact, the meanings of leisure can hardly be analyzed without reference to the role salience and segregation intended by the actor. In some situations leisure's self-contained consequences can offer opportunity for trying out identities that do not become lost in the more unyielding structures of the workplace. Further, there is some evidence that leisure may provide an alternative for those whose self-investment potential is limited in the economic sphere.[77]

There would seem to be a dialectic within leisure as well as the one between the social structure and the social actor. If the development of role identities in leisure is a major element in decisions and meaning, then what of the stress on intrinsic satisfaction said to be integral to its definition? McCall and Simmons propose that there is intrinsic satisfaction in the fulfillment of role identities.[78] In leisure, satisfactions in the experience – physical, social, emotional and intellectual – may well be contained within the event itself. Role identity may take second place to the sheer autotelic experience of cross-country skiing through quiet woods when the snow is soft and the weather crisp. Nevertheless, the fulfillment of being *able* to ski well enough for the experience is also part of the meaning of the complete event. What is suggested is that the meanings of leisure are not pure but mix dimensions of intrinsic satisfaction, social meaning and identity development. What is added to previous models here is the significance of role identity as a third dimension to the oversimple intrinsic-extrinsic division of satisfactions or motivations. Again the analysis of central leisure roles in a new town[79] and of forest recreation[80] both indicate that social and intrinsic elements are combined in the same activity. In the interpretive framework of the social actor they may come together in the role identity of self-definition and social role.

Face-to-face Interaction and Community

One danger to this approach is that the structural elements of role identity come to dominate the analysis and the processual elements are neglected. The bias toward convenience always works against research designs that focus on process and emergence rather than presumed properties of an event sequence. In leisure sociology the increased stress on the social aspects of what had been presumed to be primarily 'activity' and on the centrality of primary relationships in leisure requires examining the quality of the interaction as well as its form and environment. 'Relational leisure' in which the development and expression of the intimate relationship *is* the primary meaning of the event turns attention to the process of interaction. Just how does the leisure episode provide for that relation-building?

One evident element is the 'play' or self-containment of the episodic drama. The construction of the event and its interaction can be aimed at the process itself as well as outcomes within the episode. While there may well be a structure within the event that includes a measured outcome or *dénouement* of the little play, the quality of the interaction and the process of relating are prime meanings of the event. The reciprocal or multifaceted process containing intersecting lines of action uses the activity and environment as a setting. The face-to-face 'interchange of expressivity' is itself the most direct element of the interaction.[81]

There has been some analysis of how the setting is managed, so that interference or discrepancies are minimized.[82] More recently the processual nature of turning conversation to play with the giving and receiving of verbal and non-verbal cues has been studied.[83] The relatively fragile nature of seemingly agreed-on meanings and orientations within an episode is attested by the countless ways in which communication can be diverted or even broken off by a misread or misplaced cue. Repairing such tears in the interaction is an ongoing element of any sustained relationship. Further, cues are often misinterpreted and require either a revised replication or a shifting of the line of action to correspond with the feedback. McCall and Simmons point out that one means of directing the intersecting lines of action is by selective perception and interpretation of cues and signals.[84] Of all the possibilities in a complex situation, actors tend to focus on those that are consistent with and reinforce the role-identities perceived as being presented and that are complementary to self-presentation. In general, the fabric of relationships remains untorn as actors select and interpret in ways consistent with the ongoing meaning of the reciprocal role identities.

Again the meaning of the event is dialectical. The regularities of the relationship are built out of mutual or complementary interpretations of the interaction process. In a leisure episode as constrasted from one that has imposed external goals the process that concentrates on the relationships is most open to both direction and interpretation. In leisure we are most able to develop and enjoy the interaction with a minimum of interference from intruding institutional requirements. Cheek and Burch's proposal that leisure is the social space for intimacy would seem to be justified.

In turn, leisure may be studied processually to understand the nature of that problematic part of the social dialectic that is most open to ongoing construction and reconstruction. Not only the taken-for-granted rules and orientations, the accepted norms of the persistent role identities and the structure of the event itself, but the development of lines of action that build inward to the quality of the episode and its communication rather than outward to institutional goals provide a social space for assessing the problematic in interaction.

The Existential Balance
The social limits on freedom in leisure become essential to beginning to understand more of the existential elements. We may extol the significance of leisure's freedom for human expression and development. However, neglect of the social structures in which leisure occurs yields a temptingly attractive but unrealistic philosophy. The carryover of institutional roles into leisure role identities, the persistence of class-based socialization, the unremitting character of some familial and economic expectations and the environmental limitations of the socioecosystem are all parts of the context of leisure. For the most part, we tend to accept such contexts and work out our relative freedom within them. For example, the sequential timeframe of Western culture shapes how we even begin to interpret leisure possibilities in ways that are seldom evaluated.

Nevertheless, the existential side of the social dialectic does stand peculiarly revealed in much of leisure. There is a freedom of determination, however relative, in leisure choices. There is some openness in many leisure episodes related to their problematic and somewhat self-contained nature. Leisure is not segmented and unconnected to institutional roles; but neither is it wholly determined. As a consequence, the decision side of the social dialectic may be most discernible in leisure. So much of life is long-range in intents that research strategies that encompass meaning are difficult to develop. The more

open and episodic character of leisure suggests the possibility of following lines of action to some completion in that context without giving up
the significance of role identity development.

Too much stress on the freedom of leisure threatens to return its
study to the inconsequential. A failure to look past the structural
elements to the existential surrenders the opportunity to understand
both sides of the social dialectic as well as truncates the problematic
nature of leisure interaction. Finally, in the role identity model the two
dimensions intersect in an identifiable and analyzable frame. The role
identity model enables the sociologist to 'bring freedom back in' to the
social dialectic without discarding structural contexts.

References: Chapter 8

1 J. R. Kelly, 'Sociological perspectives and leisure research', *Current Sociology*, no. 22, 1974, pp. 127–58.
2 N. Cheek and W. Burch, *The Social Organization of Leisure in Human Society* (New York: Harper & Row, 1976).
3 J. Wilson, 'Sociology of leisure', *Annual Review of Sociology*, no. 6, 1980, pp. 21–40.
4 Kelly, 1974, op. cit.
5 R. Friedrichs, *A Sociology of Sociology* (New York: The Free Press, 1970).
6 G. Ritzer, *Sociology: A Multiple Paradigm Science* (Boston, Mass: Allyn & Bacon, 1975).
7 N. Mullins, *Theories and Theory Groups in Contemporary American Sociology* (New York: Harper & Row, 1973).
8 A. Giddons, *Capitalism and Modern Social Theory* (Cambridge: Cambridge University Press, 1971).
9 K. Marx, *Capital* (New York: Modern Library, 1936).
10 Kelly, 1974, op. cit.
11 J. Coleman, 'Relational analysis: the study of social organizations with survey methods', in *Sociological Methods*, ed., N. Denzin (New York: The Free Press, 1967).
12 R. Havighurst, 'The leisure activities of the middle-aged', *American Journal of Sociology*, vol. 63, 1957, pp. 152–62.
13 H. Marcuse, *One-Dimensional Man*, (Boston, Mass.: Beacon Press, 1964).
14 K. Marx, ed., R. Pascal, *The German Ideology* (London: Lawrence & Wishart, 1934).
15 Marcuse, op. cit.
16 H. Blumer, 'Society as symbolic interaction', *Symbolic Interaction*, 2nd edn, eds., J. Manis and B. Meltzer (Boston, Mass: Allyn & Bacon, 1972), pp. 145–54.
17 M. Weber, *The Theory of Social and Economic Organization* (New York: The Free Press, 1947).
18 G. H. Mead, *Mind, Self, and Society* (Chicago: University of Chicago Press, 1934).
19 A. Schutz, *Collected Papers*, Vol. 2 (The Hague: Martinus Nijoff, 1964).
20 Cheek and Burch, op. cit.
21 M. Csikszentmihalyi, 1980; personal communication.
22 J. Huizinga, *Homo Ludens* (Boston, Mass.: Beacon Press, 1955).
23 S. DeGrazia, *Of Time, Work, and Leisure* (New York: Anchor, 1964).
24 K. Burke, *Attitudes toward History* (Boston, Mass.: Beacon Press, 1961).
25 Cheek and Burch, op. cit.
26 R. Rapoport and R. N. Rapoport, *Leisure and the Family Life Cycle* (London: Routledge & Kegan Paul, 1975).

27 G. McCall, and J. Simmons, *Identities and Interactions*, rev. edn (New York: The Free Press, 1978), p. 65.
28 C. Gordon, 'Development of evaluated role identities', *Annual Review of Sociology* (Calif.: Annual Reviews, Inc., 1980), pp. 405–33.
29 Rapoport and Rapoport, op. cit.
30 J. Kelly and S. Masar, 'Leisure identities through a life course transition', unpublished paper, University of Illinois, 1981.
31 R. Stebbins, *Amateurs: On the Margin between Work and Leisure*. (Beverly Hills, Calif.: Sage, 1979).
32 McCall and Simmons, op. cit., p. 20.
33 A. Gouldner, *The Coming Crisis of Western Sociology* (New York: Basic, 1970).
34 E. C. Cuff, and G. Payne, eds., *Perspectives in Sociology* (London: George Allen & Unwin, 1979).
35 B. Luckman, 'The small life-worlds of modern man', in *Phenomenology and Sociology*, ed., T. Luckman (New York: Penguin, 1978).
36 E. Goffman, *The Presentation of Self in Everyday Life* (New York: Doubleday, 1959).
37 E. Goffman, *Interaction Ritual* (New York: Anchor, 1967).
38 D. Brissett and C. Edgeley, eds, *Life as Theater* (Chicago: Aldine, 1974).
39 P. Berger, and T. Luckman, *The Social Contruction of Reality* (New York: Penguin, 1966).
40 T. Luckman, *Phenomenology and Sociology* (New York: Penguin, 1978).
41 A. Schutz, 'Some structures of the life world', in ibid.
42 C. W. Mills, *The Sociological Imagination* (New York: Oxford University Press, 1959).
43 ibid. p. 165.
44 R. Turner, 'Role taking, role standpoint, and reference group behavior. *American Sociological Review*, vol. 21, 1956, pp. 855–67.
45 Gordon, op. cit.
46 C. Gordon, and C. Gaitz, 'Leisure and lives: personal expressivity across the life span', *Handbook of Aging and the Social Sciences*, eds, R. Binstock and E. Shanas (New York: Van Nostrand Reinhold, 1976).
47 McCall and Simmons, op. cit.
48 K. Wolff, *The Sociology of George Simmel* (New York: The Free Press, 1950).
49 J. R. Kelly, 'Outdoor recreation participation: a comparative analysis', *Leisure Sciences*, vol. 3, 1980, pp. 129–54.
50 J. R. Kelly, 'Situational and social factors in leisure decisions', *Pacific Sociological Review*, vol. 21, 1978, pp. 313–30.
51 Cheek and Burch, op. cit.
52 B. Gunter and N. Gunter, 'Leisure styles: a conceptual framework for modern leisure', *Sociological Quarterly*, vol. 21, 1980, pp. 361–74.
53 T. Parsons, *Sociological Theory and Modern Society* (New York: The Free Press, 1967).
54 J. Jackson, ed., *Role* (Cambridge: Cambridge University Press, 1972), p. 4.
55 McCall and Simmons, op. cit.
56 Wolff, op. cit.
57 Goffman, 1967, op. cit.
58 Jackson, op. cit., p. 7.
59 Wolff, op. cit., p. 88.
60 L. Zurcher, 'The friendly poker game: a study of an ephemeral role, *Social Forces*, vol. 49, 1970, pp. 193–6.
61 P. Brown, and G. Haas, 'Wilderness recreation experiences: the rawah case. *Journal of Leisure Research*, vol. 12, 1980, pp. 229–41.
62 N. Denzin, *The Research Act: A Theoretical Introduction to Sociological Methods*, 2nd edn (New York: McGraw-Hill, 1978).
63 Goffman, 1967, op. cit.

64 E. Goffman, *Frame Analysis: An Essay on the Organization of Experience* (New York: Harper & Row, 1974).

65 R. Lynch, 'Social play: 'An interactional analysis of play in face-to-face interaction' unpublished Ph.D. thesis, University of Illinois, Champaign, Illinois, USA, 1979.

66 G. H. Mead, ed., A. Strauss, *On Social Psychology: Selected Papers* (Chicago: University of Chicago Press, 1964), p. 218.

67 ibid., p. 217.

68 J. Coleman, *The Adolescent Society* (New York: The Free Press, 1961).

69 A. Hollingshead, *Elmtown's Youth* (New York: Wiley, 1949).

70 H. Lynd and R. Lynd, *Middletown* (New York: Harcourt Brace, 1956).

71 J. R. Seeley, R. A. Sim and E. W. Loosley, *Crestwood Heights* (New York: Basic, 1956).

72 L. K. George, *Role Transitions in Later Life* (Monterey, Calif.: Brooks/Cole, 1980).

73 Kelly and Masar, op. cit.

74 Rapoport and Rapoport, op. cit.

75 J. Kelly, 'Leisure socialization: replication and extension', *Journal of Leisure Research*, vol. 9, 1977, pp. 121–32.

76 Stebbins, op. cit.

77 E. Spreitzer and E. Snyder, 'Work orientation, meaning of leisure, and mental health', *Journal of Leisure Research*, vol. 6, 1974, pp. 207–19.

78 McCall and Simmons, op. cit.

79 J. R. Kelly, 'A revised paradigm of leisure choices', *Leisure Sciences*, vol. 1, 1978, pp. 345–63.

80 Brown and Haas, op. cit.

81 P. Berger and T. Luckman, op. cit., pp. 28–9.

82 Goffman, 1959, op. cit.

83 Lynch, op. cit.

84 McCall and Simmons, op. cit., p. 94.

Index